Weak in Body,
Strong of Heart

Weak in Body, Strong of Heart

understanding the
road of suffering

Kent & Sarah
Whitecotton

TATE PUBLISHING
AND ENTERPRISES, LLC

Published by Tate Publishing & Enterprises, LLC
127 E. Trade Center Terrace | Mustang, Oklahoma 73064 USA
1.888.361.9473 | www.tatepublishing.com

Tate Publishing is committed to excellence in the publishing industry. The company reflects the philosophy established by the founders, based on Psalm 68:11,
"The Lord gave the word and great was the company of those who published it."

Book design copyright © 2012 by Tate Publishing, LLC. All rights reserved.
Cover design by Kate Stearman
Interior design by Erin DeMoss

Published in the United States of America

ISBN: 978-1-61862-230-3
1. Biography & Autobiography, Personal Memoirs
2. Religion, Biblical Studies, General
12.03.13

Dedication

To our three sons, Brandon, Jeremiah, and Isaac: Mom and I love you all very much. Thanks for walking the journey with us!

To Sarah's mom and dad: Mom you made this book a reality by your sacrifices. And Dad, although you were not here to see this happen, rarely a day goes by that we do not remember you.

To Kent's mom: You are an example of a great woman who persevered through the trials of life. You are a great example to us both.

To Kent's dad: I regret that we had only the last ten years to really get to know you. Thanks for coming back and being my father again. We love you and miss you very much.

To the doctors, nurses, and staff of the eighth floor Bone Marrow Unit at UMass Memorial Hospital: We wish we could mention each of you by name because you deserve it; you guys are the best in the whole world. You made Sarah's journey possible by your dedication and commitment. We promise to never forget any of you! Thanks, Doctor Nath, for seeing Sarah through to the very end!

Special dedication to all the wonderful patients of the eighth floor who journeyed like we did. To your families and loved ones who walked with you, and to all of those who will come through these doors after we have left. May God be with each of you and see you through.

To our church family at Faith Assembly of God in Webster, Massachusetts, you stood by us with your prayers and support. Thanks for all the meals, cards, donations, and love that you so unselfishly gave to us during this journey.

And finally and most importantly: To our Lord and Savior, Jesus Christ, who kept His Word and gave us the grace to get us through the journey.

Table of Contents

Forward   11

Sarah's Introduction: 13
   Ready for Something New

Kent's Introduction   17

The Beginning of a Journey: 23
   Day 1—September 28, 2010

Always Remember God is Watching

over His Word   29
   Day 2—September 29, 2010

Learning to be Thankful   35
   Day 5—October 2, 2010

Faith Tested Becomes Great Faith   43
   Day 6—October 3, 2010

Learning to Know God's Character   51
   Day 13—October 10, 2010

Avoiding the Pitfalls of the Pit   57
   Day 16—October 13, 2010

Try Tears   63
   Day 20—October 17, 2010

Ears to Hear   67
   Day 27—October 24, 2010

I will Lift Up Mine Eyes 73
Day 32—October 29, 2010

Your Faith Needs to Work 79
Day 34—October 31, 2010

Sarah's Second Round of Treatment Begins 87
Day 38—November 4, 2010

Acknowledge the Lord with Your Trust 93
Day 42—November 8, 2010

Sarah's Leukemia is in Remission 101
Day 43—November 9, 2010

Allowing God to Make Needed Changes 107
Day 53—November 19, 2010

No More Quitting 113
Day 55—November 21, 2010

Feelings and Faith 119
Day 57—November 23, 2010

Thanksgiving Day...Eyes Opened 127
Day 59—November 25, 2010

The Reward for Suffering 135
Day 63—November 29, 2010

Giving God What You Love Most 143
Day 73—December 9, 2010

Be Careful You Don't Miss God

Opening a New Door 149
Day 74—December 10, 2010

Strength in Weakness 155
Day 77—December 13, 2010

A Place Called Lodebar 161
Day 84—December 20, 2010

Christmas Time is here Again   167
    Day 88—December 24, 2010

Never Panic Over Your Situation   173
    Day 91—December 27, 2010

Learning to Wait—Part 1   179
    Day 92—December 28, 2010

Learning to Wait—Part 2   185
    Day 93—December 29, 2010

Sowing and Reaping in Righteousness   191
    Day 100—January 5, 2011

Discerning the Spirit of Pride in Me   199
    Day 101—January 6, 2011

Jesus Walks in Storms   207
    Day 107—January 12, 2011

Dreams from God Do Not Die   217
    Day 117—January 22, 2011

Breaking Pride and Releasing Grace   225
    Day 120—January 25, 2011

Stop Working and Start Resting   231
    Day 128—February 3, 2011

The Call of a Servant   239
    Day 131—February 6, 2011

The Sounds of the Church Bells   245
    Day 135—February 10, 2011

To My Sweet Valentine   253
    Day 139—February 14, 2011

Learning to Trust the Love of the Father   261
    Day 148—February 23, 2011

Preparing for the Inevitable   267
    Day 155—March 2, 2011

A Book Deal   275
    Day 158—March 5, 2011

Eyes Back on the Prize   279
    Day 170—March 17, 2011

You Must Learn the Value of

Personal ME Time   289
    Day 177—March 24, 2011

Who Decides What is Acceptable?   295
    Day 178—March 25, 2011

The Transplant   303

Sarah's Final Words   311

Kent's Final Words   315

Foreword

When Kent and Sarah Whitecotton came to pastor the little church in Webster, Ma., I knew it was going to be a challenge. I never dreamed how big of a challenge! When the news of Sarah's cancer diagnosis came my heart dropped. I knew too well the path that lay ahead. My wife is a two-time cancer survivor. I was well acquainted with the demands of time, energy, emotions, finances and faith that such a journey required. As I prayed for them and the church, I wondered if they would make it. I was concerned! I became even more concerned when Kent began to blog a journal of their journey. Going public with such private information can be dangerous. My concern began to turn to amazement as I read each day's blog. The blogs came at all hours of the day and night. He wrote every day. He wrestled with the hard questions of why, where was God in all of this, did he do something wrong to cause it. Caring for Sarah, pastoring the church, wrestling with fear and doubt; it had to be exhausting. My amazement increased as I read with interest the pen of a pastor who was in a pit... a very large pit! My utter amazement moved into respect and appreciation as their journaled journey drew me into the presence of the God who walked with them through this valley of the great shadow. The journey that became a journal has become the book you are holding. Your emotions and your faith are about to take a roller coaster ride. Read and witness the presence of the One who promised to never leave us no matter where the journey takes us!

By the way, the name of the little church in Webster is FAITH ASSEMBLY OF GOD. Who better to pastor it than a couple that walks by FAITH every moment of every day?

Rev. Robert Wise, Jr

District Superintendent

Southern New England Ministry Network

Sarah's Introduction

Ready for Something New

It is the morning of February 14, 2010. I was awakened at 5:00 a.m. with a heavy heart. Being that it is a Sunday morning, my husband was already up and getting ready for the morning church service. I asked if we could sit and talk, and he was very open to it because to my surprise, he too had a heavy heart. You see this is only two weeks before we would be celebrating our twenty-fifth wedding anniversary.

I had dreams and aspirations of where our marriage would be by this time. I had felt that we were not where we could be and that God had so much more for us. In fact, I was ready for something new. After pouring my heart out to my husband that morning, we made a commitment to grow deeper together. Neither one of us knew what to expect; all we knew is that something wonderful was happening.

That morning we both cried and hugged and looked forward to what God had in store for us as we prepared to journey into our next twenty-five years of marriage.

When we arrived at the church, right before service was to begin, a woman in the congregation came up to my husband and asked if we would be willing to renew our vows for our twenty-fifth wedding anniversary. He was almost in shock and didn't know what to say. He sent her to me to get a glimpse of my response. I too was in awe and speechless. But deep down inside, I knew this was God working. This was His way of saying, it's time to let go of the past and get ready for something new. It was an amazing feeling because my husband and I just had that intimate talk together that morning and now things are already beginning to move. Our heavenly Father had heard our cry. We had no intention in renewing our vows at this time mainly because time had gotten away from us and it just seemed like it would be an impossibility. But when God is in something, the impossible becomes the possible. We had just two weeks to put this wonderful event together.

Well, in two weeks everything fell into place. I found a beautiful gown, someone bought the cake, several people made food, we had a photographer, many people set up the hall, and we were even able to do a little dancing. It was like God had it all put together ahead of time. He was just waiting on us. His timing was perfect. It was a glorious day. I felt so beautiful and so adored by my husband. I had many people say to me that I was glowing. I could feel all the heaviness slip off of me and I felt like I was a princess. Deep inside, I knew that we were preparing to go on a new journey. I felt like my love was renewed for my husband, and that he and I could handle anything that was ahead for us. We had now moved into a new place of oneness and we were truly ready for something new. Little did we realize what that would truly entail for us.

It would only be four months later when things would begin to take a drastic turn not only in my life but in my marriage. We tend to think that when God has new things in store for us that it means exciting and awesome things that we would love and enjoy. But in God's kingdom, it could mean just the opposite.

Our lives were soon turned upside down. We first found out that I had renal cell cancer, which my only option would be the removal of my right kidney. A week before I was to have surgery,

I was informed that I also had leukemia. My emotions and my mind had a hard time consuming all of this. I was in shock at the moment, but deep inside I knew I was in for a journey that only God could help me through.

As I began my chemotherapy and later began to lose my hair, my heart just sank. But I felt a still, small voice say to me, "Sarah, be still and know that I am God. I see the bigger picture. Keep your eyes on me and trust me." After that I decided in my heart that I would take it one day at a time and allow God to give me the grace that I needed for each day.

Through this journey, I have seen God do such miraculous things that I can't help but thank Him for choosing me to be a vessel to bring them all about. So many lives have been touched and changed, including mine and my husband's. Our marriage has become stronger through all of the challenges we have faced. This may not have been what we had in mind when we first asked God to do something new in our lives, but in the end we knew that it will be even better than we could have imagined.

As I write this I want you to know that the journey is not over. I am preparing to go through the roughest part of the treatment for leukemia. I will be having a bone marrow transplant within the next few weeks. I know that God is with me and I hope to end this book by saying that He has never left me and He was faithful to the end.

Kent's Introduction

In February of 1985, I married the love of my life, and we were blessed with three wonderful boys, Brandon, Jeremiah, and Isaac. Our ministry during our married life consisted of youth ministry, music, preaching, street evangelism, training leaders, and being an assistant pastor. However, in March of 2008, Sarah and I took the full-time pastorate position at the Faith Assembly of God Church in Webster, Massachusetts, where we are currently still pastoring. This book was birthed out of our own personal suffering and trials that we went through, and it is intended to be a word of encouragement to those who are suffering now and for those who have a loved one who is suffering. Our prayer is that in the same way God ministered His Word to us that He would do the same to you.

Let's start where it all began. In August of 2010, I started preaching a series of messages at church on the subject of healing. Little did Sarah and I know at the time that it was going to be the beginning of something that was going to change our lives.

One night in the middle of my studies the Lord spoke to me to read the book of Job again. I had read Job once many years ago while I was a student at International Bible College in San Antonio, Texas. At the time I had believed that I had known just about everything there was to know about this book. Besides, Job wasn't a book about healing, it was a book about suffering, and I did not want to go there. I wanted to preach on healing, not suffering. I started reading it that night, and when I got to the seventh chapter of the book I felt I had read enough and must get back to my studies on healing. I also had felt that I understood what God wanted to say to me. How wrong I was! After finishing the seventh chapter, I turned to the book of James and wanted to study chapter five, verses thirteen through fifteen. This was going to be my opening text for Sunday. However, that is not where I turned to when I opened the book of James. Instead my finger stopped on verse 11. I read this and almost fell over on my chair, "We call them happy because they endured. You have heard of Job's patience, and you know how the Lord provided for him in the end. For the Lord is full of mercy and compassion."

This was very strange to me because of what I had just read out of the book of Job. What did God want me to know? In all my wildest dreams I did not expect God to be preparing me for what was about to come into our lives.

It all started when Sarah was making a routine doctor's visit to a new doctor that we had just switched to. During her routine physical, Sarah had told the doctor that just a few days prior to her visit she had noticed a very small amount of blood in her urine. The doctor decided that he would run some tests but seemed confident that there wasn't too much to be concerned about.

He sent her to a urologist who took X-rays, and about a month later he called us into his office for a consultation and informed us that Sarah had a large mass on her right kidney, which was diagnosed as renal cell cancer. We were shocked at first because anytime you hear the word cancer you feel fear come upon you. However, he told us that the solution was very simple, they would remove her right kidney and the problem would be solved…no worries! We were very relieved at just how simple this was going to be. She would be in the hospital for just three days and then be home recuperating for the next four to seven weeks. We can handle that. After all, people live very normal lives with just one kidney. Piece of cake!

The day had finally come for her to go to Saint Vincent's Hospital in Worcester, Massachusetts, for the lab work to be done for her surgery. Since we had nothing to worry about, I decided to send her by herself. It was then that we were given the surprise of our lives. The next morning Sarah received a call from her doctor. He wanted her to go immediately to a Hematologist, a blood specialist, for a bone marrow biopsy, and her surgery would be put off for the renal cell cancer. After seeing the Hematologist, she was told that she had leukemia and the worst kind, acute myeloid leukemia. This was on Thursday, September 23, 2010. She couldn't believe it. She immediately called me on the phone and told me the news. Her doctor wanted her to rush from the doctor's office to the University of Massachusetts Medical Hospital right then without delay to begin immediate care to save her life.

After telling me the news I was stunned...she wanted to know what she was to do. Inside I felt like a truck had just run over me. Great fear gripped my heart, and I could hardly speak to her. I knew nothing about leukemia and could not believe that cancer would have ever hit my family...but it did. I wanted to be the great protector and be able to tell her that everything was going to be fine. But I had little words to say, and the shock of the news seemed to shut me down, and I felt unable to comfort her. She wasn't crying or hysterical; she was very calm which made it worse for me. What were we supposed to do? What were we going to tell our children and our families? What about the church? Was Sarah going to live? Too many questions that had no answers were bombarding me inside. I wanted my faith to begin shouting out truth, but it too was in shock. I now know that until this journey began my faith was always frozen; it was there but never tested...at least until now.

After hearing it all, I decided to tell Sarah to come home because we were not going to do anything. After all, I was a man of faith and thought for sure at the time that I knew exactly what we were to do. I told Sarah that we would trust the Lord completely and see what He would have us do. We were believers in the divine supernatural healing power of God, and this leukemia did not take God by surprise. This to me, at the time, was a test from God to show His mighty power, and I had no doubt that we were going to receive a miracle and that miracle would bring glory and honor to God. So I thought!

So we decided to tell the doctor that we were not going to do anything, we felt that rushing out in fear would result in regret and poor decision making on our part. The doctor, of course, felt the opposite. So against her doctor's wishes Sarah came home, and we were going to wait on God.

Sarah returned home and we had the painful task of telling our loved ones that Sarah had leukemia and that there was only a thirty-three percent cure rate for this disease. I called my district pastor, Bob Wise, to inform him as to what was going on and his words of wisdom still ring in my heart to this day. He told me that God uses medicine because every good gift, according to the Word, is a gift from God. I never really saw it like that before, even though I wasn't against the use of medicines, I just preferred that God would heal her in the way that I wanted Him to. I also felt I was betraying God's Word by not requiring and waiting for a miracle; wasn't faith the key to miracles and if I have enough faith God would just heal her? Was I going too far? Was I not going far enough? I felt stuck in the middle and soon realized how strong my pride really was. Was it God that wanted to heal her or me that wanted a miracle? I tried to keep the faith and felt that if I took her to the hospital for treatment that I was doubting God. I didn't know what to do.

After talking to our family and friends and praying together, Sarah and I decided that we would bring Sarah before the church on the following Sunday for special prayer and that if nothing changed by her Tuesday doctor's appointment then we would proceed to the hospital for treatment.

Well, Sunday came and our precious church people gathered around us and prayed for her healing. We stood with tears in our eyes but strong in faith believing that God was in total control. I believe that every one of us expected a complete healing that morning; however, on Tuesday at the doctor's office we were informed that her leukemia was still there. I was disappointed a little in God. I remember thinking, Why is this leukemia still here? We prayed, believed, named it, claimed it, quoted scripture, spoke to the mountain, and rebuked the devil; everything we knew to do, we did! What could we have missed? Why is she still sick? Remember, she also still had the renal cell cancer as well; what was going on? I felt that somehow I had failed in my faith and I would now have to face this giant. But what did I have left to fight with? I did not know what to do!

I became filled with both fear and faith at the same time. What was going to happen to us? What was she going to have to endure to get this disease out of her body? And of course, my greatest fear was…would she survive this? I wanted to be strong for her, to be strong for our boys, and to be able to say without a doubt that God was going to bring her through this. I became very selfish in my heart. God had to heal her, and I gave God no choice in the matter. I only knew God as a healer; I never knew God as a sustainer. Therefore, I gave God no alternative. Looking back now, I now know why God had me read the book of Job. But what were we going to have to face? Was I going to have to lose Sarah?

From that point on God began speaking to me in a new way, different than I have ever experienced before. His voice and His words became very personal to me; they were words coming from a Father speaking to a son. I had never experienced that from God before, I had always been a little afraid to get that close to Him, because I only understood Him as this Mighty and Powerful God who demanded perfection from me, and I always seemed to fail in giving Him what I thought He wanted. I then knew that this journey was not going to be with just Sarah, our boys, and myself, but it would include closeness with our heavenly Father as well. Something amazing was beginning to unfold; we never felt such a peace like that before. A confidence rose up within both of us, so we knew from that moment on that Sarah was going to be all right.

I then felt led of the Lord to begin writing a daily journal in the form of a blog that was intended to keep our friends and family updated on Sarah's progress. Every day, at all hours of the night, I sat at my computer wrestling with God, hoping to better understand the purpose of suffering. After writing for several months I began to receive countless e-mails from all over the world of people who had experienced the same journey as I did. It was then that I was encouraged to put this blog into a book. I have never written much before nor did I have much desire to do so. But as you will hear later in the journey, God uses life's experiences to direct us into paths that He chooses for us to go. These paths become life-changing experiences that produce great godly character. God was going to send us both on a journey that would change our lives. A journey that would give Him the opportunity to reveal Himself to us in a way that we have never known before; it will be a journey of faith, trust, and hope.

In this book, I have written these experiences as they have happened in our lives. It was intended to be only a daily blog, but Sarah and I have taken some of the entries and written them in this book. I pray that it will bless you in the same manner it has blessed us.

The Beginning of a Journey

Day 1—Tuesday, September 28, 2010

The journey has officially begun for Sarah, the boys, and me. Today is the day that Sarah goes to see her doctor to be retested for leukemia. Remember, Sarah and I had made a promise to the Lord that if she tested positive for leukemia today then we would consent to the treatments in hope for a cure through medicine. We are at peace with whatever God would have for us to do.

We just returned from the doctor and the test results have said that she has the worst form of leukemia—acute myeloid leukemia. And it's still there! I couldn't believe what he said; our hearts were very heavy, and the news took my breath away. I have to admit, I expected a complete healing, but I also knew that God expected my complete trust. I was sure hoping that I could trust Him. I always thought I did, but that trust was never really tested like it is being tested right now. What choice is He giving me? I have always been able to trust Him but it was always with little things. Now I have to give Him, Sarah, and I am not really as confident as I wish I could be. Why Sarah? Why Sarah?

After getting the news we were told that they wanted her to be at the University of Massachusetts Medical Hospital first thing tomorrow morning to begin immediate chemotherapy. I know that starting today I will be forced to search my faith with all my heart. My heart is broken and I feel despair in my spirit; however, I have never been let down by God once in my entire life and I know that it will not begin here. My faith is being tested, and I will remain faithful.

During the past week I have learned that the healing process of God takes on many different avenues. There are instant miracles and they cause us to rejoice in God, and there are also healings through the medical profession, and this also causes us to rejoice in God. I know that to go through the process of healing will require much more faith and trust than a miracle will need, but the experience will become life changing. I also know that to be able to trust the words of God during trials is the ultimate act of love, faith, and commitment on our part. I am willing to do it or at least try to. I ask the Lord to please give me greater faith.

I am reminded that like Job, we seldom, if ever, get to choose what we go through in this life. I have asked myself several questions today like, Is it fair that as Christians we are never asked to suffer? Is it fair that we would rather that others suffer instead of us? Can we say that when we do suffer that God has forsaken us? The answer is, "No!" For God to allow us to go through suffering and trials becomes His way to test our faith and allow faith to be perfected in us. It also opens up our ears and hearts to those who suffer around us.

Sarah and I are prepared for tomorrow, although we wished there was another way out of this, we have decided that we will go forward with the power and authority of His Word, which is filled with very precious promises. The surrender to proceed for the treatment is not a white flag; however, we are certain God will bring us to the fulfillment of all His promises. He will not forsake us or His Word! He will never leave us alone, and sorrow may last for a day or two, but joy comes in the morning!

I am writing this today in faith! Knowing that my God is with Sarah and He will guide her through this unknown journey that's ahead. In the process we will become more like Him in every way and our Father has our permission to guide us through to the end.

Tomorrow is going to be here before you know it. The family right now is very quiet and trying hard to encourage one another; no one knows what to expect, and it just seems easier to stay busy so you don't have to think about it. We are not really sure what to say to each other, and a few times I have seen our boys fighting to hold back the tears. I know they are afraid. So am I!

Sarah is upstairs packing for a five- to six-week hospital stay away from all the things she loves; away from her boys; her family; her dog, Toby; and away from her church. She is extremely worried about the church. She loves them so much and knows just how much they love her. What will happen next? We do not know. We do not even know if she will survive. We have all heard the horror stories of the effects of chemo and pray to God that she does not have to go through that nightmare. It is going to be a very long journey.

Having to put Sarah's bags in the car tomorrow and then drive her to the hospital is going to be unbelievably hard for me to do. Yet tomorrow morning at 8:00 a.m., I will have to do this. I feel like I am abandoning her and leaving her alone. It is awful to think about. We feel the helplessness of the situation.

It is times like this when I find my secret place with God and get a word of the Lord that is for me. I am left with no answer, no solutions, and no great ideas. God has seen fit to allow us a journey that will only require faith and trust on our part. There will be no secret cures or magic potions. She is left to the mercy of medicine and prayer. For the first time in my Christian life I can't intervene in the plan, I am left helpless and at the mercy of God alone. It is here in this passage of scripture God spoke to my heart and reminded me that my eyes must stay on His Words.

> My child, pay attention to what I say. Listen to my words.
> Never let them get away from you. Remember them and
> keep them in your heart.
>
> Proverbs 4:20-21

When you do not know what to do and all you have is faith, you are brought into another world. I have heard all the Bible stories and listened to the miracles that others have experienced. But now Sarah and I have to stand on them ourselves for perhaps the first time in our lives. This passage is so important to remember, because it is foundational to my faith in God. I am first instructed to listen and pay attention to what is being said to me. It is easy to get sidetracked and miss what God wants to tell me. Fear will do that to you. There can be no greater truth spoken than what comes directly out of God's Word. Sometimes it takes the Holy Spirit to open our eyes to see what God is saying to us. The Word spoken is already breathing and only when placed in the heart can they be kept safe from being forgotten. Verse 22 tells me just how important these words are:

Proverbs 4:22:

> They will give life and health to anyone who understands
> them.

For those who receive them in the way for which they are given, it brings powerful change to them. Imagine words so powerful that it can bring to you health and life just by understanding them. I must believe! I have to take God's Word seriously as if He was talking directly to me. This is important to do.

> Be careful how you think; your life is shaped by your
> thoughts. Never say anything that isn't true. Have nothing
> to do with lies and misleading words. Look straight ahead
> with honest confidence; don't hang your head in shame.
> Plan carefully what you do, and whatever you do will turn
> out right.
>
> Proverbs 4:23-26

Whenever you are obeying God's Word you will always hear other voices around you, you have to be careful not to be led in the wrong place by those who do not know the Lord. My obedience to His Word will be seen in my actions and in the words that I speak forth. It is easy to speak against the promises of God and not realize it.

> Avoid evil and walk straight ahead. Don't go one step off the right way.
>
> Proverbs 4:27

This is the final word of instruction here. Evil talking is always talking against the Word of God. It is rooted in unbelief and will quickly make void all the promises of the word God had given to you. Although we do not know what to do, we do know that God is the One we want to trust.

No one really ever realizes just why we go through the things we go through in life. Sometimes we are left confused because God never really tells us what is coming. He just asks for our simple faith and trust and our obedience to His Word to get through.

I will not pretend that I know Sarah's outcome, because I do not. Neither am I sure that I will be able to hold on to all of God's promises. But I will try hard to. What do you do when the hope runs out? Can you still believe in the promises? I believe you can.

I have a promise from God that this journey will change my life and I have to become willing to obey today...right now... to obey and do so without any doubt. I have nothing more than the promises of God; that should be enough. It seems fitting that God wants to test our faith, and tomorrow we will find out just how much testing we will have to go through.

So, when you read a promise in His Word, begin to react like you hit the medical jackpot. Write it down, quote it every day, keep it in your heart and mind. And never doubt His promise...just wait for it! The absolute worst thing is to quit and give up hope.

Always Remember God is Watching over His Word

Day 2—September 29, 2010

This is it...the journey of the unknown has begun. I was up early this morning and helplessly took Sarah's bags out to the car. I slept in my bed last night while my mind raced most of the night hoping that this was all a bad dream. I awoke constantly praying for her and asking God to be with her. Not knowing what to expect is the worst part of any journey, and the idea of just trusting God can be fuzzy at times. Today was the first time I broke down and cried for her! I was supposed to be the one who was bringing strength to Sarah, and it was me, not her, that seems to be having difficulty in holding things together. But I am all right now thanks to the peace I see on Sarah's face; it is the face of an angel.

I drove the forty minute drive into the city of Worcester, and we arrived at UMass Memorial Hospital at 8:00 a.m. to meet with Doctor Nath at the clinic. He took his time and explained everything that Sarah was going to have to go through. Even though he spoke with such confidence and kindness, he gave us no promises of a cure and informed us that her treatments would be very hard physically. I kept looking at Sarah for a response, but she said very little. I know that she was expecting me to be the one who asked all the right questions for her, so I did my best to do that. After our one hour consultation, I had nothing else to say, so I asked Dr. Nath if I could pray over him. After all, Sarah's life was going to be in his hands, and I wanted God to help him. I prayed a simple prayer of faith, asking that God would bless this man and be with him in his care for Sarah. I prayed that God would be with his staff and those patients who really needed him. So many hurting people are being left into his hands, and I knew it must be a difficult place to be for him at times. After praying for him I felt better knowing that I was able to bless this man like this. He then thanked me for the prayer and told us that he would do his best.

When our meeting was over, we were sent to the eighth floor of the university hospital. We took elevator C as high up as it could go onto a very lonely and quiet floor. Once pushing the button to release the secured doors we walked onto the bone marrow transplant unit. It was a very scary place. There were only eight rooms there, and each room was isolated and shut up so that no one could see inside. I then felt the fear that I am sure that other patients feel when they arrive. I knew that leukemia was a lonely disease that brought much uncertainty. I was very nervous watching them prepare Sarah for the treatments. I remember feeling afraid that I might never see her again, but I remembered God's Word! That wonderful, trustworthy Word of God that has never failed me yet. I immediately took time to re-focus on His Truth and His love for us; by doing so I would gain much needed strength and faith, without it the only option would be to be sucked into fear, and I hate that place, so I chose to stay focused.

It is during these times that it is very easy to allow yourself to be afraid or to not understand why God is allowing you to go through these things. At times I needed Him to speak to me with a revelation or a voice that sounds like thunder. But I know He will not do that! Not for me or for you. The reason why is because he has already done that in His Word; that Word He spoke is so powerful that to repeat it again would be useless. His Word is His very voice speaking to you and me, and what He said then He means now, and you and I do not need anything more than what He has already spoken. God wants to reveal that very Word to us through our spirit and it is to be received by faith. Only when we are left without a choice can we at times see what He is able to accomplish.

This is the reason that we must make time to just sit and wait in His Word. It is these times that God shows us or reveals to us a scripture verse and the Holy Spirit says, "That's for you!" In Jeremiah chapter one, verse twelve you see God speaking. "You are right," the LORD said, "and I am watching to see that my words come true." Do you know what you just read? God just said that He is watching to see that His words come true!

God's Word is filled with promises from the Lord, and this one is one that God used to speak to me today. What a great promise from God for the start of any journey! God tells us that He is watching to see that His Words come true. This is why we must seek revelation from His Word every single day so that we have ammunition to fight doubt and discouragement.

Now, I am sure that when Jeremiah was hearing the Lord he was afraid and unsure and uncertain too, just like we are today. But God used His Word to assure him that what He said would come to pass, and He will do that for you and me as well. His Word becomes living in us as soon as we believe it.

Today, I am also asking God to use this journey in our lives and to open doors of ministry to the hurting here. After Sarah got settled in her room, I went home to be with the boys; in a few hours I will be going to see Sarah again. On the way to that floor are people who are there to visit loved ones or to care for them, and they too are hurting and afraid. I pray that God will not allow me to have blinders on and think only of myself as I

The LORD is my light and my salvation; I will fear no one. The LORD protects me from all danger; I will never be afraid.

Psalm 27:1

It is so wonderful to know that the Bible says 365 times to not be afraid, enough for every day of the year.

If you were to come here for a visit you would be unable to bring flowers or fruit. You may also have to wear a mask and rubber gloves. And you would not be allowed to visit if you were sick in any way. So, many of these patients feel the isolation the moment they hear the wooden door lock shut. But they need you, they need you to care to touch and encourage them.

I have many times wished that it was me going through this rather than Sarah, but I now believe that it is much harder to watch a loved one suffer than to suffer yourself. I can only imagine how difficult it was for God to watch His Son giving His life for us.

Learning to be Thankful

Day 5—October 2, 2010

We probably had nearly a hundred phone calls along with e-mails and posts from our friends on Facebook, all encouraging us and praying with us. We need this! People who go through suffering need to know that you're out there even if we seem too tired to listen. Many sick are abandoned when journeys go on too long, and I feel that before this journey is over that Sarah and I will also experience this. I noticed that the majority of patients on this floor do not have many visitors. Not sure why. Maybe the journey has gotten too long and it has become too difficult to bear. I pray this is not the case, because this is a hard journey to go at alone.

Inside the deepest part of my heart I am afraid, even though God is constantly pushing my eyes to see what His Word says. I have become confident that if I will see His Word, believe His Word, and act on His Word that I will receive the daily strength to help Sarah and I through this journey.

Here is my word of strength for today:

> Whoever offers thanks as a sacrifice honors me. I will let everyone who continues in my way see the salvation that comes from God.
>
> Psalm 50:23

This passage is one about honor. To truly honor God is to believe in every word that He speaks. If you and I honestly believe that the words that are spoken in His Book are true, then no matter what we face, we will offer thanks to Him in advance in the form of a sacrifice. In God's eyes, that is how we honor Him. How important it is for us to thank God no matter what the situation is. Many only thank Him when they are doing well and when things go in their favor...this is not at all the case for this scripture. David said that we were to offer thanks as a sacrifice to God and in doing so we would honor Him. But sacrifices are always costly. Costly because they are to be given in faith; it is to be done before we get what we are seeking. It was also to be done regardless of how our circumstances were going or what the outcome would be. Think about this, have you been able to thank Him before you knew the outcome? To thank your Heavenly Father that He is watching over you or your loved one? Thank Him even if you go through loss or devastation? This is the only kind of sacrifice that will honor God. I often used to think that every situation had to turn out the way I wanted it to and then I was able to praise the Lord for the outcome. But learning to praise God for the storm you're in is hard to do and requires a faith that is true!

Have you ever thanked Him for your healing before He healed you? Or, what about thanking Him when you do not get what you were hoping for? That is the very step of faith that He wants us to have. Why? Because when we believe His Word we believe Him! When we trust Him, we honor Him. We sometimes want that instant miracle, but by God allowing us to go through the trial or the suffering our faith becomes stronger and it is perfected. He is God in the storm! Stand on those promises He gave you; your faith will push the Word of God into reality! I too speak this in faith. I know now that Sarah's outcome is ordered of the Lord. Do I believe in her healing? Every day! But I also trust where He chooses to take us...even if it ends in death. In death, my Father will take her home to be with Him, and there can be no better place. The thoughts of this are real right now, but it is settled in my heart that God is her Father and He cares for her.

I am well aware that I might not have the outcome I want. There are times I must admit that I feel that if God does not heal her in the manner that I want Him to, then God would have failed me. I have walked into her room when it was filled with doctors and specialists and nurses thinking that they are going to turn around and say, "It's a miracle…she is healed!" But is this God's will for us? If this was to happen will faith become totally perfected in all other areas of our lives? That is why I must keep my eyes on something more than just complete healing. God may have plans to do something even greater. He may intend on bringing us on a life-changing journey that will bring more honor and glory to Him than we think or understand. I have to trust Him for that!

I cannot believe what powerful promises have been given to us from His Word so far! And that is exactly how God wants us to see His Word. Do you trust what His Word says to you? It is written to you and to me, and God wants me to see it as His very voice speaking to me. He says, "Do not be afraid, Kent…I am with you, Kent! I will keep you and I will watch over Sarah! Therefore offer me praise and in return I will show you my salvation!" You can make His Word personal, because it is personal!

You see, I have been given His Word, and that Word will come to pass and when I praise God in advance for that fulfillment of His Word, then the devil cannot steal it away from me. My thanks are what waters the promises, defeats the enemies of fear and unbelief, and releases the Word to live in me! So, I thank Him for this trial of faith and I trust Him to bring me through for the glory of God.

There is another part to that verse I just quoted to you, and it is very important that you don't miss what it says. God always blesses sacrifice! The great thing about sacrifice is that God will always give you something in exchange for what you give. This Word promises you something in exchange for your thanks. Look at the last part of Psalm 50:23, "I will let everyone who continues in my way see the salvation that comes from God." God says that if you will continue in His way, the way of gratitude, then He would allow you in exchange to see the salvation that comes from God. What a great and precious promise we have here! My sacrifice of thanks gets in return the salvation that comes from God, Himself. He said I will get to see it! This salvation may come in different ways than you expect; however, they will be glorious because they will come from Him. There are great rewards for faithfulness during struggles!

I know that these words are encouraging, but like Sarah, you are still surrounded by your circumstances, and I promised myself that I would be honest with everyone about what I was feeling when I started writing. So I will tell you right now exactly how Sarah and I are doing as well as our children. It is hard! Our entire lives have been turned upside down. Things that were important aren't so important anymore. Life has taken on a new meaning. There is both fear and faith at work all the time, but never, not once have we doubted the purpose and plan of God for our lives. He is and will always be our Father and never will we back away from that. We know His eyes are always watching us to work in us His purpose and plan. But we are still very afraid. No one seems to be able to guarantee that Sarah will be all right. She is hooked up to so many machines and confined to her room. There is no socialization except with the medical staff. When I visit I do not know what to say. Our boys are afraid that we are not telling them everything and constantly ask to pray together. Isaac is looking up scriptures and calling Sarah to encourage her with the promises of God. This journey we are on is the pits! I wish it would end and we could bring Sarah home. There, I said it!

I am saying this because in some journeys it is not supposed to be easy. Lessons are never learned on easy street. They are learned through tough and difficult situations. As hard as it is, we must remain faithful to His Word. We have little choice. You either have faith or fear, and we are choosing faith. This is when my thanks is given to God, not while it is all going well, but when I am uncertain and afraid. I thank Him for what He is doing in us even when I am unsure and afraid. Our trials and fears will last a while and there will be days when we are afraid of what is happening, but we still praise Him for who He is. The outcome has nothing to do with how we must see His faithfulness.

I will share with you some of the difficulties I have personally faced so far: Starting today hardships really began to show. I went grocery shopping for the first time in twenty-five years. Sarah had always taken such good care of us, and besides, she loved to shop. But while shopping I felt broken inside...alone...I felt so abandoned and afraid. Feelings had surrounded me while in the store. Even though there were people shopping all around me I felt afraid. Many thoughts ran through my mind, and knowing that my best friend was not going to be home when I got there made it harder to want to go home. I wondered if Sarah was all right; what if something went wrong with the chemotherapy? What if I never see her again? I was fighting the tears as I pushed the shopping cart down each aisle. I tried to shop and in a way that would honor her. I bought the things she bought. I even checked the receipt for mistakes, because that is something she always did. But I hurt inside. I questioned whether or not I was honoring God by having these feelings. I wanted to be a super Christian and never have these thoughts, but I wasn't. I was just Kent Whitecotton, husband of Sarah, and father to Brandon, Jeremiah, and Isaac. I felt vulnerable and weak. I didn't want anyone to know that I was having these emotions, but I was. I am afraid inside!

The second thing that happened was exhaustion. You get tired of hearing from everyone. I had to tell the whole story of what is going on a hundred times a day. You get bogged down with everything and you become unsure of who to talk to. You begin screening your calls because you hate to repeat the story all over again. Sound familiar?

You also hear from people who want to give you advice and counsel. I call them the friends of Job, and if you have read the life of Job you will understand what I am talking about. In fact, I received an e-mail from a dear friend. She informed us that this sickness will be healed as soon as we deal with the offence that caused it. I was a little offended to hear this. I began to question God, "Is all sickness a result of sin?" Or does God use it to punish those who have issues or wrong concepts in their lives? If this was totally true would not the whole world be sick? Now I do believe that there are sins that cause sickness, but how do you explain the sickness of Job other than God wanting to test Job? God Himself said that he was perfect, yet God had little to no problem in allowing Satan to afflict him.

In suffering you will have two choices: (1) to trust God and believe for the fulfillment of His Word, (2) or to become angry and bitter towards God and others, and to lose your faith. In the case of Job, we find that it was God who brought up Job's sinless life to Satan. He said, "Have you considered my 'servant' Job?" Why did God do this? It was like God sent Job out and ordered His suffering. But God did this for a greater purpose, one that honored both God and Job. He knew Job's faith would stand. You may not understand why God allows sickness or even death, but I know that His plan is always perfect. Does He want to heal? Yes! But through sickness we have the opportunity to push our faith to the front and show the world that even though I am sick, I will not deny Him. This kind of faith is the highest level of faith that we can give to God and for God to ask this of us is not punishment, but honor. Such was Job's case!

God never once said that Job had sinned or that there were issues in His life that needed to be dealt with. He tested Job to show His own mercy and compassion. Was it hard? Discouraging?

Fearful? Yes! You see, there are Christians all over the world who are imprisoned, put to death, tortured, and mistreated. Did God forsake them? No! But the world has been unable to shake the faith of those who truly love Him; regardless of what they are asked to go through they remain faithful to the end.

The third thing that has happened to us is that at 3:00 p.m. this afternoon Sarah got very sick and had severe pain; they had to give her morphine to help her. She told me that she literally thought that she was going to die. Unfortunately, this is what cancer patients both young and old have to cope with, and their loved ones suffer too! They are the ones forced to watch and are unable to do anything. I find it easy to have the great faith (or at least think I have great faith) that I spoke about when everything was going well. But it becomes very difficult to believe fully when things are not going so well. What if I would have lost her? I felt like I could relate to David when he spoke this psalm. "My heart is sorely pained within me: all the terrors of death are fallen upon me. Fearfulness and trembling are come upon me, and horror has overwhelmed me" (Psalm 55:4-5, kjv).

I am saying this because I know there are those who can relate. I am not trying to be mean because no one is intentionally trying to discourage me. They want to help, but I think sometimes we are misguided when it comes to what God is doing. This is reality not just for Sarah and I, but for thousands all around us. Over 127 people die every single day in the US from cancer. Leukemia is the number one killer disease for children. Sickness affects everyone. It hurts the whole family. Everyone cries inside and worries regardless of where their faith is. This is why we need the Word of God and the encouragement of others so much. His Word is His way of comforting us, and Jesus sent the Holy Spirit to reveal the Word of the Lord to us during these times. I have found that by writing this journal it has become the constant reminder of His promises to my family.

Sarah and I will offer daily sacrifice of thanks, today and every day. We will do it when we are hurting and we will do it when we are rejoicing. He will perfect this Word in us through our trial and we will see His salvation! Oh, great is His faithfulness to all generations!

Faith Tested Becomes Great Faith

Day 6—October 3, 2010

We have made it through the first six days of our journey. It may not seem long to you, but to Sarah and me it feels like forever. Our boys seem to be holding out pretty well, none of us know exactly what is going to be next, so every day has become precious to us. I have noticed that the boys seem to be quieter, more concerned about each other's feelings and of course still very worried about their mother. It has been nice watching them come together and help each other take up the slack for their mother not being here.

We all went to see Sarah last night, and she looked so beautiful sitting in her chair all cozy in her flannel pajamas. Her smile gleaned ear to ear as she hugged me and each of the boys, of course being careful not to get too close. She was hooked up to a lot of monitors and machines, and the boys and I were relieved that she was in such good spirits. I watched as each of the boys took pictures of themselves standing next to her; she seemed so proud of her boys; they were all becoming young men and I know that Sarah felt what I felt as they hugged her and took the pictures. Leaving was hard to do last night, maybe harder for Sarah than for me. As we gathered our things and said our good-byes, we all seemed to know that she was going to be fine. But I was going back to the familiar and she had to stay not knowing what to do expect.

The boys and I headed to the elevators and walked outside, laughing and happy. As we got near the parking garage we turned around and could see Sarah's room on the eighth floor. Although we could not make her out we knew she was watching us because the curtains were moving. I had tears of joy in my eyes and wondered just what she must have been feeling. Was she crying? Was she sad? Was she happy? Too often she really never shows her feelings, but tonight I think she was very happy.

Today will be the first Sunday that I will be attending church without Sarah; I hope I will be able to keep my focus on what God wants to do in the service. We will have to struggle through our worship time because she was our worship leader and it's hard when someone you depend on for so much no longer is able to be there; after all, Sarah was my biggest supporter; she laughed at all my jokes and always encouraged me with kind words when the service was over. Boy, is today going to be difficult to get through! I am hoping to see her immediately after the service is over; Marlene Ogden has offered to do the service tonight so that I can be with Sarah. When I see Sarah I know she will ask a lot of questions about how the service went. Trials are never easy; like many of you, I too hate trials and testings. This one is especially hard because it involves someone I adore with all my heart. Sarah has been what I lean on in life. She has blessed my life with her passion for Christ, her love for music, and the fact that everyone who ever meets her finds a best friend. I believe this is why God has raised up people all over the world to pray for her... people like you! We have received countless e-mails and postings on Facebook telling us that you are praying. So many from all over the world and from people we never met. We even received an e-mail from one of my heroes in the faith, David Wilkerson.

My mother-in-law e-mailed him a prayer request for Sarah and he sent us a personal e-mail in which he told us of his own family struggles with sufferings. His wife and daughters had all struggled with cancer and he now has a grandson with stage four cancer. He reminded me to remind God of all his promises and to never give up. It was then that I knew that God was no respecter of persons. You do not get to choose what you go through, but you do get to choose your attitude and your level of faith.

Her first rounds of chemo are almost over and so far Sarah feels great. After she has completed her first round they will allow her body to respond. After a few days they expect that she will bottom out physically and because we are unsure exactly what that means we wanted to keep praying for her. They are also very concerned still about her right kidney and hope that somehow the growth on her kidney is related to the leukemia so that this treatment might just treat them both. But they are not sure.

God is in control and His Word is working in her, and like the scripture in Jeremiah 1:12 says, "He watches over His Word to make sure it comes to pass!" This promise excites me so much I just want to shout! My Father is watching Sarah; she is on heaven's watch list! God has ordered it from His Word. Even when your faith struggles or freezes up, you still are able to rely on the promises of God's Word. What great power His Word releases when we hold on to them. And there will be times that you will feel yourself doubting His promises due to things that you are told and things you see and feel. So just remember this great promise in what Paul said to Timothy:

> If we are not faithful, he remains faithful, because he cannot be false to himself.
>
> 2 Timothy 2:13

He is who He is no matter what! His Word is going to win in the end, and we will do our best not give the devil one opportunity to say that we shrank back in our faith! God has triumphed!

For those who are walking this journey with us, I want to share one of the most important verses in all of scripture that you must try to remember. It is found in Peter's first epistle. The apostle speaks of the necessity of having our faith tested:

> Be glad about this, even though it may now be necessary for you to be sad for a while because of the many kinds of trials you suffer. Their purpose is to prove that your faith is genuine. Even gold, which can be destroyed, is tested by fire; and so your faith, which is much more precious than gold, must also be tested, so that it may endure. Then you will receive praise and glory and honor on the Day when Jesus Christ is revealed.
>
> 1 Peter 1:6-7

This passage is very powerful, yet overlooked by many who are going through trials. Testing is very important for the purifying of body, soul, and spirit; without it we never are able to become completely Christ-like and therefore unable to bring the kingdom of God to earth. Peter said this testing was more precious than gold tried with fire, and it brought praise, honor, and glory to Jesus Christ. Fire purifies and removes all impurities. When finished it multiplies itself in value and purpose. It becomes an asset to the one who owns it. The testing will also give you the ability to stand in coming adversity. Much like David was able to do when he faced Goliath. Because he had killed the lion and the bear, David was able to know that he could stand against Goliath. Testing and trials, prepare you for great victories.

It is always important to know that God is not a merciless dictator who demands our love, quite the opposite, in fact. It honors God when we give Him our love and it honors Him more when we trust Him when suffering. The fact is, suffering ranks you in a special class of the great men and women of God; read Hebrews 11 and look at the lives of all the apostles. Paul said that those who suffer with Him shall also reign with Him. Paul understood that suffering would rid him of his sinful flesh and prepare him for the service of God. That is why it is important that you keep your heart and eyes on the Lord; your trial may be preparing you for His work. Great things can be produced in our lives if we will understand that God is still the One who is in control.

So, God is not going to ever use sickness as a method of forcing you to obedience, but like Jonah He very well might send you through a storm to redirect the path that you're on.

Remember that when Job was tried by God we see that God tells us exactly how He saw Job:

> "Did you notice my servant Job?" the LORD asked. "There is no one on earth as faithful and good as he is. He worships me and is careful not to do anything evil."

> Job 1:8

Look at the very words of Job:

> I have never trusted in riches or taken pride in my wealth. I have never worshiped the sun in its brightness or the moon in all its beauty. I have not been led astray to honor them by kissing my hand in reverence to them. Such a sin should be punished by death; it denies Almighty God. I have never been glad when my enemies suffered, or pleased when they met with disaster; I never sinned by praying for their death. All those who work for me know that I have always welcomed strangers. I invited travelers into my home and never let them sleep in the streets. Others try to hide their sins, but I have never concealed mine. I have never feared what people would say; I have never kept quiet or stayed indoors because I feared their scorn. Will no one listen to what I am saying? I swear that every word is true. Let Almighty God answer me. If the charges my opponent brings against me were written down so that I could see them, I would wear them proudly on my shoulder and place them on my head like a crown. I would tell God everything I have done, and hold

my head high in his presence. If I have stolen the land I farm and taken it from its rightful owners—if I have eaten the food that grew there but let the farmers that grew it starve—then instead of wheat and barley, may weeds and thistles grow.

Job 31:24-40

Not only does God lack a problem with Job, but we see that Job himself can't find what he could have possibly done to warrant this suffering. But none the less it is God that tells Satan in Job 1:8 that Job was His servant, there was none like him, he was perfect and upright and he feared God and hated evil. God is literally bragging about Job to Satan.

However, Satan wasn't so sure of Job's true commitment; after all anyone will serve God when everything is given to him. So God allows Satan to take Job on a journey that tested every part of Job's life. God also knew that this journey would forever alter the life of Job.

I have heard many people ask me, "Why Sarah?" They say, "Of all people, why her?" Maybe it is because God sees a bigger picture for her than we see. The trying of her faith is going to produce something of greater value when the testing is completed. Maybe this is not meant to be bad but to produce good in her.

Now understand I do believe that there are those who suffer as a result of sin, but Job was not the case of that. Sin has consequences! These consequences could result in severe suffering and even death. That is why you must search your heart when the trial begins and seek the Lord to find out what the purpose of this trial is. If it was caused by sin, then only true repentance can change the outcome. This type of sickness may be God's last resort in trying to bring you to true repentance, so you must seek the Lord earnestly.

We also must remember that sickness takes a lot of time to get through. It's not like a cold that you will get over in a few days; it could last years. The reason for this is when it is over there is little guarantee that you will return to life the way it use to be. So, why does God allow this? Because change is difficult for all of us, and ridding ourselves of the barriers of the flesh is even more difficult. The result of suffering faithfully will allow a greater increase and release in faith and enable your life to find greater and deeper meaning and fulfillment. At the start of Job's journey he questioned God, and at the end of the journey he says,

> In the past I knew only what others had told me, but now I have seen you with my own eyes.
>
> Job 42:5

This was the transformation that Job received as the reward for his suffering. He came into a revelation of God, a place where God is not just believed by explanation. He is believed by visitation. Job saw the true nature and character of God! There is a difference between the Jesus that walked on the earth and the Jesus that is seated in heavenly places. One is earthly and physical and visible by our senses. The other is a resurrected Christ that goes from the physical to the spiritual. This can only be revealed through revelation. It is usually suffering that brings us into this revelation of His glory. Paul said that we are seated in heavenly places with Christ Jesus. To totally understand this; we must be given a deeper spiritual revelation and that can only be done when the flesh is subdued and in subjection to the spirit. If you really desire to know God, He might just have to bring you through suffering.

I do not know why journeys need to take as long as some do, but I do know that those who keep their faith receive great grace from God both during and after the testing. And when the journey ends they walk in a new realm of faith that others do not understand.

Keep your eyes on Him and all His promises. His plan for you is not over; it is just beginning. I know that the doctors may have told you one thing, but God says you will live! His promises are powerful and He will never forget what He has told you. I challenge you to believe, doubt your doubts, and trust His Word. He will bring it to pass!

Learning to Know God's Character

Day 13—October 10, 2010

Take a look at these wonderful promises for us today:

> He brought me forth also into a large place; he delivered me, because he delighted in me.
>
> Psalm 18:19 (KJV)

> I sought the LORD, and he heard me, and delivered me from all my fears.
>
> Psalm 34:4 (KJV)

> He sent his word, and healed them, and delivered them from their destructions.
>
> Psalm 107:20 (KJV)

> For I know that my redeemer liveth, and that he shall stand at the latter day upon the earth.
>
> Job 19:25 (KJV)

There is no better way to start your day than to hear the Word of the Lord. It is God's way to prepare you for whatever you are going to have to face that day.

Well, it's been thirteen days and Sarah seems to be doing very well today. She is still very weak due to a low blood count, but nonetheless, the Father is watching over her and He has been there every moment of every day. It's hard at times visiting her because she tries so hard to put up a strong front and I know she is tired and weary; thirteen days can seem like months when you're sick. I try to understand just how much she needs to rest, so I make my visits as special as I can.

Tonight the boys and I are all going up to see her, because this is a special day. Today is our son, Jeremiah's nineteenth birthday. Nineteen years ago, today, my wife gave birth to our second son who came a month early. Due to this early arrival he was forced to have to stay in the NICU for two extra weeks. I remember how hard it was for Sarah to see her little boy suffering and so very helpless. I feel many times it is the way God sees us when we are hurting, so helpless and in need of Him. It was hard for Sarah to leave the hospital and go home without this precious little guy. I remember waking up to her getting ready extra early, so that she could go and be with him. Now, nineteen years later he is the tallest in the family, so I know Sarah is excited to be able to see him.

Too many people have such a wrong concept of our Father and therefore it takes a long time for them to understand God's plan for them. This is why so many of us do not understand the purpose and meaning of trials and sufferings. We assume that God has dropped the ball on us or is punishing us for something we have done. It is a reason why many will fail to follow God or trust Him. Now, I do not understand all the ways of God when it comes to suffering, like why do children have diseases and die, or why do car accidents take away the people we love. I do not have your answers for that. But we have to by faith develop an attitude of trust in the Lord. What we go through He is able to use and He is able to sustain us to get through it.

When the children of Israel were in the wilderness, they had a wrong concept of God; even Moses had one. They saw God as angry and powerful. He brought fear to them. Moses himself at one time said he too was afraid of God. But one day God allowed Moses to be given a true revelation of who God was. God led him to the cleft of a rock and allowed him to look through to see His hind parts as He passed by. Moses saw His glory and that vision never left him. He saw God in a way that changed His life. That cleft and that experience represented the revelation of Jesus Christ. God sent to us, Jesus, to show us His true nature. He wanted us through Jesus, to understand His love, His mercy, and His compassion for His people. Jesus became the message from the Father to the world. When Jesus healed the sick He was showing them the Father's heart concerning their sickness. He spoke in love and not wrath, so that the world would see that God wanted them to know that He loved them and that He was moved by their sufferings.

In John 14:8-9, Philip said to Him, "Lord, show us the Father; that is all we need." Jesus answered, "For a long time I have been with you all; yet you do not know me, Philip? Whoever has seen me has seen the Father." You see, Jesus came to show us exactly what the Father was like. God wanted to show us through Jesus that He cared and that He loved them. Wrong concepts allowed people to see the side of God based on what they thought. But Jesus said, "This is how God is…Just like me!"

David, in Psalm 145:7-9, had a revelation and understanding of God's true nature. "The Lord is gracious," he said. This is God saying that He wants to touch you and meet your needs. He is not angry! Before true healing can begin you must understand His nature. He wants to heal not because He is all powerful, but because He loves you. Nowhere in scripture does it say God is power, but it does say God is love and full of compassion. Even when suffering is allowed by God it is under His watchful eye.

Another thought from the above scripture tells us that God is "Full of compassion." Compassion has an awesome meaning: "to suffer with another." In other words, He feels your pain with you. Your hurt is His hurt. In Isaiah 53 it reads, "In all their affliction he was afflicted." He demonstrated this through His death on the cross. There is great comfort for Sarah and me knowing that our Lord suffers with us. He gives us the strength we need when we need it. We do not always understand why He doesn't just heal, but we do know that when we go though something it allows us to be tested by fire. Do you want to be useable in His kingdom? "Then count it all joy when you go through testing and trials because they produce godly character in you" (James 1).

All through scripture it reads how Jesus was moved with compassion and healed all their illnesses and diseases. He is moved with compassion over your suffering!

> As he saw the crowds, his heart was filled with pity for them, because they were worried and helpless, like sheep without a shepherd. So he said to his disciples, "The harvest is large, but there are few workers to gather it in. Pray to the owner of the harvest that he will send out workers to gather in his harvest."
>
> Matthew 9:36-38

You should never think that God could ever abandon you. You are His love and He has set His affection on you. So, before you go on from here I challenge you to place your hope back in His love.

Remember the leper came to Jesus in Mark 1. He said to Jesus, "If it be thy will, you can make me whole." This is such the faith of the church today. They do not know how much the Lord wants to touch them. Jesus said to him, "It is my will!" And the scripture said that Jesus touched him! Why? Compassion! Jesus knew that his critics were watching. Jesus also knew the law concerning leprosy. No one would ever touch one who was considered so unclean and so useless and helpless. Yet He still touched him! Why? Compassion!

Too many are facing suffering alone while the church plays the game of caring for one another without touching them. Listen, when someone is suffering, your calls matter; your prayers are urgent; your faith is required; but your touch is what gives them the most hope. Oh, that we might care more and learn to touch!

Yesterday, while sitting with Sarah the Lord allowed me to see something and I saw the words, "I am with you always." They were the words I wrote on Sarah's marker board the first day she arrived at the hospital. The words I am really spoke out to me. It was the same words that God spoke to Moses when Moses asked God, "Who shall I tell them sent me?" God said, "Tell them 'I Am sent you!'" There can be no greater comfort than knowing that "I Am" is with you! To all of you who are suffering, "I Am" said He would never leave you!

Avoiding the Pitfalls of the Pit

Day 16—October 13, 2010

It's 4:00 a.m. and I am up because I could not sleep. Having to adjust to sleeping alone has been difficult especially with the uncertainty of what Sarah is going through. Sarah now has to suffer through some of the effects of the chemotherapy. She is extremely tired and her hair has begun falling out. This is the part that most people with cancer fear the most. It becomes the evidence of cancer to those who go through it, and it can be devastating for anyone, especially a woman. I know that Sarah was praying earnestly that God would spare her from this, but the Lord has decided to allow her to go through it.

She is now in the full effects of the chemo and is very exhausted. She told me that she doesn't want to have anyone visit her, including me, until she feels better. We were told these things would come, but were praying they wouldn't. We have also gotten her test results from the sonogram and it shows that the cancer on her kidney is unchanged. They were hoping that the chemotherapy would treat both cancers, but it has not. It is another day to refocus on the Lord.

I keep thinking of the scripture that says, "Shall the clay say to him that formed it, 'what are you making?'" (Isaiah 45:9). It's hard to know what God is doing and why He has chosen us to go this way. I do see my life changing in many different ways. I just wish He would have chosen other ways to teach me. Watching and waiting are often the most difficult ways to learn from God. Often times I imagine what Job went through! How long was God going to make Job suffer? Job didn't even know why he had to go through it. All he could do was to trust God. I too feel this uncertainty at times.

Many of you are going through tough things as well, but in different ways. Please, never be mad at God! He chooses because He knows us each individually. The potter knows the clay, and he is forming something of value. Stand on His Word, because when He is finished a precious prize will come forth.

I have had many responses on Facebook and through phone calls and e-mails as to how to deal with what we are going though. My brother found this great illustration that describes it quite well:

The Pit
A poem that has been circulating from an adaptation of Kenneth Filkins's The Wittenburg Door.

> A man fell into a pit and couldn't get himself out.
>
> A subjective person came along and said, "I feel for you, down there."
>
> An objective person came along and said, "It's logical that someone would fall into the pit."
>
> A Christian scientist came along and said, "You only think that you are in a pit."
>
> A Pharisee said, "Only bad people fall into pits."

A mathematician calculated how he fell into the pit.

A news reporter wanted the exclusive story on the pit.

A fundamentalist said, "You deserve the pit."

A realist said, "Sure enough, that's a pit."

A scientist calculated the pressure necessary in pounds per square inch to get him out of the pit.

A geologist told him to appreciate the rock strata of the pit.

An evolutionist said, "You are a rejected mutant destined to be removed from the evolutionary cycle. In other words, you cannot produce any more 'pit-falling' offspring."

A tax man asked who was paying taxes on the pit.

A government inspector asked who got the permit to dig the pit in the first place.

An evasive person came along and avoided the subject of the pit altogether.

A self-pitying person said, "You haven't seen anything until you've seen my pit."

A gambler said, "Chances are nine to five that someone else will fall into this pit."

A charismatic said, "Just confess that you're not in a pit."

An optimist said, "Things could be worse."

A pessimist said, "Things will get worse."

Jesus, seeing the man, took him by the hand and lifted him out of the pit!

When you go through suffering many people will be speaking into your life. This is because they care for you. Some of what you hear will not match what God has spoken to you, so you must keep your focus. God's promises will always outweigh the depth of your pit, and He will make a way out for you. But you must listen to the right voices.

I am often amazed at how Sarah sees her pit. She told me yesterday that God gives her enough grace for just one day at a time. When she awakens each morning she goes to the Lord and asks for her grace for that day. Sometimes it will come in the form of a visit from me and the boys, and sometimes from an encouraging e-mail or a phone call from a friend. It also comes from reading and remembering the words of the Lord and sometimes just sitting before the Lord. Tomorrow He will give her the grace for that day and it will become the grace she needs.

You have to go through your struggle daily with God, but never take the whole journey in just one day because it will overwhelm you. Get daily grace and your strength will be renewed. Be careful not to shut people out; it is easy to do when you're suffering. Remember grace might come through someone you least expect.

I do want to share with you a very special e-mail we received yesterday. This woman called herself "a fellow journeyer." She shared her own battle, three years of fighting cancer and the hard battle of losing her hair. She even sent a picture of herself during the journey without hair. I want to thank this brave person for sharing this. My wife lit up with joy knowing she was not alone; this lady became Sarah's grace for the day. Coming to the place of being able to share your journey with others is life changing, and it is grace giving. Sometimes we try and take our spiritual journeys without the help of others, but I think they were meant to go through them together. When we share of our own trials and sufferings we bring hope to others. I am not sure if Sarah would ever allow anyone to see her without hair, but I know that she now sees that God could use her journey to brighten someone else's. Thank you, my sister, so much; your battle is now your victory and we will be joining you soon with our own victory celebration.

So if you are in the pits of suffering or trials, we want to challenge you not to see it from the eyes of those who have never been there, but through the eyes of the One who cares for your journey. God is able to give you a peace and a joy that those around you do not understand. The Word says in Hebrews 4:16, "Let us have confidence, then, and approach God's throne, where there is grace. There we will receive mercy and find grace to help us just when we need it." This place of grace is always available to you just by asking for it. Never feel like you have to earn it or even have to have a certain attitude to get it. It is available only on the condition that you need it. With this asking comes mercy and help from the very throne room of Almighty God Himself.

Sarah tells me about this place of grace all the time. The place where she goes to when she is overwhelmed with her sickness and all the things that come with it. When His grace and mercy is released she says it brings about a peace and comfort that no one else is able to give her. She told me that many people do not even know about this place because they have never been taught nor had a need to go there. We become so confident in ourselves and keep everything inside, not knowing there really is a rest given to us by God. I am amazed by this insight she has been given, and now I too have learned to go there every day, and she is right…God had been waiting there for me.

By the way, this place is located at the very throne of God. Think about that! God Himself is the one releasing it to you. He does not trust anyone else to do this. This throne is not a throne of performance or works or judgment, it is a throne of grace and help for all of us to be able to go to. So go there, right now and get the grace you need for today. Then watch how your day will change and become productive and godly. You will become, like us, amazed!

Try Tears

Day 20—October 17, 2010

I recently remembered a story that I heard about General William Booth, founder of the Salvation Army. He had received a letter from a minister overseas who had all but given up. The minister said that he had tried everything to reach the people where he was for Christ and nothing had worked; no one cared or was interested in what he had to say. He had felt that he could go on no longer and that he had failed as a minister. William Booth wrote back and said just two words, "Try Tears!" Several months had passed and William Booth got a response back from the Pastor. He too wrote just two words in response that said, "Tears Work!"

No one can understand what it's really like to suffer until they have suffered. There are things we learn through suffering that can only be taught through suffering. God could have chosen a million ways for Christ to redeem man, but He chose only one. "It was the road of suffering" (Isaiah 53). Isaiah 53:10 says, "Yet it pleased the LORD to bruise him..." God chose His Son to experience the life and hurts of man. He chose Him to experience loneliness, fear, hurt, joy, pain, and suffering. Jesus saw them for Himself and listened to those who had lost all hope. He experienced all of the feelings of our infirmities, and He did it without sin. This was done so that we would know that He felt what we felt. It's love in the deepest form. On His own hands are the scars that allow us to know that He is with us when we are sick, with us when we are alone, and with us when we are hurting inside and can't go on.

You may feel alone today, but you're not! One day your trial will end, and because of what you went through, God will be able to use you to reach out to someone else. Your trials will produce the tears that impact people's lives...tears work! Your trials will produce your ministry, and the way you go through them will be your testimony.

Sarah and I have learned that we can sit here in her room and sing "Kumbaya" and feel sorry for ourselves and even blame God, or we can look at the Word and realize that great things are in store for us when this journey is over! The day that it is finished will begin a new journey with God that only opened up because we completed the one we are on.

Here is my Scripture for the day:

> Let us, then, hold firmly to the faith we profess. For we have a great High Priest who has gone into the very presence of God—Jesus, the Son of God. Our High Priest is not one who cannot feel sympathy for our weaknesses. On the contrary, we have a High Priest who was tempted in every way that we are, but did not sin. Let us have confidence, then, and approach God's throne, where there is grace. There we will receive mercy and find grace to help us just when we need it.
>
> Hebrews 4:14-16

He is with us. You may ask me, why then does He not just deliver you? That is a fair question that I can only respond to by saying that it is by trials and suffering that Christ is perfected in us. The Chinese Christian Martyr Watchman Nee once said that you can never become fully used by the Lord unless He is allowed to bring you into suffering. We also see that the apostle Paul said in Philippians 3, "That I might know Him...and the fellowship of His suffering." The question is, can God trust Sarah and me to suffer? Will we remain faithful? Will we allow Him to do a work in us that can only be done through a complete and utter trust in the Father's will for us?

The three weeks Sarah has been in the hospital seem like months. Sarah is constantly tired and now she has developed a fever. She has also lost most of her hair and chooses to wear a hat. I know that the loss of her hair was the hardest part for her thus far. Every day I see the grace of God upon her. Is she frustrated? I am sure she is inside, but she never shows it. Even though trials seem to last forever they will have an ending. Today, I am reminded of another great Scripture of encouragement.

> The LORD is my strength and my shield; my heart trusts in Him, and I am helped.
>
> Psalm 28:7

Help comes as a result of allowing your heart to fully trust in who He is. If we fail to trust our Father, then our strength will come only when we receive good news. Faith in His Word is a powerful source of strength. How? By believing in who God says He is. The Word says that He is our strength. So when you're weak, lean upon the Lord through prayer. Ask God for His strength to come upon you. I have found that He gives strength to me, when I worship Him, and when my mouth is filled with praise (Psalm 71:7-8). There you have it; the source of His strength comes in praise and worship. Try it!

Some have asked me where I am getting my strength from. That's easy, from the Lord! Without knowing His Word daily I would be a mess. His Word sustains me and I am daily watching my Father keep His Word to both Sarah and me. The psalmist said "Oh taste and see that the Lord is good..." (Psalm 34:8). I have! He is good and His love for me is ever present every day.

I am finding that through this journey He is allowing me to feel His heart for the hurting. Oh, if you only knew how much He cares for you! We are His creation and He so loves us and hears our every cry; not one tear that is shed goes unnoticed by your Father. You may wonder why you are going through your battle. I assure you this, if you will get away with God and His Word, your Father will show you the secrets to winning wars. Why spend all your time worrying? Has worrying changed the outcome? Has fear made things better? Get alone with God and you will find your strength to face Goliath. The army of Israel had fear and worry, and it caused them to hide in their tents. All they heard was Goliath's threats. But David knew the Word of God and had experienced God's help in the past. It was because David daily meditated on the Word of God that he knew that this giant was coming against the people of God and that God wasn't going to stand for that. Like David, you too must know that the enemy of sickness is coming against the people of God and God doesn't want to allow that. So stand up and face your giant with the truth, and stop crying in the mud and hiding in your tent. This is true faith. The size of your enemy doesn't matter. David had a rock and a sling shot while Goliath had a sword and a spear; remember the outcome of the fight? People said that the rock was too small to hit and kill a giant, but David said the opposite. He said the giant was too big to miss. So when the giant went down David was not shocked...Israel was! Why? Because Israel had lost their faith; David had not!

Try tears! The outcome of all our sufferings will produce godly tears for those who hurt. These tears water the promises of God in the hearts of others. No amount of counseling will replace tears.

Ears to Hear

Day 27—October 24, 2010

The day has finally come. Today Sarah is coming home from the hospital. We were all up early excited, because it feels like Christmas morning. It was a day we have looked forward to for many weeks, and now it is here. The past twenty-seven days have seemed like months and even though she is still very sick she will at least be home where her family can be with her. I have to say that as excited I am about picking her up and taking her home, I am grieved because there are seven other rooms here with patients who are not able to go home yet. They have to stay and continue treatment. A big part of my heart hurts for them, because I am so aware of what they are going through. By tomorrow there will be someone else taking Sarah's bed; perhaps they will be every bit as uncertain as we were on our first day. I pray for their well-being.

We have met many hurting people here on this floor since we first arrived. It is not a happy place to be. Many are afraid and unsure if they are going to survive their treatments. Hope and optimism run very high as the nurses and doctors do their best to help bring healing to so many. There are also the family members who come to visit that you find in the waiting room. Many are huddled together crying for their loved ones. Long treatments take time to know if they are working, and that extended time brings a lot of uncertainty to people who have to wait. Today as we leave here we want to pray for the many who will lie in this very bed that Sarah is vacating. May God touch them and comfort them. Thanks to all the great staff here who have dedicated their careers to helping all of us. Even though Sarah will be returning home we pray that those who remain will find the peace that we have.

Since being here we met a young woman named Nicole. She too had two forms of cancer, only hers was much worse than Sarah's. She was only twenty-one years old and all alone. She seemed too young to have to go through all of this. A few years back she had a falling out with her parents and even in her condition it was not enough for her parents to come and visit with her. She also has a two-year-old little girl that she is unable to see, because no children are allowed on this floor. It grieved me to know that she has been here for six weeks without a single visitor; no wonder she lit up when we went to her room to see her. Sarah and I had such a wonderful opportunity to share the Lord with her and our willingness to visit her brought such a joy to her.

We also met Scott, whose wife was not doing well. They are a young couple facing the failure of a transplant. I met Scott in the hall way when I noticed him crying. There was the fear that he was going to lose his wife and the mother of his children. When you see this you are lost for the right words to say to them. After all, what could you possibly say to them? Sometimes you just have to let them see your concern in your eyes. Oh, that I could bring them hope! All I could do was ache inside for them. I let him know that I was going to pray for him. I see such a difference in people when they know you are going through the same thing as they are.

There was also Carol, who was next door to Sarah. She was an elderly woman, and every day her husband came to be with her. I can tell they have a love for each other that is so special. I would see her light up just through the cracks of the door when her husband walked into the room. She was always so glad to see him, but many times she was too weak to get out of bed to sit with him. But he came on a regular basis to support his best friend. I can only imagine the fear that they both must have as to the outcome of her disease. I was so glad to be able to talk with Carol one afternoon when she was walking the hallway to regain her strength. She wore a hat to cover up her loss of hair, but her smile was so contagious and confident. She had the look of life in her and I can only believe that she brings that wherever she goes.

All of these precious people have different stories of life. They are, however, all loved by someone, and they all want to live. There is a silent cry among the hurting that few people outside their world ever hear. A cry to want to know that everything will turn out all right and that their loved ones will be comforted. There is a cry for us not to reject them or forget them. There is a cry to be seen and to be remembered. It is a cry for you and me to hear as well. I often wonder why I never heard it before. Maybe I have closed my ears and shut my eyes when I saw and heard it off in the distance. I believe that when Jesus was on earth it was the silent cries of the hurting that caused Him to go to the places He went. When He went to Samaria in John four it was because he heard the cries of a harlot woman who had searched for something more in her life. Everything she tried turned bad. She was rejected by the community in which she lived, rejected by family because of the choices she made, rejected by the church because of her past. Jesus saw past all of that and went to her. We should never underestimate the hurts in people's lives, their need to be heard and cared for.

We too often judge others by what we see. For example, you see a long-haired, grungy fellow walking towards you late at night, what do you see? Trouble? Are you nervous? You may have an opinion based solely on what you see with your eyes. But somewhere this man has a mother who sees potential, hope, and a future. She prays for him to have a good life and to be protected. He is loved just like you and I are. We see what we want to see! How many of you would have spoken to the woman at the well?

All around us there is the silent cry of the hurting. It is the cry that Jesus wants us to listen for. I never heard it till now, but now I hear it almost everywhere I go. I hear it at Walmart when I see someone confined to a wheelchair. Many disabled have been forced to move into an alternate world because we have silently learned to reject them. We never notice them trying to reach things on top shelves with no one there to help them. I guess it's easier to not look or make eye contact, that way we won't become responsible to help. I'm grieved over this. Why have I not noticed just how many are hurting around me? Next time you go to a shopping center and you see a disabled person I want you to notice that they will intentionally not make eye contact with you. They are tired of being hurt by our stares and lack of compassion. It has become easier for them to pretend that you are not there than to have to explain with their eyes that they too need love. So they will go about their business without needing your help. The sad thing is that they have grown accustomed to us rejecting them unintentionally.

My question is, has the Church of the Lord Jesus Christ shut the door to His compassion because we are not hearing their silent cries? Many times even in church, people bypass the disabled, the elderly, and the sick. They will see them and fail to open the door for them, fail to pick them up for church if they have no ride, fail to call them for special events or to visit with them when they're ill. It is as if they don't see them or don't want to see them.

Failure to love past the history or the condition of someone's life is a great sin in the church. It is also the message that we have sent to our children. Failure to teach them true godly love allows them to neglect the needs that are in others and reject them. It is why the sinner does not want to go to church—all he hears from us is what he has done wrong; he rarely hears about God's forgiveness, mercy, and loving kindness. Jesus seemed to be drawn to those who had nothing to give back. The hurting were able to get the closest to Him and Jesus never pushed them away. The reason was because He heard their cries.

I see another example of Christ hearing the cries of people in scripture. There was the cry of the centurion in Matthew eight. He went to Jesus on behalf of his servant who was sick and grievously tormented. He knew that Jesus could just speak the word and his servant would be healed. He came in great faith on the behalf of someone else. This centurion heard the cries of his servant and those cries went through him and into the ears of Jesus. There are too few like this centurion. Not many care for those around them because they have too many cares of their own to worry about.

Suffering has a way of opening a door to the very heart and soul of someone. Rarely does the sinner ever think about eternity until they face it. When facing it, the devil will always show up to bring in a heavy heart; would this not also be the opportune time for someone to share Christ? To show up on the behalf of Jesus! I promise you that when you go out of your way to touch someone that God blesses that.

> I called upon the Lord in distress: the Lord answered me, and set me in a large place. The Lord is on my side; I will not fear.
>
> Psalm 118:5-6(KJV)

This new place is a place that God will open up for you will be the result of what you have gone through in your life. Many times our Father uses our distress as a way to "Bring us into a larger place." This is a new place, one that we would not have found had we not had distress. This place comes as an answer to your distress and with it we have no fear because we have the Lord's presence. It takes His presence to help us to understand its purpose.

I heard of a story about a man who had found a cocoon with a butterfly trying to get out of it. He felt so sorry for the butterfly because he seemed stuck and was struggling so hard to get free. So he decided that he could help him by cutting away the cocoon so it would be freed. Once he did the butterfly flew for about twenty seconds and then fell to the ground and died. The man was so disappointed that it had died. Sometime later he had found out that God purposely made it so that the butterfly would have to struggle to get out of the cocoon. In doing so it would build the strength it needed to survive. This is so true for us as well. God uses conflict, struggle, and suffering to build the needed character in us to be like Jesus. It allows us the ability to hear what everyone else misses.

Allow God to take you deeper than you're able to understand. To see things around you that others miss. To hear the cries that are only cried inside of those who are hurting. To feel what others do not feel. These will be the result of that special place and it will open doors for you and opportunities to bring hope that so many will never have.

One last thing; the reason why God allows you to hear their cries is because in you are the healing words of Jesus Christ. The comfort that God wants them to have is found in the Words that dwell in us. We are His voice and His hands but only if we hear the cries they are crying.

I Will Lift Up Mine Eyes

Day 32—October 29, 2010

About two-thirty this morning I was awakened by Sarah's little dog, Toby. I knew something was wrong, because Toby was acting very strange. He is very attached to my Sarah, and his actions made me get out of bed to check on my wife, who was in the bathroom. As I entered the bathroom, Sarah stood there looking at me with tears in her eyes. She was had awful pain in her arm where the pick line was located. Her arm had swollen up so much that she could not raise her arm at all. I knew that she was struggling earlier in the day, but now she was in rough shape. My son Brandon and I rushed her to UMass Memorial where they gave her pain meds to help with the horrible pain. It turned out to be a very bad infection, and her pick line needed to be removed.

I am learning that in this journey we will have to always be prepared to deal with the unexpected. David said in 34:19: "Many are the afflictions of the righteous, but the Lord delivers them out of them all." As this journey now seems to be d-r-a-g-g-i-n-g along it becomes more difficult to deal with. It seemed so much easier when you knew what was coming next; at least then you could brace yourself for it.

Are we tired? Yes...tired of hospital visits, nurses coming daily to the house, return hospital stays, medications (Sarah and I look like we are peddling drugs). Yes, it's a real burden to bear. Our lives have changed, but not for the worse, for the better! We are better for this, because all of this is making us "more than conquerors through Christ Jesus our Lord." Conquerors are battle winners, because they have fought and won! We have become more aware of His love for us and we are being made aware of His ways. How can we not say, "It is well!"

It is knowing that He is with us and He will not forsake us that allows us the strength to fight another day. You might say, but you're still sick! Listen, His deliverance in us has taken on new meaning. He is delivering us from the power and attractions of this world. Healing can come in an instant, but the life that is changed by His dealings in us take time. Affliction can work in us the same way they worked in Job. We know that God is still the healer! But in His time, and for now, His grace is enough, and we will run with patience. Do I still have faith to see Sarah completely healed? More now than ever! It is because He has proven Himself to me through this journey. How could I not believe after all I have experienced?

David said in Psalm 121:1-8:

> I look to the mountains; where will my help come from? My help will come from the LORD, who made heaven and earth. He will not let you fall; your protector is always awake. The protector of Israel never dozes or sleeps. The LORD will guard you; he is by your side to protect you. The sun will not hurt you during the day, nor the moon during the night. The LORD will protect you from all danger; he will keep you safe. He will protect you as you come and go now and forever.

I read this passage this morning after I got home from the hospital, and it brought my heart so much joy and comfort. Why? Because once again I can count on His Word; His Word is who He is. David wrote this psalm because he had found through experience that nothing else worked. It was the help that came from God that caused him to be sustained through his trials. Today I want you to know that David's source of strength is yours as well. Sarah is still at the hospital, but my heavenly Father has decided to stay there with her so that I could go home and tend to the boys. That is the faith He wants to see in us. We know that He is there and that He is in control.

David said, "I will look to the mountains" (Psalm 121:1). Trials and suffering will cause you to become heavyhearted and David knew that the first thing he needed to do was to re-direct his focus. It is easy, as you know, to keep your emotions on your feelings. David said, "I will." It had to be a part of his will to look beyond everything he was going through. We do not always understand the purpose of God, so we must trust Him. Many think that by trusting in God you will receive what you are seeking. That is not always the case. I became quite aware that God could take Sarah home if He chose to. It was hard for me to allow this thought to enter into my mind. But it has and is a real possibility with this disease. However, I am confident in the plan of God that should that be the outcome of this journey then I will still trust in the Lord. Why? Because "I am looking to the mountains."

Remember when Job was tested and he lost everything, this included his children. His wife said to Job that he should just curse God and die. She had encouraged him to bring this to an end because it was too much for him to handle.

In Job 1:13-15 we see Job living a normal life and having dinner at his brother's house. All of a sudden dinner is interrupted with the horrible news of an attack that killed all of Job's servants. Only the messenger survived the attack and came to Job with the news.

Then, in Job 1:16, while still sitting at the table, another servant runs in and says that lightning struck and killed all the sheep along with the shepherds. Again, just the messenger was spared.

Imagine what Job must have been thinking. There was no warning, it just happened.

Moments later, before he was finished hearing the story about the sheep and the shepherds another escapee runs into the house to tell Job that there was another attack that killed all his servants and they took all the camels.

Then came the most devastating news of all. In Job 1:18-19, his children were having dinner and a storm hit and blew the house down and killed them all. The one survivor was able to bring Job the bad news.

> Then Job got up and tore his clothes in grief. He shaved his head and threw himself face downward on the ground. He said, "I was born with nothing, and I will die with nothing. The LORD gave, and now he has taken away. May his name be praised!"
>
> Job 1:20

What? "May his name be praised?" Are you serious? Is it possible that anyone could speak those words after hearing the reports that Job had just heard? I bet Satan was shocked! After all, the devil made sure that one person was able to survive each attack so that they could go and tell Job exactly what had happened. Satan will always arrange for a messenger to come and bring you the devastating news. That is where the fear originates…in the news you're given.

He went into mourning as any father would. This is evident by his actions. He tore his clothes in grief. He shaved his head and threw himself to the ground. But he understood the Lord was in control. His attitude was amazing. He says, "I was born with nothing, and I will die with nothing. The Lord gave, and now he has taken away. May his name be praised!" Wow! I bet this aggravated the devil a little! God was right about Job thus far! Look at the next verse and you will see his attitude.

> In spite of everything that had happened, Job did not sin by blaming God.
>
> Job 1:22

You must admit that what Job just did was something to be admired. He held his tongue even through his grief and pain. This was however just the first wave of attacks for Job. When Satan had seen that Job was able to withstand this onslaught he decided to make his second request to God in chapter two.

The Lord again asks Satan about Job and asked Satan to notice his faithfulness and worship. This must have frustrated Satan.

This victory must have made God proud of Job. Notice in Job 2:3 that God said, "He worships me..." You see being able to stand for truth is worship. There can be no higher form of worship than this. To worship the Lord when you have lost everything only shows that those things were never what you worshiped. Job never allowed anyone to take God's rightful place of being worshiped.

So, we have Satan coming up with another plan of attack against God's servant...

> Satan replied, "A person will give up everything in order to stay alive. But now suppose you hurt his body—he will curse you to your face!" So the LORD said to Satan, "All right, he is in your power, but you are not to kill him." Then Satan left the LORD's presence and made sores break out all over Job's body. Job went and sat by the garbage dump and took a piece of broken pottery to scrape his sores.
>
> Job 2:4-8

Poor Job, little did he know that things were about to get worse. That usually seems to be the road for those who suffer. When you suffer you are usually believing and praying for a great outcome and then something else comes along. What more could

he be made to endure? The toughest part of suffering can often come from those closest to you. Look at what his wife said:
Job 2:9:

> His wife said to him, "You are still as faithful as ever, aren't you? Why don't you curse God and die?"

Now you see why Satan left his wife alone. She begins to feed Job's fear and unbelief, and even offers him a solution to all his problems. Just get it over with she tells him…Curse God! It's His doings; God is responsible for all of this. It is Satan's ultimate goal, just like in the garden, to switch blame away from him and onto God. We must always be aware of this tactic of the devil or we will fall into a trap set to cause an offense against God.

In Job 2:10 Job refuses to listen to her and stays focused in his trust of his God. This is astounding to me. Job watched what he spoke against God and refused to lose hope. I pray that each of us can do the same through our trials. It is not always easy to maintain this attitude, as you will see if you read more out of the book of Job. But this was the attitude that honored God the most. When we do not understand God we respond in the same manner as Job's wife did. To understand God is a faith that will trust Him in everything.

God allowed Satan to test Job, but never did God intend to forsake Job. His plan was designed for Job's good and God has your good in mind too, and He will never leave you or forsake you.

Your Faith Needs to Work

Day 34 —October 31, 2010

Sarah is doing well! She was supposed to go to the hospital tomorrow, but God has granted us a few more days together. Guess what? Her test results from her bone marrow biopsy have come back, and we are happy to say that there are no bad cells in it. In other words, her body is producing all good cells! What a mighty God I am serving! He teaches me His ways and then He demonstrates His Word.

As a pastor I have found that we are often guilty of preaching to our congregation truths that we expect them to live by and yet struggle to live by ourselves. I often feel that if people would just listen to the Word of the Lord and obey it that they would experience its benefits. But this applies to the preacher too. We must also trust the Word with total obedience to it. During this time of trial in our lives we have seen just why it is often hard to trust God. We are surrounded by so many voices telling us what is going on and those voices change as the prognosis and treatments change. But the Word of God never changes no matter how much the situation does. This leaves me to believe that we must continue to trust the Word above all things. The book of James is a foundational book for understanding trials:

> My friends, consider yourselves fortunate when all kinds
> of trials come your way.
>
> James 1:2

Getting excited about trials is not normal behavior in my book. But we are told to do so because we must understand that trials produce something of greater value in our lives. It is both a trust issue and a training issue with God. He must trust you to go through it and to complete it and to do so with an understanding of its purpose. However, He may not tell you what that purpose is because He expects you to trust Him. And when you have completed it you will have come into a fresh and new revelation with God. Sounds better than it feels, I'm sure. But it is no less true.

> For you know that when your faith succeeds in facing such
> trials, the result is the ability to endure. Make sure that
> your endurance carries you all the way without failing, so
> that you may be perfect and complete, lacking nothing.
>
> James 1:3-4

When your faith succeeds in the trial, the result is the ability to endure. That endurance is what will make you perfect and complete in the things of God. Is this easy to do? No! That is why James tells us in the next verse to seek for His wisdom in the matter.

We see in scripture that God allows Satan to attack the apostle Paul in the form of a thorn in his flesh. We have all had thorns or splinters in life and they hurt and they are aggravating. This thorn we are told in 2 Corinthians 12:7 was a physical ailment which acted as a messenger of Satan. Its purpose was to keep Paul from being proud and puffed up. It was also designed to cause him to suffer and be out of his comfort zone.

The Word said that three times Paul prayed that the Lord would take it away from him. This kind of prayer was also prayed by Christ in the garden. Three times he went into pray and he finally finished with "Nevertheless, not my will but thine be done" (Luke 22:42). Your request for removal is allowed by God, but in the end it has to be settled as to what you are going to do. Jesus prayed three times and then settled the matter in His heart. Paul prayed three times until God told him the purpose of this thorn. This is something we must also learn to do. It is never wrong to ask God why you are going through suffering.

God tells Paul why, and Paul like Christ had to settle it in his heart to accept the purpose of God for him. God tells him in 2 Corinthians 12:9 that all he needed to get through was His grace. This was settled with Paul, he was now able to concentrate on the fact that God was allowing this for a greater purpose. He then proceeded to continue in his ministry.

> But his answer was: "My grace is all you need, for my power is greatest when you are weak." I am most happy, then, to be proud of my weaknesses, in order to feel the protection of Christ's power over me. I am content with weaknesses, insults, hardships, persecutions, and difficulties for Christ's sake. For when I am weak, then I am strong.
>
> 2 Corinthians 12:9-10

The result was that Paul would now understand the purpose of trials, hardships, sufferings, and all the rest. When he was weak he found the source of strength through Christ. Our weakness forces or allows us to seek after and tap into the very strength and power of God. To do this in your own strength has only human results and human strength.

> But when you pray, you must believe and not doubt at all. Whoever doubts is like a wave in the sea that is driven and blown about by the wind. If you are like that, unable to make up your mind and undecided in all you do, you must not think that you will receive anything from the Lord.
>
> James 1:6-8

It is all right for you to pray for the purpose of your trial, but you must do so in faith. That faith may not be the kind of faith you understand. Most of the time we pray that God would do exactly what we want, and only if He gives us what we want we are happy. This faith is not that kind of faith. This faith is faith in what God wants to do through trials. God's outcome may not be the outcome you are looking for or expecting. Paul was not praying for understanding of this thorn, he was praying for complete removal. This is why God may not have answered him the first two times he prayed. God had a different purpose in mind than Paul did. Paul thought that life and ministry would be so much easier without it. He felt that without it he would accomplish more for the Kingdom of God not having to be hindered. But God in the long haul knew that without this thorn Paul would be shipwrecked in his faith. We also know that God allowed Paul to be imprisoned and without the imprisonment we may not have much of the New Testament. It was in prison that Paul wrote or had the time to write. But only God knew that.

There is much to understand when it comes to suffering and lack. James uses this book to help us to understand it.

> My friends, as believers in our Lord Jesus Christ, the Lord of glory, you must never treat people in different ways according to their outward appearance. Suppose a rich man wearing a gold ring and fine clothes comes to your meeting, and a poor man in ragged clothes also comes. If you show more respect to the well-dressed man and say to him, "Have this best seat here," but say to the poor man, "Stand over there, or sit here on the floor by my feet," then you are guilty of creating distinctions among yourselves and of making judgments based on evil motives.
>
> James 2:1-4

Many people despise the poor or those who do not meet their personal expectations. I have seen some preachers exploit the poor into giving what little they have so that the preacher would

Kent & Sarah Whitecotton

have more. These ministries claim it to be a providence of God to have much, all the while encouraging you to send it to them in faith. I am not against blessings of wealth and prosperity as long as it is in balance to the Word of God. Many have robbed the people of God by building kingdoms of man and not the true kingdom of God, and much of it is financed by the poor.

James informs us that many will have the tendency to despise the poor and honor the wealthy. For us to distinguish between the two as one being better than the other is a sin. There is a blessing that the poor possess that the rich have lost sight of. That blessing is the blessing of faith and the possession of the kingdom of God.

> Listen, my dear friends! God chose the poor people of this world to be rich in faith and to possess the kingdom which he promised to those who love him. But you dishonor the poor! Who are the ones who oppress you and drag you before the judges? The rich! They are the ones who speak evil of that good name which has been given to you.
>
> James 2:5-7

This knowledge is given by James to help us keep focus of what has greater value. Being wealthy is not a sin. But with wealth you must understand what the purpose of your blessings is for. Do you help the poor and the oppressed? Do you advance the kingdom of God? Are you using your influence to reach the lost? Storing up for personal gain is wrong (Luke 12:15-21). I believe that even when it comes to good health we have a responsibility to help the sick and to show them the love of God.

Let's look at another area produced through faith found in this book.

> My friends, what good is it for one of you to say that you have faith if your actions do not prove it? Can that faith save you?
>
> James 2:14

Many of you will say you have faith and trust in God. However, until that faith and trust is tested, how do you know for sure? Do your actions when you suffer prove your faith in God? James says that faith is only demonstrated by your actions and if you have no actions to go with that faith then it will not work. Below he gives us an example of what he is talking about.

> Suppose there are brothers or sisters who need clothes and don't have enough to eat. What good is there in your saying to them, "God bless you! Keep warm and eat well!"—if you don't give them the necessities of life? So it is with faith: if it is alone and includes no actions, then it is dead. But someone will say, "One person has faith, another has actions." My answer is, "Show me how anyone can have faith without actions. I will show you my faith by my actions."
>
> James 2:15-18

James goes on to show us another example in the life of Abraham.

> How was our ancestor Abraham put right with God? It was through his actions, when he offered his son Isaac on the altar. Can't you see? His faith and his actions worked together; his faith was made perfect through his actions. And the scripture came true that said, "Abraham believed God, and because of his faith God accepted him as righteous." And so Abraham was called God's friend.
>
> James 2:21-23

His faith was only complete through his actions. He did this before he climbed Mount Moriah, the place where God sent him to sacrifice Isaac, not after. Faith is not hindsight but foresight.

> You see, then, that it is by our actions that we are put right with God, and not by our faith alone.
>
> James 2:24

So then, as the body without the spirit is dead, also faith without actions is dead.

James 2:26

So, believe God that regardless of the situation you are facing that He is in control. Pray and ask for wisdom, pray until He shows you the purpose. Then trust with all your heart. Many people have changed the course of circumstances just through faith and the authority of the Word of God. God will hear your cries and He will keep His Word.

Sarah's Second Round of Treatment Begins

Day 38—November 4, 2010

W ell it has finally happened—at 6:30 pm last night the hospital called and said that Sarah had to come in right away because they had a bed for her. They will be starting her second round of chemotherapy tomorrow, but this will only last about a week and she can come home. This was quite the surprise because we were already settled down for the evening and now we have to rush to get all her things together and get her to the hospital. I guess that part of the journey involves expecting the unexpected. Even though they said she would only be in for about a week, as you know a week could seem like a month.

This past week with Sarah being home has been so special to me. After twenty-five years of marriage you think that love can't get any stronger but without a doubt it can. I often would look over to her sitting in her chair with little Toby watching the 700 Club and think how blessed I was to have her in my life. She seems to be in such a state of rest and relaxation. We're not in a hurry much anymore; I guess because we have come to a greater place of peace and rest in the Lord. I am going to miss seeing her in her chair for the next week.

I met with a group of local pastors yesterday morning for breakfast, and my dear brother Pastor Gary Collette said to me something that really made me think. He said, "This journey with Sarah involves your own personal journey as well." It really does! This book has actually helped me to see that. For all of you who read this book who have someone you love going through something hard, I want to say that I know how hard it is for you personally. To watch your loved one go through sickness, pain, hurt, long visits to the doctor's office, shots, pills, daily nurse visits, and the responsibilities of life in general has to be the absolute hardest thing you are ever asked to go through. You seem to feel all their pain in ways that I can only describe to those who have gone through it themselves. Many think they understand what I am talking about, but how can you know until you go through it. I am not saying this because I am hurting inside right now, because I am not. I have received great grace from the Lord that has sustained me every day, and His strength is carrying me in ways that are unexplainable. I watch daily in amazement the wonderful grace of the Lord upon Sarah, and that allows me to know without a doubt that He is with us. But it is a journey for me as well, because Sarah has to look to me for strength and wisdom that is from the Lord. I must keep my eyes fixed on the Healer and allow His process in our lives to go unhindered. He will get us to the other side, and we will arrive standing up in victory; we may have battle scars, but like a woman who finally delivers the baby, she no longer remembers the labor pain. You see, labor pains open the womb to make delivery possible; we need it, otherwise delivery is hindered.

At the breakfast yesterday, I felt surrounded by great friends who have been praying for Sarah and me every day; no wonder I have received such grace from the Lord! These men have offered to fill in at the church for me if needed, or to sit with me if I needed to talk; this is certainly Christianity in action!

Brother Bill Button so graciously said to me something else that I want to pass on to you. He said, "Do not go through your journey alone! You need the body of Christ to surround you and hold you up." I know for many who go through wilderness journeys it is lonely even when you're in a crowd. This is understandable! For me, I personally needed time to process everything in my own heart before I was able to share it out loud. These journeys begin with just you, but you must make sure it doesn't remain that way and that Satan does not draw you into isolation. If he does then you will cease to receive the grace that you will need from others to get through the journey in victory.

Encouragement is one of God's ways to give you strength. God wants you to taste your victory by faith before you even get it; Satan wants you to fear and draw away into hopelessness. Therefore, you must take a faith stand and see the victory party waiting to celebrate with you, in doing so your faith will please God and strength will come into you like you never imagined. This is what Job did. He took a stand when he said, "Though He slay me, yet will I serve Him" (Job 13:15). He settled in his heart that regardless of the outcome he was still going to stay faithful to God. Not only was this settled in his heart he also silenced the wrong voices that were around him.

You see, when Jesus was asked what the greatest commandment was He summed it up by saying:

> Love the Lord your God with all your heart, with all your soul, and with all your mind. This is the greatest and the most important commandment. The second most important commandment is like it: Love your neighbor as you love yourself. The whole Law of Moses and the teachings of the prophets depend on these two commandments.
>
> Matthew 22:36-40

Think about what Jesus is saying here. I know that you, like me, want to please God in everything you do. The way to do that is to obey what He commands. So here, Jesus tells us what the Father is looking for in us. First, to love Him with all your heart, with all your soul, and with all your mind. That is absolute trust, to push God to the front of everything in your life. This sounds easier than it is to do. This level of love is something that most people may never reach and yet most people think that they do, but with all your heart, soul, and mind?

Then He does something even more difficult. He says we are commanded to love our neighbor as much as we love ourselves. He tells us that the second commandment is just like the first one. That means that in the eyes of God that loving our neighbor is as important as loving Him. If you fail in the second commandment you will automatically fail in the first one. And yet in just about every church I know there are people who do not love one another! They do not care for the sick or the oppressed. Their ears are shut to the needs that surround their churches. All of Christianity is wrapped up in these two commandments and until we get these two commandments right we will always hinder the true workings of the Holy Spirit through us.

Paul said to the church: "What good would it be to have a gospel that is hindered and doesn't work? I have found through this journey that this Gospel does work and I am not running it in vain." Paul instructs me in Philippians 2:13 to hold forth to that Word because it is life. Life lives! What has life in it has breath and movement. It is so very worth all my energy and all my courage to labor for the continuance of this message of life until all the world hears it. I understand why so many believers throughout church history were willing to lay their lives down for this gospel message. So, if you hate testing and trials think again; it is in your testing and trials that God will use to bring you to a place of awe concerning who He is, and you will be able to stand up, run faster, and run with joy like never before. It is because you truly love Him that you will trust Him regardless of the outcome.

My wife always tells me that no one can call Jesus "Lord" and say no to what He asks.

Your testing may render you weak or fallible, just like Jacob's testing, which left him crippled, and the Word said he walked with a limp the rest of his life (Genesis 32:25). This weakness was given to allow him to rely only upon the strength of his heavenly Father. He became better, pure, and righteous before the Father, unwilling to compromise any longer. The man he was before that night he was no longer. This is my cry as I write this, "Make me like You, Lord; make me like You."

My faith has become stronger during my journey and my fears have rested in the Father's love; my hope is no longer being tested because I now know He is with us! When we arrive at the finish line our testimony will be, "God is faithful!" So, do what you were commanded to do and love one another, comfort those in need, and show the compassion of your Heavenly Father. You will change a life!

Acknowledge the Lord with Your Trust

Day 42—November 8, 2010

I woke up this morning with a headache. However, I have great expectations as to the plans of my heavenly Father. Sarah is still in the hospital and has two more rounds of chemo to go before she can go home. She is doing well so far, much better than the first round. We are praying that she will be able to be home for Thanksgiving. It's funny how important things become when you go through trials. Holidays become more meaningful and precious. I will have much to be thankful for this year, my wife, three awesome sons, great church family, great friends, and perhaps something even more greater than I may have ever realized...a great God. I have heard many say over the years that it was trials that caused them to lose faith in God. It was something that happened unexpected or something that someone had done to them that caused them to lose their faith in God. We have not had that experience. I believe it is because we stayed focused on the Word of the Lord and not on our own expectations or wants. So many miss out on just how close you are able to get to the Father when you're hurting. It's like the story of the three Hebrew children in the book of Daniel who refused to take the easier road and chose suffering over blessing. Once in the fire they found that they were not alone. God walks with us in the fire, but we have to look for Him and by faith see Him there. He has been like that for us. We have not found discontentment or frustration; we have found peace and comfort in the Lord. It truly is amazing.

We have asked for you to believe with us for Sarah's healing of her kidney. I refuse to box God into any corners, but I cannot help but stand on His Word that He heals all of my diseases. My trust is in His Word! This Word is something that heaven and hell must abide by...it is the Law of heaven and earth. Jesus said, "Thy Kingdom come, Thy will be done, on earth as it is in heaven" (Matthew 6:10). God's kingdom comes when His will is done here on earth. I know that we can experience all of the glory, power, and presence of the living Christ when we can submit and surrender to His will. I do want His will in my life and in the healing of my wife, and if He chooses to heal through the removal of the kidney, that is fine with us. Or if He chooses to heal so that she does not have to go through the surgery, then we will be grateful as well. I can't seem to find any disappointment in God no matter what we have to go through.

Therefore, I must start to pray His Word and to speak His Word. The Word says life and death are in the power of the tongue; therefore I will speak the Word's of life on Sarah's behalf. She shall live, her body shall be made whole and she shall have health to all her bones. Sarah and I have taken Proverbs 3:5-8 as her Scripture to trust in.

> Trust in the LORD with all thine heart; and lean not unto thine own understanding. In all thy ways acknowledge him, and he shall direct thy paths. Be not wise in thine own eyes: fear the LORD, and depart from evil. It shall be health to thy navel, and marrow to thy bones.
>
> Proverbs 3:5-8(KJV)

Now, it is important that you understand everything that God says concerning the matter. You cannot just take what you want out of scripture; you must obey its content. It says: "Trust in the Lord with all thine heart." God requires that we trust Him, no matter what we feel or what we are going through: everything starts with complete trust in the Father.

The second thing you must do is "not lean on your own understanding." This is such an area of weakness in us. It is so easy to think about it in the flesh or to make a decision without consulting the Father or waiting upon Him. Oh, I am so guilty of this sin! We think that we know what to do so we proceed without ever asking God what His will in the matter might be.

The third thing clarifies this when he says, "In all thy ways acknowledge him, and he shall direct thy paths." Herein lives the promise of our obedience to acknowledge Him in all my ways and then allow Him to direct me where to go and what to say. Oh, how much my Father wants to be a part of my life if only I will just learn to trust in Him. It is so easy to say to Him, "Come, tell me what to do," and then fail to wait upon Him for guidance, as if we know more than He does. We must ask God to forgive us for such a great sin!

I believe that many times God will delay things in our lives so that He can test us to see what we will do. Will we trust the Lord? Will we be content with what His Word tells us? Will we be content with His will for us even if it is not what we are wanting? It's easy to say "yes" until we have to face something that He has for us that we do not want.

The next part is kind of amazing because all it does is explain what was already said, "Be not wise in thine own eyes: fear the Lord, and depart from evil." What evil? It is the evil of not trusting in the Lord but trusting in ourselves. And it is a great evil! We too often think that we "know" what to do, and we move forward only to find ourselves in trouble. But God does know what to do, and to fail to wait upon Him is to commit evil in His sight.

Here will be the results of your trust, "It shall be health to thy navel, and marrow to thy bones." This passage is amazing because bone marrow produces the blood cells for your body if they are unhealthy your body sickens and dies, this is the case for Sarah. But this Word says that our obedience for trusting the Lord will produce "healthy bone marrow!" Hallelujah! What a Savior that He would send us such a wonderful promise!

This is both physical and spiritual. Too many lack good spiritual bone marrow. They have become weakened in their spirit, and they are spiritually unhealthy. To wait upon the Lord is the most perfect form of worship that we can offer God. It shows that we are loyal to His Word over everything else. Oh, that God would bring us all to this place of obedience to the faith.

So, if you are reading this scripture, obey its content, all of it! In doing so, God will send health into your bones, both the physical ones and the spiritual ones. By the way, the words "health to thy navel" means health to your body. Physical, mental, and spiritual health is the result of trusting the Lord with all your heart. God wants you healthy, but He would rather have you obedient! So repent for doing it your way and failing to trust His way. Ask God to teach you to wait for Him. Begin to see His purpose and plan in your life, just as you are. Then wait on Him with a thankful heart and praise Him in your storm.

Look quickly at the example in the life of Jonah:

> One day the LORD spoke to Jonah...He said, "Go to Nineveh, that great city, and speak out against it; I am aware of how wicked its people are."
>
> Jonah 1:1-2

This was the voice of God speaking to Jonah to go and preach the word of repentance to a city that was known for its violence and wickedness. No one could blame Jonah for not wanting to go there.

Jonah decided to run from God and disobey the Lord. So God rose the sea up around the boat that he was on. It was so bad that the sailors were terrified and began throwing cargo over the sides to lighten the ship. The Word says that each of them began praying to their own god, all of this while Jonah slept down below.

It seems typical that when you're in disobedience to God that you could sleep in a storm. Sin takes away the sensitivity to God around you. When you have unconfessed sin you don't pray, you don't worship, you don't hear God, and you just begin to live life selfishly.

When it was realized that Jonah was the cause of the storm, Jonah made a startling comment. He said, "I worship the Lord, the God of heaven, who made the earth and the sea." In the King James Version, he said, "I fear the Lord." Did Jonah really fear the Lord? Did he really truly worship God? If Jonah had really feared the Lord he would have obeyed the Lord.

Jonah told the men that he was the cause of the storm and told them to throw him overboard and everything would be all right. I am not sure if Jonah knew what the outcome of being thrown overboard from a ship away from land during a raging storm would be like. I think I am convinced that storms have a great purpose in them. I also find it thought provoking that God had him jump into the storm rather than calming the storm down first. What seemed to be easier, obeying God and going to Nineveh, or jumping into the ocean during a storm? The second act of obedience is always harder.

His obedience calmed the sea. Your obedience will calm the sea around you, but you will still be in the center of the ocean. The lesson God wants you to learn is going to cost you a little.

> From deep inside the fish Jonah prayed to the LORD his God.
>
> Jonah 2:1

There are times when the only thing you can do is cry out to the Lord. You must do what Jonah did, pray!

> In my distress, O LORD, I called to you, and you answered me. From deep in the world of the dead I cried for help, and you heard me. You threw me down into the depths, to the very bottom of the sea, where the waters were all around me, and all your mighty waves rolled over me. I thought I had been banished from your presence and would never see your holy temple again. The water came over me and choked me; the sea covered me completely, and seaweed wrapped around my head. I went down to the very roots of the mountains, into the land whose gates lock shut forever. But you, O LORD my God, brought me back from the depths alive. When I felt my life slipping away, then, O LORD, I prayed to you, and in your holy Temple you heard me.
>
> Jonah 2:2-7

I often think that it's in the depths of despair that brings us to our senses with God. Why didn't Jonah just obey the Lord in the first place? I love the fact that God can be found even though we put ourselves in bad positions with our disobedience. It's because He has a great love for us. Look at what Jonah does after he prays. He makes an act of faith to God before God does anything on his behalf.

> But I will sing praises to you; I will offer you a sacrifice and do what I have promised. Salvation comes from the LORD!
>
> Jonah 2:8-9

What sacrifice could he have possibly made? He was still in the belly of the fish. God hadn't delivered him, and I don't think that Jonah got a word from the Lord. He just knew enough about God to act in faith. That is exactly what you and I have to do, to act out of faith to His Word. Jonah knew that God had a hard time staying angry for long periods of time. He also must have known that God has a weak spot for praise! Imagine, Jonah singing while in the belly of the fish! But it was enough to make God act.

The story doesn't end here, because we see that whale spit him up back at the place where he started. He still had to be obedient to the first calling.

It's easy to want your own outcome of the plan of God. It's not always easy saying "Lord, Lord" when we are asked to go through suffering or hardships. But God would rather have my obedience than my sacrifices and offerings. Make it your goal to always obey the will of God no matter what you have to go through.

Sarah's Leukemia Is in Remission

Day 43—November 9, 2010

Once again, the Father has kept His Word. I just got a call from Sarah about 5:30 p.m., and she told me that her doctor, the one I had the opportunity to pray for when we first heard the news of Sarah's leukemia, came into her room and told her that her leukemia is in complete remission. He was amazed and said that during the first round of chemo they thought that it was in remission but they were not sure, but after the second round they are now sure. No leukemia!

Sarah and I thought that this was great; the journey is almost over and we can go home for good. Not so! I was let down a little when Doctor Nath told us that this was good, but there is much more to come. He said that eighty percent of leukemia patients will go into remission after chemotherapy, however, Acute myeloid leukemia always comes back. So we will now need to proceed to the next phase.

I have almost daily asked the Lord about the purpose of this journey and many things come to mind. I feel that this journal was one of the plans of God. I have received reports from so many people about how our story has touched their lives and brought comfort to them. Should that had been the plan of God then Sarah and I both rejoice, but I feel it goes even deeper than that. God has a purpose in all His doings. He has taught me to hear the cry of the hurting and to know the compassion of the Father. I now see that I am His vessel to show the world how much He loves them. I am His voice of love to those who hate; His eyes of compassion to those who suffer; His feet to bring the lost the message of His Son. I am His ambassador to carry His message to the world, and so are you! This is your calling too.

I have been asked many times, "Why did God allow this to happen to Sarah in the first place?" I believe that it was an answer to our prayers. Our heavenly Father is always working for the purpose of making us like His Son, to become pure before God you must go through the fire of testing so that all the world and its effect is burned off your life. Only then are you truly useable. So many fail during testing because they failed to see the Father's willingness to go with them in it and they tried to go alone...they listened to the wrong voices and allow fear and worry to be their guides through the trials rather than faith and hope. You can always rest assured that when you are going through something God has allowed that there will be those who have been sent by the devil to encourage you. But their encouragement goes against what God has spoken to you. We know Sarah has been allowed by God to go through the whole ordeal. This is not what we wanted, but there is no going back. So we have to guard ourselves against those who do not understand this journey that God has chosen for us.

Please understand, some need words of faith, so in having that God will give you an instant miracle. We are not against that, and we suggest that everyone ask God for it in faith. But when you are not healed, you must seek the Lord for the right answer for you. Sarah and I did this in total faith. We wanted a miracle too, but God knew that He could very easily sustain us if we would follow with Him in obedience. The results for us have been amazing.

But this is our journey! God is using it to change us. Your journey will be different, and it will be used to change you.

Better to trust in the Lord than to put confidence in man.

Psalm 118:8

Why is this scripture so important? It is the verse that is located in the very center of the Bible. I believe that this verse is the key to the entire Christian life regardless of what you are going through. The one thing we must never lose sight of is the fact that God is all powerful; man is created and given a limited amount of power. God is all knowing; man is limited in what he knows. Why then would we not wait on the Father's wisdom and direction before we assume what we are to do?

Someone shared with me yesterday about a man who after seeing children stricken with cancer swore that he could never serve a God who allowed this to happen. I must agree that to see children suffering is about the hardest thing to witness in life. But why is this something that God allows? What about those who say that tragedy is a result of the sins of the nation? Hurricanes and natural disasters is the judgment of God on us for our sins. Sadly, I do not know the answer. It's better to trust in the Lord! I do know that when man fell in the garden, sin entered, causing sickness and disease along with separation from God. This was not God's plan but rather a result of a fallen race. It's the result of man doing only what he wants to do and thereby pulling God out of the picture. It can never be said that this is the will of God, because it is not. If it was, God would have never sent Jesus to die for man's sin.

Sickness, death, sin, and suffering became the reason why God sent Jesus and the reason why God raises you and me up. We are called to bring the restoration of the kingdom of God through healing, deliverance, and salvation to this fallen world. We are the world's hope. It is why the Great Commission is for all believers. "Go ye into all the world and preach the gospel to every creature" (Mark 16:15-17). We are told to cast out devils and to heal the sick. Why? Because the world is dominated by the fall of man and the devil is head over the fallen creation of God. When we cast out devils, heal the sick, and preach the gospel, we are bringing the kingdom of God to the world, thereby destroying the works of the devil.

Let me give you an example: Jesus said in Matthew 12:28, "But if I cast out devils by the Spirit of God, then the kingdom of God is come unto you."

Jesus was saying that when you bring light into darkness, the light wins. Try it. Go into a dark closet and light a candle. Instantly the darkness leaves. Jesus said that you and I are the light of the world. If we take that light into the darkness of sin the light will eliminate the darkness. Those of us who have accepted Christ as our Savior are the answer to man's sin, because we have the light living in us. It's time to take that light and release it into people.

Too many Christians want entertainment and rejoicing to music rather than seeing the oppressed go free. No one wants to be in the trenches fighting the enemy. We are being told that we have to have the good life, now! Blessings...blessings...blessings, but this is why there are so many sick and dying. The church who is the carrier of truth is dead. They are growing, but not producing. Living, but not breathing on their own, their on life support and living in a spiritual coma. No one's preaching outside the church. We say we love our church, but what is it that we love—the fellowship, the worship, the people, or the pastor? What about loving the lost, the sick, the disabled, and the imprisoned? Is that not what we were commissioned by Jesus to do? I even worry that today's method of outreach is no longer preaching the message of deliverance, but rather "blessing the community." We pour out clothing, food, toys, bikes...this is good, but we are not seeing much lasting fruit with it. Jesus showed us the true method of reaching a community; it was preaching the Word so that the captives would be set free. It was miracles! Light confronting darkness, not light blending into darkness, but rather an outright confrontation with it! During the life of Jesus crowds came from everywhere to see the miracles that this man was producing. They brought the sick and blind, the deaf and possessed, and Jesus healed them all. Now, I am not against outreaches that bless the community, I just want to see ministry that produces change.

If we are going to see a true, lasting revival, we must bring light and confront the darkness face-to-face and stop playing silly useless church games to get people to leave their church and come to ours. We must fight in the right war! It may feel good right now to see your churches growing through fellowship, activities, and music, but will it survive the fires of tribulation and suffering?

I want you to know I speak the way I do because it is how God is dealing with me personally. I want more! I must go deeper and seek the true riches that are eternal. It's the only thing that will last! Go deeper, seek all that God has. I have only one goal in my quest, it is to reach my city with the gospel of Jesus Christ. Till they all hear and know! Then I will rest. "Better to trust in the Lord than to put confidence in man" (Psalm 118:8).

There is one other thing I want to share with those of you who are suffering. Suffering does not give you the right to become unfaithful. God still expects the best that you have. I have seen many come up with every little excuse that they can to not honor the Lord the way God desires them too. The cares of life and even the burdens of suffering is no excuse to not place God first in your life. Nothing should hinder you from walking deep with God, nothing!

Well, I got to get dressed and go and pick Sarah up today.... she is coming home and I am going to cook her a fresh haddock dinner with cabbage, corn, fresh potatoes and maybe a peach pie. Oh, how much I love Him! He is an ever present help in my time of need.

Allowing God to Make the Needed Changes

Day 53—November 19, 2010

I cannot help but recall how far Sarah and I have come in our lives together. In February we will have been married for twenty-six years. When we first got married we were all excited about coming together, raising a family, and then growing old together. We soon found out that living together wasn't so easy. We were different in every way. We grew up with our own ideas and our own priorities and ways of doing things. Once we came together in marriage we began to conflict with each other. She needed things from me that I never learned how to give. I did not know how to be a husband or a close friend. I was selfish and self-centered. I had my own ideas of how life for me and my wife was suppose to be. But she had an idea too. We didn't match, not even close. In a very short time we grew apart from each other; not intentionally, it just happened, and it happened quickly. She began to feel that she married the wrong person. I felt great rejection, because I could not understand just what she wanted from me. The marriage was breaking apart, and the only thing that seemed to hold it together was our firstborn son, Brandon. We both knew that he needed a mother and a father…parents! So we hung on the best we could.

This type of marriage describes what it is like when a sinful man gets saved and comes into contact with the holy God. There is conflict. Like our marriage it was more than just agreeing to change and making promises that you will do better. It takes conflict to make change a reality. God needed to break Sarah and me and rebuild our lives on the right foundation. This is one of the purposes of suffering and trials. It allows God to get our attention refocused on the right things. We have learned that it is not my way or her way that we want to follow, it is God's way. Those ways have always kept us in harmony with one another and with Him.

It was the reason why God allowed young David to kill a lion and a bear when he was watching his father's sheep. The conflict allowed David to gain the faith and courage to challenge a bigger enemy in his life. One named Goliath. He did it without fear because God had used previous battles to prepare him for bigger ones.

I have learned that there are two ways to go through every journey: You can ask God to send you on the easy road, but you must remember the fact that being easy is the only reward that He will give you for your journey. Easy journeys have short lasting testimonies. Or you can allow God to take you on the road marked with challenges that will redirect and change your life. Do not misunderstand me. I am not saying that you should ask to suffer; I am saying that you should tell your Father that it is His choice. That choice could very well be a miracle in which He would be glorified. He will reveal to you things you never dreamed, doors will open for you to bring in His glory. And more than anything else, that conflict in your journey will change you to become like Him.

Our journey has brought Sarah and me into new heights. God prepared us for this a long time ago when we allowed Him to break down our whole marriage and rebuild it on the right foundation. The conflict of building our marriage brought lasting change and long-term healing. And it prepared us for the journey we are now on.

I have an amazing little brother named Robert. Robert and his wife, Tammy, pastor a church in Maryland, and they have three daughters. The oldest daughter has been diagnosed with multiple sclerosis. One day she had to be rushed to the hospital because she had gotten very sick. After a few days there, Robert said to me that what he and his wife were going through was not fair. I could not believe that he said that to me. My wife has leukemia and he wanted to say that it was not fair for his little girl to be sick! I have seen children killed in car accidents and die of cancer; how could he say such a thing? Who has the right to say what is fair or unfair? Why is it fair for us in America to throw away more food than some third world countries have to eat? Why is it fair that our children have the best education and the best medical facilities in the world while many countries lose their children to disease and famine and war? Is any of it fair? Who decides this great question before us? What is fair? Do I have the right to never suffer? Will I dare stand before God and say to Him, "Why me?"

Is it fair my dear friends for me not to suffer in any way and yet not to care that you have to suffer? I told my brother that I daily thank God that He saw fit to test us with this leukemia! You might be saying, "What? Are you serious?" Yes, I am. It has given me the understanding of God's mighty and powerful grace that is available to me when I need it. It has taken our marriage to the next level, maybe even higher. It has opened countless doors to minister to people, it has brought our church together as a family; it has brought me to the cross and I have found the One whom my soul longs for. Is it fair? No, it will never be totally fair until the day we all get to heaven and we have no more pain or sorrow and no sickness or suffering. But until then, we must level out the playing field. To do that is to learn how to suffer with one another so that we are all suffering together. We must learn to carry one another's burdens and to bear one another up when they hurt. Galatians 6:2 says, "Help carry one another's burdens, and in this way you will obey the law of Christ." This is the call to the church to true suffering. When one hurts, we all hurt. I told my brother that God will open to him the true ministry of compassion for those all around him. Compassion means "to suffer with." I should weep for those who suffer, because in doing so I am fulfilling the very law of Christ.

When Sarah is in the hospital I go to visit her and anyone else that the Lord will open the door for me to visit. I have removed the blinders of self-pity and opened my heart to the world around me.

I have even practiced this as a pastor. I no longer pastor the Faith Assembly of God Church...I now pastor the city of Webster, Massachusetts. I have 26,480 people in my congregation. There is every race and nationality, every type of sickness and disease, all ages from infant to elderly. We have hospitals, nursing homes, retirement homes, parks, and schools—all a part of our church. This is our mission field; to reach this city for Christ. Our personal sufferings make us qualified to bring them this gospel. Sin, suffering, and sickness rendered us all hopeless and in need of Jesus, just like the rest of the people in our huge congregation. Although many of these people haven't been to the services yet, we pray for them and care for them.

God promises that the suffering we endure will produce glory. For me it has. I am passionate for more of Him and I am more convinced that He is changing me for the purpose of being useful and fruitful (John 15). So much is gained when a grain of wheat goes into the ground and dies, and so little when the grain stays in the comfortable package. Imagine a package of seeds that you buy from the store; as long as those seeds remain safely inside the package they will forever remain just seeds, totally useless, unless planted. They are, however, very comfortable and safe and have the ability to look productive and have purpose when you look at the package. I can look at the package and dream about what kind of wonderful fruit it will produce one day and how good it will taste. But unless it is planted and faces the conflict of change, it will remain useless. But if you take those seeds and bury them in the ground and allow the soil to invade them and transform them they will begin to grow and that growth will produce glory. One apple can either remain alone or become millions and millions of apples, just by planting the seeds. But it must go through the process of death.

I remember a story I heard many years ago about a missionary who gave the ultimate sacrifice to God. The missionary was Jim Elliot. He, along with four other missionaries, was brutally martyred in Ecuador while trying to bring the gospel to a tribe of natives. This tribe was so violent that the word love was not even in their vocabulary. After her husband's death, Jim's wife, Elizabeth, went to a church in the United States to share her story about the passion that her and her husband had for these people. After she spoke a young reporter came to her and said, "I am so sorry that your husband died in the jungle." She replied by saying, "My husband did not die in the jungle." He said, "Elizabeth, I know you must be grieving, but you have to come to grips with what really happened to Jim. He died in the jungle!" She said, "No, young man, it is you that must understand; my husband did not die in the jungle. He died when he was a high school senior by the side of his bed." It was there that Jim Elliot laid it all down and surrendered to the will of God. Life was never taken from him in the jungle because he had already given up his life for God's best. Some of his quotes are among my most cherished:

> "He is no fool to give up what he cannot keep, to gain what he cannot afford to lose."

"Father, make of me a crisis man. Bring those I contact to a decision. Let me not be a milepost on a single road; make me a fork, that men must turn one way or another on facing Christ in me."

He made life count both in life and in death!

Elizabeth Elliot took the gospel message back to these people who had murdered her husband, and that tribe came to know Jesus. Her husband became the seeds of the mission, along with the other four men who gave themselves, so that these people could find God. No regrets!

I can spend all my time in being frustrated or angry over situations, or I can rest in the fact that I am in my Father's heart. Look at what the apostle Paul wrote concerning what He went through:

Romans 8:18:

> I consider that what we suffer at this present time cannot be compared at all with the glory that is going to be revealed to us.

Do you not like the will of God for your life? Is it because you are selfish, or because you do not know that God has something great in store for those who allow Him to lead the journey? I am well aware as I have mentioned before that God has the power to heal and to deliver you. But what if that is not His choice; will you allow Him to bring you through it so that your journey can bring in the right amount of conflict to produce the right changes in you? Like I said, miracles are instant. Journeys are life changing and produce more miracles. Both are rewarding!

No More Quitting

Day 55—November 21, 2010

A few days ago I was saying just how good Sarah was doing, but yesterday Sarah had a fever of 100.5 and the chills. This is never good. Any fever over 100.3 is an instant five-day hospital stay. So last night we had to take her in and she was admitted. My heart is broken for her because it never seems to end. The question of "why her" comes to my mind often, but I know better than to say that out loud. I find it hard to say one day she is doing well and the next day she is suffering. The journey is so much more than we realized it would be. I do not know how people who do not know the Lord make it through such trials. We, however, are forced to endure whatever comes our way, but we will do so in faith that God is with us. We will, like yesterday and the days before that press on in faith because there is no other way to go. Our journey is in forward progress only and there is no retreat; we have no alternative left but to finish it. Maybe today I am learning about quitting, after all, it had been my weakness throughout my life. To start and not finish, to begin and quit before God was done with me. I had always allowed opposition to discourage me and even when I would get bored I would begin to look for new challenges somewhere else. It became easier for me to start over than for me to press through. This journey is no exception. I would love to quit right now, but I am forced to continue on. In some ways I am relieved to know that I have no choice in the matter. I will have to muster daily faith and daily grace regardless of what comes, and in some ways this is good. I know that it will be one thing that I will be able to say, that I finished from beginning to end. But I also know it is being used to teach me to finish in all areas of my life. To persevere through hardships and fight wars that lead to greater victories. Maybe I'm not as sad today as I thought I was…Maybe I now know that this journey is going to change this weakness in my life. After all, greater men than I have been brought down the road of hardship in order to produce the godly character needed to win.

What about David, who was anointed king of Israel by Samuel? I am sure that he did not realize what he was about to face in order to be King. When anointed by Samuel, I am sure he felt flattered, but he was still just a boy. He needed to become a man and not just any man—a man after God's own heart. David never realized that Saul would try to kill him and then chase him through the wilderness in an effort to end his life. Promises from God are guaranteed, but the road to their fulfillment can be long and unsure. Why? Because it all goes back to God wanting to build in us the character of righteousness, a character that has learned complete trust and faith in the one who gave the promise. No one is up to the true challenge that God has for them, and the Bible said that if we are to follow Christ then we must take up our cross daily and deny ourselves. That is not a simple task to perform. Crosses are heavy, and to deny yourself is often humiliating or costly. But it produces godliness and faith in those who obey it.

Joseph had the same lessons to learn as well. In the book of Genesis, we see that Joseph was a dreamer and his father's favorite son. He was spoiled and didn't have to do the work that his brothers had to do. One day Joseph had a dream. He saw all his brothers and family bowing down and worshipping him. Of course he did not understand what it meant even though it was from God. To make matters worse his family despised him for thinking such things.

Sometimes God reveals to us some of what he has planned. I often wonder why God doesn't tell us everything upfront, maybe because He knows that we would mess it all up if we knew. But learning a little at a time can be just as frustrating as knowing the whole story. But Joseph none the less became hated by his brothers and they ended up throwing him into a pit, then selling him into slavery, then telling his father he was dead. The last words from his brothers were, "Now let's see what will happen to his dreams" (Genesis 37:20).

Those who suffer feel the pressure of losing their dreams every day. They feel the weight of the world come down upon them and no help to get out from under it. I understand this; every day I wake up and wonder if Sarah is going to be all right. Will she be sick or need to go to the hospital? It's hard to be away from the house long and I worry if she doesn't pick up the phone by the third ring. Dreams are often put on hold and even forgotten when you're suffering. Pretty soon people even stop asking how she is. It's hard to experience that because the journey is not yet near being over. But it's all right because it is just the way it is.

Every day people suffer all around us. They go through pain, suffering, and hardships. I think that it is easy to forget what it feels like to experience major hurt or loss, and this causes us to lose compassion. When we lose compassion we stop trying to heal the hurts. Laughter is said to be a medicine, but not caring is a disease and a pain far worse than most. It brings us away from the very plan of Christ to touch the hurting and to bring His healing touch to people. Maybe this is why there are so few healings in the church anymore. At one time doctors used to go to people's homes and care for them; they demonstrated great compassion.

Jesus came with a purpose and He would not quit until it was finished.

> Whoever continues to sin belongs to the devil, because the devil has sinned from the very beginning. The Son of God appeared for this very reason, to destroy what the devil had done.
>
> 1 John 3:8

This must also be the reason we are preaching on Sundays; to see to it that Satan's work is destroyed, especially in the body of Christ. Jesus said, "Upon this Rock I will build my church and the gates of hell will not prevail against it" (Matthew 16:18). These are powerful words, and Jesus meant them. I am going to break out of my comfort zone and who knows what might happen if I dare to believe God! I am going to hold Him to His Word to heal the sick, cast out devils, raise the dead…"the lame will walk, the deaf will hear, the blind will see and the victim will be set free" (Mark 11:24). If we are not going to preach it and do what it says then we are not much different from the religious Pharisees that Jesus contended with while He was on earth. We must stop hindering the Word from being fulfilled with our lack of faith. Have you noticed that fancy sermons sound good but have no power? When someone is healed or set free you have a living, breathing, impacting, walking, talking testimony that proclaims the glory of God where ever they go. You know how Jesus spurned revival? Not through preaching (although he did preach); he spurned revival with the demonstration of the power of God. He did not just preach about it, He demonstrated it.

When John the Baptist was in prison he sent his disciples to Jesus to ask Him if He was the Messiah. Jesus said, "You go to John and you tell him the things that you saw…the deaf hear, the blind see, the poor have the gospel preached to them" (Matthew 11:2-6). In other words, the proof was in the manifestation, not the words. When Jesus healed the sick the crowds came and they followed Him.

It is so easy to follow the norm and miss the spectacular or to follow man's ways and not listen to the Spirit. You must learn to pray for your pastor. Pray that God would get a hold of him reveal to him more of His Son. Please, do not fight against him. That is always the work of the devil. Pray for Him!

Today I have made up my mind. No distractions! I am going to finish my course and fight a good fight! I will not quit!

Feelings and Faith

Day 57—November 23, 2010

Well, here is another lesson about faith. There is so much to learn about faith that I believe that it would take many books to teach us all there is to be learned. I also believe that if there is anything keeping us out of the precious promises of God it would have to be our faith. Much of a person's truth is based upon what he believes, because of that he becomes limited to just how he will express himself in his actions. If he believes that God is angry with him he begins to doubt God's love when he fails or sins. He is less likely to go to the Father in repentance because he feels the Father is angry with him. Therefore we must all allow the foundation of our truth to be based on the Word of God rather than just what we feel or think.

According to Hebrews 11:6, we know that it is impossible to please or honor God without faith being present. But faith in what? Is faith based on what I believe? Or is faith based on what He says?

Hebrews 11 tells us a lot about it when it says it is "the substance of things hoped for and the evidence of things not seen." It is hoped for and yet remains unseen (seems unfair almost, yet it is necessary in God's plan). Faith is the substance of what I want. Everything I am asking for exists in the faith for what I am ting. That faith is not seen and is not touchable or tangible, either is it due to arrive at a certain time. It's just based upon what I was promised. Faith is based on what I have been told by God. Faith is knowing it's coming because it relies on the confidence you have in the one who spoke the promise. If you believe in God then you place your faith in what He has said.

> Our great desire is that each of you keep up your eagerness to the end, so that the things you hope for will come true. We do not want you to become lazy, but to be like those who believe and are patient, and so receive what God has promised. When God made his promise to Abraham, He made a vow to do what He had promised. Since there was no one greater than himself, He used his own name when He made his vow. He said, 'I promise you that I will bless you and give you many descendants.' Abraham was patient, and so he received what God had promised.
>
> Hebrews 6:11-15

Promises are not always instant with God, because then faith would never be required. Many receive much from God that others miss because they stood firm on the promise by believing in it. That belief though needs faith to respond and that faith kicks the promise into action. Check out the rest of this:

> When we make a vow, we use the name of someone greater than ourselves, and the vow settles all arguments. To those who were to receive what he promised, God wanted to make it very clear that he would never change his purpose; so he added his vow to the promise. There are these two things, then, that cannot change and about which God cannot lie. So we who have found safety with him are greatly encouraged to hold firmly to the hope placed before us. We have this hope as an anchor for our lives. It is safe and sure, and goes through the curtain of the heavenly temple into the inner sanctuary.
>
> Hebrews 6:16-19

There are many things written here that you must take into account. Hebrews says that God would never change His purpose, and because of that He added His vow to the promise. God's vow means He will honor what He said in His Word. It is a promise He vows to keep. He then says that we have found safety with Him; in other words, we can trust what He said. This hope is an anchor for our life…safe and sure!

It is for this reason that I am confident to say that even though it may feel that everything has turned upside down that you can still know that God will bring it about to our good. Satan intended it for your destruction, but God will turn it for your good. The key to winning is faith in the Lord. That faith must hold on regardless of what is experienced in our lives because only those who can hold out to the end will receive the promise and the reward that God has to offer those who endure.

There is one more great promise written in this book:

> Do not lose your courage, then, because it brings with it a great reward. You need to be patient, in order to do the will of God and receive what he promises.
>
> Hebrews 10:35-36

Learning to walk in the obedience of what God wants is important. What we might want or expect may change during the course of our journey, but it will change for the purpose of what God wants in us.

What about my feelings? Why do journeys like ours come with pain? Could not God have brought us through without so much suffering? You can't help but allow your feelings to dictate the success or failure of your journey. When times are good we feel we are on the right road. But when times get hard we wonder if we missed something or got off the right track. Wasn't God supposed to protect us from that? My feelings involve so much of who I am and what I think. It's hard to experience anything without feelings. Much of what we do or don't do is based on whether or not we felt like doing it. With that in mind it leads me to believe that God takes my feelings into account with what I am going through. David understood this,

> From the end of the earth will I cry unto thee, when my heart is overwhelmed: lead me to the rock that is higher than I.
>
> Psalm 61:2

Knowing this about David leads me to believe that having similar feelings is not where my sin lies. It does not mean I have quit, failed, or raised the white flag. It's normal! David's prayer was that when he would become overwhelmed that God would lead him to the rock that is higher than he was. That rock is the place of stability and security. It is a shelter where I can go to be protected from the war that surrounds me. So, to look at my feelings first before I trust my faith is a part of the journey. But to stay with my feelings is a mistake. I must find the place of shelter and go there and wait out the feelings until the faith kicks in.

I use to love to go camping. A few years ago my father-in-law and I took a group of boys from the church to a Royal Rangers campout for a weekend. It was going to be a great time teaching the boys survival techniques and sitting around the campfire. However, the unexpected came up. It poured rain the entire week. What we did was build a shelter to protect us and we stayed dry even though it still rained. Only the boys who ventured out from the shelter got soaked. When you're in the midst of a trial God has built for you a shelter, the Rock, Jesus Christ. That rock is a place from the Lord to protect you and to allow you to regain your confidence. Look at the next verse that David wrote:

> For thou hast been a shelter for me, and a strong tower from the enemy.
>
> Psalm 61:3

Part of the promise given to us through the death of Jesus Christ was the wonderful gift of grace. In the Old Testament, the rock and shelter represented this gift. Grace is God enabling us to handle what we need to go through; it carries us through trials and hardships and equips us with His strength, might, and wisdom. However, this grace must be accessed in order for you to have it. Like David who prayed, "When my heart is overwhelmed lead to me the rock." We too must walk into the place of this grace in order to have it. Look at what Paul tells us:

> Now that we have been put right with God through faith, we have peace with God through our Lord Jesus Christ. He has brought us by faith into this experience of God's grace, in which we now live. And so we boast of the hope we have of sharing God's glory! We also boast of our troubles, because we know that trouble produces endurance, endurance brings God's approval, and his approval creates hope. This hope does not disappoint us, for God has poured out his love into our hearts by means of the Holy Spirit, who is God's gift to us.
>
> Romans 5:1-5

Here is the key to receiving the help you need to get through everything: It is knowing how to get the grace of God to be activated in your life.

First, Romans 5:1 said, I have been made right with God by faith which results of course in my having peace with God. This is salvation, and you must have that first in order to understand His grace.

Second, Romans 5:2, through Jesus Christ and His salvation, we have grace made available to us into this grace. In the King James Version, it says I have access, not entrance in His grace. In other words, it's like being given a debit card to purchase what I need. But I have to go and get it. Faith is the key, or the debit card, to open that door. I must see it in my heart if I am going to have it in reality. Only after I know what I have been given will

I go and obtain it. It is there! I must however realize that there is only enough for today, and sometimes there is only enough for right now. You must learn to constantly go into His grace if you are going to be sustained through your trials, but it works! It is powerful and life changing, and it is God's wonderful gift to us! It requires your faith for it to work.

The key is this: take all your feelings and emotions and go into your prayer closet, call upon the Lord your God, and rise up and claim your vision. Here is what I did when Sarah first got sick. This has sustained me from the very first day. I went to my prayer closet and prayed this:

> Father, I come to you in the name of Jesus Christ. He Himself has given me access into Your grace so that I might find help in my time of need. I am here on the behalf of my wife, and I need You to sustain me, uphold me, and encourage me. Help me to see Your purpose in this and help me not to interfere in any way. I trust you completely. Help my unbelief! I bind any and all spirits of darkness and sickness against Sarah. I bind the spirits of discouragement against her, and I renounce all fear in the name of Jesus. You are my hope, my rock, my loving Father, whom shall I ever fear? You are Alpha and Omega...Almighty God...What do I have to be worried about? I remind You of Your promises and of Your love for us. Thank You for Your grace; I take it! I will make it! I receive Your peace, Your joy, Your hope, and all of Your grace. In Jesus's name, Amen!

But be warned of this one thing; it is one thing to struggle with our feelings, it is quite another to not believe. Unbelief will kill your faith, and it is the same as calling God a liar. You must see only through the eyes of faith and allow your Heavenly Father the right to bring you through it.

I find it amazing how much my faith has grown from the time I started writing about this journey to now. All discouragement has turned into hope; glory be to my Father; He has not forsaken me or Sarah! He will not forsake you either! I am living in His great provision of grace. Thank you, Father!

Thanksgiving Day...Eyes Opened

Day 59—November 25, 2010

This past Tuesday Sarah came home from the hospital. The family was so excited to know that we are going to be able to have Thanksgiving together. It really is an answer to our prayers, and even though we are unable to have family members and friends over to enjoy it with us, we were just grateful to know we were all able to be together. The past few days were spent watching Sarah prepare the food list, and I was overjoyed watching her put all this together for us. I took several opportunities to peek around the corner to see her smiling face shining with the joy of the day. She was happy knowing that the family was together. It was so special. It was a gift from God.

But late Wednesday night Sarah had started bleeding very heavily. At first we were not too concerned because on Thanksgiving morning she had a nurse that was scheduled to stop by and check her out. We could only pray that by then she would be better.

We woke up early today because the smell of that fifteen pound turkey filled the house, and it was a smell of celebration and excitement. Sarah was home today and we were all together;

what could go wrong now? But by 11:00 a.m. joy turned to sorrow. The nurse had informed us that the hospital wanted Sarah to go there right away. Even though dinner was almost done, we had to put everything on hold. So not fair! The boys and I agreed not to eat until we could have this meal together with Sarah. The mood in the house turned sad, and we all pitched in to put dinner away, unsure if we were going to be able to enjoy this together. I walked her out to the car and drove her to the hospital feeling so sad for her. She had so wanted to have this special day with us as we had been planning it for several weeks and now it was being taken away. I knew she was sad inside even though she was the one encouraging all of us.

On the way to the hospital I asked the Father what His reason for this was. After all, it was just one day a year, just one day that we could have had together after going through so much. Soon after we arrived at the hospital I was given the answer to that prayer.

Taking Sarah to the eighth floor required me to walk through most of the hospital. I saw families coming and going that were there to see loved ones who could not be with them this Thanksgiving. I was saddened to see so many there, all who had someone that wished they too could have been home for Thanksgiving. I realized just how small my compassion for the hurting still was. I truly thought I had gone further than I did. While preparing to enjoy such a feast year after year I was forgetting to pray for those who suffer. In the halls and rooms were families who had loved ones who needed their visit.. I felt so sad for each of them. After all, they too were suffering; it was no longer just me or Sarah. I wiped tears away from my eyes this morning asking God, "Why have I allowed myself to be so blind to the needs of the suffering?" Where did they all come from, and how is it that I never really noticed them before? I get so caught up in football and friends and food that I forget that I am an ambassador for the Lord Jesus Christ. I represent Him—

His goodness, His kindness, His healing, His compassion, and His love. God forgive me for being too busy to have compassion especially this time of year. Every day we should not hesitate to show the compassion of Christ, to smile and make conversation with others so that the true love of Christ can touch them. My attitude shows my trust in the Father and rather than complaining and getting restless I have learned that God has a purpose for everything and He is in complete control.

The trials that I go through will test me and purify me in every area of my life; like Job said:

> But I know there is someone in heaven who will come at last to my defense. Even after my skin is eaten by disease, while still in this body I will see God. I will see him with my own eyes, and he will not be a stranger.

> Job 19:25-27

When the trial is finished, God will prevail. Job did not understand why he was suffering in the manner that he was, but he knew that when it was over he would be rewarded with a fresh revelation of God.

To those of you who are not suffering or going through trials, remember those who are; stop being too busy to see those around you. If you are a Christian you must repent for your blindness and open your eyes to your calling. It is true, it may cost you something. Hungry people cannot eat on your good advice; you must feed them. But this is your calling and responsibility as His ambassador; will you heed to it? As bad off as you might be yourself, you can trust me when I say that there is someone out there close by that is worse. Care for others the way you would want them to care for you. This is the mandate of what Christ taught us while He was with us here on earth.

I read something in the Word this past week that really intrigued me. God speaks to Elijah in the book of 1 Kings 17 in the middle of a major famine and tells him to go to a widow in Zarephath and that He had commanded this widow there to sustain him. So he goes to see this widow only to find out that she only has enough food for one meal for her and her son. She told the prophet that she was going to fix this last meal for her and her son and then they were going to die. She had it settled in her heart that there was nothing else left to do but to prepare it, eat it, and die. She seemed to have settled her affairs and prepared for what she saw was the inevitable. But God had a different plan, a test perhaps. That test was to take what she had for herself and give it to someone else who had need of it. Look at this amazing story:

1 Kings 17:13-16:

> "Don't worry," Elijah said to her. "Go on and prepare your meal. But first make a small loaf from what you have and bring it to me, and then prepare the rest for you and your son. For this is what the LORD, the God of Israel, says, 'The bowl will not run out of flour or the jar run out of oil before the day that I, the LORD, send rain.'" The widow went and did as Elijah had told her, and all of them had enough food for many days. As the LORD had promised through Elijah, the bowl did not run out of flour nor did the jar run out of oil.

Now, this seems odd to me! Why would God send Elijah to get a meal from a widow woman who is getting ready to eat her last meal? How was she going to sustain him when she was unable to sustain herself? The key was through the obedience of the Word spoken to her by the prophet of God. Many times we miss the Lord because what He asks us to do does not make sense to us. This passage is filled with that.

First, Elijah is told to go to a widow woman who would be able to sustain him physically with food and shelter. Widows were usually poor; they had little means of support as it was there was no welfare system in place. Plus, she had a son she was supporting.

Second, this widow had only one meal left! Not enough to sustain a hungry prophet of God. And there was a famine in the land, people all around were going hungry and were in need; how was she going to accomplish this?

Third, the prophet told her to feed him first. To take what she had for her last meal and to give it to him. Why? The answer was easy. Elijah had a word of the Lord he was operating on. The Lord said that she would sustain him and that meant God was going to see to it that she had what she needed. This woman though had to act in faith and obedience to the words spoken to her. Look at the results of her obedience.

It did not fail, "according to the word of the Lord, which he spoke by Elijah." You see, as bad off as the widow might had been, she still allowed herself to see the needs in someone else; that my friends will always produce the favor of the Lord for your own life. Sacrifice honors God!

How much we miss by not obeying in faith the Word of the Lord. Jesus spoke in the New Testament about this very story in the book of Luke.

> Listen to me: it is true that there were many widows in Israel during the time of Elijah, when there was no rain for three and a half years and a severe famine spread throughout the whole land. Yet Elijah was not sent to anyone in Israel, but only to a widow living in Zarephath in the territory of Sidon. And there were many people suffering from a dreaded skin disease who lived in Israel during the time of the prophet Elisha; yet not one of them was healed, but only Naaman the Syrian.
>
> Luke 4:25-27

Listen, you are that voice to your cities! It is time to stand out and speak His Word. When you pray over the sick or speak faith to the needy, you are bringing light into darkness. You may not think that it is effective, but it is. Elijah spoke from God to the people and those words were just as powerful as if Jesus said them Himself. There are results in the spiritual world that you do not see with your natural eyes.

While I was waiting for Sarah to get treated, I decided to go into the chapel and check it out. While there I noticed a guest book and I decided to look in it and see what people wrote. I expected it to be like a guest book where people just signed it with their name and where they were from. But I found that it was something more than that. It was a book full of prayers, and it really touched my heart. There were prayers written by dads asking for God to heal their sick child; prayers from children asking God to heal their moms or dads. Tears filled my eyes as I wondered if just maybe this was the same kind of prayers that the widow in Zarephath was making for her and her son. They were humble prayers asking God to send His healing touch; all I could think of was, "Where are the Elijah's today?" Maybe you and I are the answers to their prayers! Is this the reason I was supposed to come here today, to see this? I know that, as a church, we have the gift of healing to body, soul, and spirit, but it is useless unless we speak it out. Many widows will be feeding their families their last meals if the church doesn't come out of their buildings and go to them. Imagine the power that could be released if the body of Christ would speak forth God's Word in every hospital in America! If we would begin to pray for every sick person we meet instead of just comforting them, heaven would be released and the darkness would be broken! My prayers today have changed and now I pray, "Here am I Lord, send me to the widow!"

So I end today by saying to the Lord, thank you! Sarah and I were still able to have our Thanksgiving dinner together. The nurses worked hard at getting everything done quickly so that our day would still be wonderful. We arrived home by 3:30 p.m., and Sarah put together dinner for all of us to enjoy. It tasted wonderful and we all sat at the table and thanked God we were all still together. We thanked God for His many blessings and prayed for those who were unable to be home; for the many who were forced to be separated due to sickness and suffering. We feel like this was a milestone for us to have gotten to and for that we are so thankful to the many that have prayed for us, counseled us, encouraged us, visited us, fed us, and even those wonderful doctors and nurses that took such great care of Sarah while she was in their care.

The Reward for Suffering

Day 63—November 29, 2010

Sarah is doing so well this morning. She got up and cooked us a special breakfast, and I could only think about how blessed we truly are. It was a time to be thankful to the Lord. We have experienced so many wonderful blessings even when going through our trials. I have seen so many when they go through hardships get angry with God and accuse God of not being there for them and for not giving them what they wanted. But for Sarah and me, He has been more than there for us, maybe because every day we look for what He wants to teach us.

It is strange how God has to use life's situations to teach you powerful truths. Some things cannot be learned any other way than for God to bring you through it. The process of going through trials teaches us the most important lessons from God, lessons that can never be learned from books or the experiences of others. I have found that God's goal in miracles, healings, and sufferings all have the same outcome; that outcome is Christ being glorified. I never understood this before, because I had always felt that only a miracle would be the sign of God's intervention. I now know a secret about God, the secret to truly knowing Him more is to understand suffering like the apostle Paul said in Philippians:

But all those things that I might count as profit I now reckon as loss for Christ's sake. Not only those things; I reckon everything as complete loss for the sake of what is so much more valuable, the knowledge of Christ Jesus my Lord. For his sake I have thrown everything away; I consider it all as mere garbage, so that I may gain Christ and be completely united with him. I no longer have a righteousness of my own, the kind that is gained by obeying the Law. I now have the righteousness that is given through faith in Christ, the righteousness that comes from God and is based on faith.

Philippians 3:7-9

The most important thing that Paul felt he wanted to possess was to know Christ more. There seemed to be only one way to gain that knowledge, and that was to let everything else go in life. While today's TV preacher is telling you to get more Paul was telling us to let go of what we have. The only true thing that has any real value is to know Christ! Paul saw something greater in suffering; it was something more precious and valuable than anything he could ever have; it was something that could only be gained by going further and deeper than others were willing to go; something that could only be gained by the loss of something else.

All I want is to know Christ and to experience the power of his resurrection, to share in his sufferings and become like him in his death, in the hope that I myself will be raised from death to life.

Philippians 3:10-11

This was his passion. I have seen the passion of great men and women who wanted to do more for the kingdom of God. Paul wanted that as well; but it could not compare to this passion he had to know Christ more intimately. This is where most of us fail when it comes to ministry; trying to do more and build bigger and better ministries and yet fail in our passion for more of Him. The ability to do more should never outweigh the desire to know Him more.

Paul said in verse ten that he wanted to know the power of His resurrection and he wanted to share in His sufferings. This is not your average request! The reason for this was simple; in sufferings we find the side of God others never find. It is why those who are martyred are able to release things in the spiritual world that were never released before. Jesus made it clear by saying that unless a grain of wheat goes into the ground and dies it abides alone. Death and suffering releases us from our flesh and brings us into a new relationship with Christ. Paul knew that understanding this would bring him into a place of greater revelation of who Christ was and that revelation would make him more like the one he loved. He was willing to suffer so that in return He would win the ultimate prize of all...Christ.

> Yea doubtless, and I count all things but loss for the excellency of the knowledge of Christ Jesus my Lord: for whom I have suffered the loss of all things, and do count them but dung, that I may win Christ.
>
> Philippians 3:8 (KJV)

> I press toward the mark for the prize of the high calling of God in Christ Jesus.
>
> Philippians 3:14 (KJV)

The place He wants for you is the place of excellence. To be able to go to a spiritual level that most will not even go after. I never understood this before my journey started. I thought I did, but now I know that for God to reveal Jesus to Sarah and me, He had to allow us to go through the journey to the very end. It is a place of commitment to something greater than we are, something that requires us to be what we are not comfortable being, all the while we are being used by the Lord as His vessels. This is the excellence that God wants from us. Vessels that are useable are vessels that have been filled with the anointing of the Holy Spirit. 2 Corinthians 4:7 (KJV) said, "But we have this treasure in earthen vessels, that the excellency of the power may be of God, and not of us."

Those that live this path have found its excellence through sufferings and sacrifices that they were willing to make. It was worth it all! This is exactly what had happened to Job. Look at the scripture again that God gave us the first day our journey started.

> Behold, we count them happy which endure. Ye have heard of the patience of Job, and have seen the end of the Lord; that the Lord is very pitiful, and of tender mercy.
>
> James 5:11

What exactly did God do at the end? I thought after thirty-five years of ministry I knew what that was. I always believed that at the end God just restored everything that Job had lost and doubled it, kind of like a bonus for hanging in there. I was wrong.

After reading Job I have found that this passage has more to it than I first thought. I even thought it meant that God was going to greatly reward Sarah and me at the end of this trial (and He is). But that is not what God wanted us to see here. There is something that happened to Job that you rarely will hear any preacher preach about because so many miss its message.

First, I will tell you that God never did tell Job why he had to suffer. But He does reveal to Job just how little Job knew about Him. This revelation was the purpose of the first journey, the journey of suffering, but the purpose of the first journey was to get us on to the true journey that He has called us to. The second journey is the true one. It is the journey that God had to use the suffering for, so that we would be prepared for what is coming. Like Paul, God has to use something in our lives to get us prepared for what He wants to do in us. Is it all worth it? Absolutely yes!

When Job started suffering, God never told Him why he had to go through this. We do not know how long Job was afflicted; we know that during that time God never spoke to him or answered any of his prayers or requests. It wasn't until chapter thirty-eight in the book of Job, after who knows how long, that God finally was going to speak to Job and clear everything up. But despite how frustrated Job was during his sufferings, God did not address him compassionately; instead He dealt with Job's understanding as to who He was! Look at the Word here with me.

> Then out of the storm the LORD spoke to Job, Who are you to question my wisdom with your ignorant, empty words? Now stand up straight and answer the questions I ask you. Were you there when I made the world? If you know so much, tell me about it.

> Job 38:1-4

After such a long period of time where Job begs God to speak to him concerning why all these things have happened to him he finally hears God's voice. Here God speaks in such a way that Job is stunned. God begins accusing Job of speaking about things he did not know or understand. He says, "If you know so much, tell me what you know!" In all of Job's understandings of who God is, he is being told that he knew nothing at all about God. Read the rest of that chapter and notice how God reveals just how little Job knew.

Job never expected God to speak in the manner in which He spoke. Job wanted answers. God wanted trust. How often we think we know God! Job was now being required to shut up and listen so that he would realize that the ways of God are not understandable; we only know what He wants us to know and that's it.

Here God demands Job to answer Him as to why he thought the way he thought. Job was convinced that he was an upright man and that God was unjustly punishing him. God demands that Job listen so that Job would know that God answers to no one. He is not required to tell us anything!

God goes on to say,

> The LORD responded to Job, "Will the person who finds fault with the Almighty correct him? Will the person who argues with God answer him?" Job answered the LORD, "I'm so insignificant. How can I answer you? I will put my hand over my mouth. I spoke once, but I can't answer—twice, but not again."

> Job 40:1-5

After reading this I began to understand that God wants a complete trust from me. Like Job, when he heard the Lord saying these words vowed to shut up and not speak any longer. I too have decided that to speak against God would be foolish.

> Then the LORD responded to Job out of a storm.

> Job 40:6

Why out of a storm? It was because God wanted Job's complete attention. The lesson being learned here was important to Job and to you and me. It is the voice coming from the storms that speak the most volumes. That is why we must learn to listen for God when we are in the middle of trials and sufferings. He so often speaks during the storms of our lives because it is in the storms that we are most vulnerable!

Like Job, we too never realize just how little we know about God. Too many times we become too spiritually advanced in our own eyes only to find out that we are mere infants in the eyes of God. Who is man that God is mindful of him? Does a man or woman who accomplishes great things for God truly know all of Him? Can he truly know Him more than just what is written in the Word of God? The true revelation of God reveals only one thing! Just how vile and insignificant we truly are. To stand in the presence of God should bring us to our knees.

The understanding of this helped me to understand another purpose in suffering. Job's suffering opened the door for God to reveal His true nature. It was what Paul was after in the book of Philippians. After God is finished speaking, Job gives God his answer to what he heard:

> Then Job answered the LORD. I know, LORD, that you are all-powerful; that you can do anything you want. You ask how I dare question your wisdom when I am so very ignorant. I talked about things I did not understand, about marvels too great for me to know. You told me to listen while you spoke and to try to answer your questions. In the past I knew only what others had told me, but now I have seen you with my own eyes. So I am ashamed of all I have said and repent in dust and ashes.
>
> Job 42:1-6

Now we see what God wanted to do in Job at the end. Everything about Job changed. His whole life was spent knowing God only by what he had heard from others. His sufferings allowed Him entrance into knowing God face-to-face. This makes the suffering worth it.

After reading this I too have repented. This knowledge caused me to reflect all night last night and I repented for my pride and self-reliance. I need Him more. I will stop trying to speak without hearing from Him. I don't want to go without going with Him. Oh, that God would show me more of Him today and less of me. We must become truly humbled when God gives to us insight and revelation. Pride has carried our leaders into a false prosperity that will one day be burned with fire to test its truth. Tears must return to the pulpit and to the true people of God. It's repentance to God that opens the door to true and tested blessings, and these blessings will stand in the fire. May our eyes be on the prize of being "found in Him, not having our own righteousness" (Philippians 3:9), so that we too might gain what is the only thing worth having…Jesus!

Giving God What You Love Most

Day 73—December 9, 2010

This morning at 5:00 a.m. we got up, and I took Sarah to the hospital to have the surgery to remove her kidney. This was a day we had been waiting quite some time for. The surgery was to be taking place in a different part of the hospital. We were used to going to the bone marrow floor, so we took the elevator up knowing that they were waiting for her when we arrived. It is 6:00 a.m. in the morning and we are supposed to be first in line. I do not know why I am more nervous than Sarah is, but I am. She is always cool, calm, and collected; it is her confidence in the Lord that makes her so strong; it is amazing how much I am learning about her faith.

I hate having to go through this with her. Her doctor who is treating her leukemia will be putting off her treatments until she recovers from this surgery, which they guess it will take six to seven weeks. Oh well, just another day in the trenches. Still confident in God, but still wishing it would end.

I am just now leaving the hospital to go home and wait for the doctor to call and let me know all is well. As usual, God has once again spoken a new truth into my heart that I want to share with you.

I grew up with a mother who used to love to tell stories. She had this amazing ability to keep the attention of six small children while she told stories from the Bible and made them come to life. I guess it is her story telling that helps me to see things around me so well. The Bible is filled with amazing true stories written to help us to understand God and what God is like. Because of my mother's story telling I have had a love for Bible stories and today I want to share one of my favorites, the story of Abraham and Isaac.

Abraham had been given a miracle son from God named Isaac. This son was a miracle because Abraham was too old and his wife was barren. One day God sent to him an angel of God and told him that he was going to have a son. He thought that it would be impossible, but God honored His promise, and Abraham had a son. When Isaac was about twelve years old God decided to test Abraham:

> Some time later God tested Abraham; he called to him, "Abraham!" And Abraham answered, "Yes, here I am!" "Take your son," God said, "your only son, Isaac, whom you love so much, and go to the land of Moriah. There on a mountain that I will show you, offer him as a sacrifice to me."
>
> Genesis 22:1-2

The scripture tells us that God was testing Abraham here. So God calls him, and in complete trust and obedience he answers with, "Here I am!" God says to him to take his son, the one that he loved so much. Now, God knew how much Abraham loved

Isaac, maybe a little too much perhaps. You see, it is easy to love something so much that God gets jealous. The Bible says in Exodus 20, that God is a jealous God. He does not want our affections on something or someone else; He wants to be the object of our worship.

So, God says to Abraham, take Isaac and go to the land of Moriah and offer Isaac as a sacrifice there. Can you even imagine that? I can just see Abraham watching his son playing outside and knowing that God was going to require that he kill his son to prove his obedience to God. I can feel this in my heart as I write this. He had to have felt like something had punched him in the stomach, because he knew that he had to obey God. Or did he? Could Abraham now choose to disobey Him? I think Abraham would have gladly given up anything and everything God would ask for except maybe his son. But it was his son that God wanted. It may have been the very thing that was in the way between God and Abraham.

So many things in life can relate to how Abraham must have felt. Oh, my heart grieves as I write this. Right now Sarah is preparing to be cut open for surgery; I feel hurt inside as I sit here helpless knowing I can't do anything to help her, like Abraham I had to just wait. Why could God not just have healed her so that she would not have to go through all this? This is the question that most of us would love to ask God, knowing that someone you love is about to suffer. Then of course you have to wait... and wait...and wait. You have thoughts going through your mind: "Is she okay?" "Did they find anything else in there?" "Is she in pain?" "Is she afraid?" I hope this is all normal thoughts and not thoughts of unbelief and fear. But who can say they don't feel the hurt of what their loved ones have to endure?

Abraham sure must have felt this.

> Early the next morning Abraham cut some wood for the sacrifice, loaded his donkey, and took Isaac and two servants with him. They started out for the place that God had

told him about. On the third day Abraham saw the place in the distance.

Genesis 22:3-4

Abraham is not even questioning God. He takes time to cut the wood for the sacrifice and to prepare for the journey that is going to take away his own son. So, is this how we are to understand the testing of the Lord? No questions? Then to make it even harder, God has him going on a three-day journey to Mount Moriah. Plenty of time to think about what God was asking him to do. After three days he gets to the mountain, and now he has to still go up to the place where the sacrifice was going to take place.

> Then he said to the servants, "Stay here with the donkey. The boy and I will go over there and worship, and then we will come back to you." Abraham made Isaac carry the wood for the sacrifice, and he himself carried a knife and live coals for starting the fire, as they walked along together.

Genesis 22:5-6

Did I read this passage correctly? Did Abraham say that they were going there to worship? Was this an act of worship in God's eyes? Then he said another astonishing thing. He said that we will come back to you...we! He believed God was going to allow him to keep his son somehow. This is my faith for Sarah! I pray that God would allow us to finish our lives together when our testing is finished.

They prepared to head up the mountain, and Abraham had Isaac carry the wood, but he himself carried the knife and the coals for the fire. Maybe he was praying that God would change His mind...but notice that God never speaks during this journey. There is no encouragement from God helping Abraham to cope with his emotions. God doesn't say, "Do not be afraid, it will all turn out all right!" No, he just says go and offer Isaac up as a sacrifice and that's it! Just obey Me! Was God going to make him go through with such a sacrifice?

To make matters worse, Isaac speaks to him about the sacrifice.

> Isaac spoke up, "Father!" He answered, "Yes, my son?" Isaac asked, "I see that you have the coals and the wood, but where is the lamb for the sacrifice?" Abraham answered, "God, himself, will provide one." And the two of them walked on together.
>
> Genesis 22:7-8

He obviously kept the word that God spoke to him a secret. God will provide it, he says. I wonder what Abraham was thinking? Was God asking too much? To want all of Abraham's love and all of his affections seemed like too much for most of us today?

> When they came to the place which God had told him about, Abraham built an altar and arranged the wood on it. He tied up his son and placed him on the altar, on top of the wood.
>
> Genesis 22:9

Once again Abraham built an altar to God. This time he had to lay on it the thing that he loved the most…his son. Even the blessings from God had to be laid down as a sacrifice to God. He could not allow even God's blessings to interfere with his obedience to God. So he did what he knew he must do and tied Isaac to the altar on top of the wood: this was it, no going back.

> Then he picked up the knife to kill him. But the angel of the LORD called to him from heaven, "Abraham, Abraham!" He answered, "Yes, here I am." "Don't hurt the boy or do anything to him," he said. "Now I know that you honor and obey God, because you have not kept back your only son from him."
>
> Genesis 22:10-12

Can you believe this? Who do you really think was being tested here? God never needed to know that Abraham would obey; He already knew that he would by his willingness to cut the wood, take the journey, and climb the mountain! But it was Abraham that needed to know that God had his true allegiance. You never know what you're able to do for God until you are tested and have to choose who and what to obey. You may be surprised!

> Abraham looked around and saw a ram caught in a bush by its horns. He went and got it and offered it as a burnt offering instead of his son. Abraham named that place "The LORD Provides." And even today people say, "On the LORD's mountain he provides."
>
> Genesis 22:13-14

Sacrifice is always required in true worship. Only when it costs you something will you understand the true value and power of worship.

Back to Sarah: after waiting for what seemed like forever the doctor finally came out and said everything went well, she did well, and I did well, and as you all know God too did well! They gave me about ten minutes with Sarah and we both cried together; it was an amazing moment for both of us. I cried because she was safe and in no pain, she cried because of the medication. All I could think of was how much I wanted her to be well and how I wanted to take her home and protect her; I love her so much. Abraham must have had the same feeling on the lonely mountain when God spared him the pain of the death of his son. All your fears turn to joy, and your joy turns into tears!

Be Careful You Don't Miss God Opening a New Door

Day 74—December 10, 2010

Sarah is still at the hospital after having her kidney removed. She is doing well today even though she asked me not to visit. Don't worry; she is fine. She is very tired due to the medication she is taking and she needs her rest.

As the end of the year approaches I always feel that it is important to evaluate the past year and then look toward the new one. I am feeling a strong push toward the need to seek for more of the Spirit of God, to allow the Holy Spirit to re-baptize me with a fresh, new impartation and vision for 2011. Already I am sensing in my spirit that God has something new in store for us if we can only allow Him the freedom to make needed and necessary changes in our lives.

Remember when Joshua was preparing to take the city of Jericho? The city was walled in with huge thick walls that were too tall to climb over and impossible to go through. But God wanted Joshua to take this city, and He wanted Joshua to trust that He would give him the way to do it. I am sure that when the people of Israel saw the city and its huge walls that they questioned whether or not it was even worth the effort to take.

Why not skip this one? Let's just go and take the next one. God wanted them to see that it was without a doubt impossible for them to do this. In so doing they would know that it would only be through God that they could take this city.

Life comes with challenges to face huge immoveable circumstances and situations that we do not know how to overcome. For some it is dealing with the past hurts in their lives. They have become constant reminders that we will never amount to anything or become who we were meant to be. Soon walls of bitterness, anger, hatred, failure, and such are built around us and begin to separate us from the Lord. We never knew that if we allowed God to take down these walls that we would be able to enter into a new life with Him.

For others, the walls are made out of pride, self-reliance, gifts, and talents, causing us to never need to depend on the Lord for much. Our ministry is like building houses on the sand, not realizing that when storms and trials come that the house will be washed away.

Some have walls that were built because of sicknesses or disabilities. They are designed to keep people who we think will hurt us away; all the while we are led to believe that we are never accepted because we are different.

There are so many of us that have huge walls built around our lives that we have built in order to protect ourselves from getting hurt. Unfortunately, these walls not only keep hurt out but they keep us in so that we cannot get out either. These walls do not bring us the freedom we were hoping for, instead they made us prisoners. What a great trick from the devil.

And there are even some who have built thick walls of tradition and structure that keep the undesirables out and only allow those that meet their qualifications in. They have allowed rules and regulations to become God's laws when they are not His laws at all.

I am finding that upon seeing all of this that there are times when God wants to take me in a completely new direction with a new passion and a new vision so that those who need Him can find Him. We miss the plans of God when we allow ourselves to stay behind walls that were manmade by the wrong influences or fears that have come into our lives.

> Then came to Jesus scribes and Pharisees, which were of Jerusalem, saying, "Why do thy disciples transgress the tradition of the elders? For they wash not their hands when they eat bread." But he answered and said unto them, "Why do ye also transgress the commandment of God by your tradition?"
>
> Matthew 15:1-3 (KJV)

Here is a good example of what I am talking about. Washing hands before they eat bread was not an Old Testament Law. It was a law that the Pharisees had come up with, and they placed that law higher than God's law. We can miss the purposes and plans of God just because we hold onto the wrong traditions.

Many times revivals are hindered because we keep up the walls of denominational barriers. Relationships are hindered because we keep up the walls of unforgiveness. Churches are ineffective because we don't want to change to meet the needs of those in our communities. Wrong traditions will keep you away from what God has for you. It is change that will help us to not get stuck in the wrong hole. Change also allows God to use something else to get us from one level to another. That something else may not be all that comfortable to deal with, but it will produce the right change if we let it.

For example, the death of Moses opened the door for Joshua to become Israel's leader. Moses was only able to take them so far, so God rose up a new leader. This new leader would have what it takes to complete the plan of God, but the people had to get behind him and understand that God had something new in store for them.

It was the death of Christ that released the power of the Holy Spirit into the heart of men. After His death, the power of the Holy Spirit moved into man's heart so that the work of Christ would become more powerful. But the disciples had to allow themselves to let go of the Jesus born in Bethlehem and hold onto the Jesus who was resurrected from the cross with power. It took on a new meaning and experience. Sometimes we have to let one thing go in order to receive something else. Until we are willing to do that we will remain ineffective and useless.

Remember in the book of Kings when the prophet Elisha was on his death bed? Look at this amazing story with me:

> The prophet Elisha was sick with a fatal disease, and as he lay dying, King Jehoash of Israel went to visit him. "My father, my father!" he exclaimed as he wept. "You have been the mighty defender of Israel!"
>
> 2 Kings 13:14

To Johoash, this was a major disaster. Elisha had been mightily used by God to protect Israel from her enemies. Now with him getting ready to die who would lead Israel into victory over their enemies? The fear of the unknown is hard, and it has the power to blind you, but the failure to trust that God has a new plan can be disastrous. I know that with every change God allows comes a new plan. But in order to know what it is you have to seek the Lord and listen very carefully or you will miss it altogether.

> "Get a bow and some arrows," Elisha ordered him. Jehoash got them, and Elisha told him to get ready to shoot. The king did so, and Elisha placed his hands on the king's hands. Then, following the prophet's instructions, the king opened the window that faced toward Syria. "Shoot the arrow!" Elisha ordered. As soon as the king shot the arrow, the prophet exclaimed, "You are the LORD's arrow,

with which he will win victory over Syria. You will fight the Syrians in Aphek until you defeat them."

2 Kings 13:15-17

Your attitude will always determine your outcome. If you are not listening and if you are assuming that what the Word tells you won't work in your situation, you will not receive its benefits. The king had to get his eyes off the problem and listen to what the prophet was telling him. These arrows that Jehoash was ordered to shoot represented something, and he was going to miss it because he didn't accept it as truth. The king only saw one solution to his problem and that was Elisha. He refused to think that anything else was possible. His faith was not in God, but in a man, and this is always bad.

Each one of these arrows represented a victory over the enemies of God. All he had to do was to act in faith and listen to what the man of God was telling him and do what he said. But no, he does just enough to make Elisha think he's listening; what a shame! Failure to hear will cause you to miss the plans of God. The king had the solution being spoken to him right from the words of the prophet. These words were enough to give him peace for the rest of his reign as king of Israel. But he missed it!

God has done the same thing for us today. He has given us the Word as a voice of truth and direction for all of our lives. Our failure to be effective lies in our unwillingness to obey His Word! When God speaks you must shut up and let go of all your own ideas and thoughts and do what He says, or you will fail and come up short of what God wanted to do!

> Then Elisha told the king to take the other arrows and strike the ground with them. The king struck the ground three times, and then stopped. This made Elisha angry, and he said to the king, "You should have struck five or six times, and then you would have won complete victory

over the Syrians; but now you will defeat them only three times."

2 Kings 13:18-19

No! Failure to hear the Word of the Lord brought a problem to the future of Israel. The king gave up, didn't hear the Word, and failed to obey it. He had his mind on the obvious situation in front of his eyes and not on the words of the Man of God. History records that Jehoash had three victories against Syria and then they were defeated in battle. There are consequences when we fail to hear and do the Word. The amazing thing here is this: God never planned to leave Jehoash without help; God had his future set in the Words of the Prophet. I too must remember to keep my ears and eyes on the plan of God so that I do not miss it either. Always remember the words of Jesus, "I will never leave you or forsake you!" He meant it! Regardless of what is going on around you, you must learn to look for Him, because His promise to be there has been given through His Word! Do you not believe His Word?

So, the next time you come face-to-face with a closed door due to a situation or circumstance, begin to look for the Word from the Lord as to where to go and what to do next. You may be surprised what God may have for you to do. Just remember, He does have a plan.

Strength in Weakness

Day 77—December 13, 2010

I am so grateful to the Father because Sarah was able to come home today and the kidney surgery was a success. Now the renal cell cancer is completely behind us with only a scar left to remind us of what the Lord has done. She is having a hard time being comfortable because of her pain, but she is happy to be home. It is becoming quite the ritual of having Sarah leave to go to the hospital and then come back home to be with us. When she came home last night I had a real war with my feelings and emotions because it is the holiday season and we have not even had the opportunity to get into the Christmas spirit. We plan on really hitting the stores soon together so that we can enjoy this special season with our boys. I was so proud of how the boys worked together to help get everything ready for Sarah's return. The Christmas spirit however is yet to show up here. The reality of her weakness is a constant reminder of our need to care for her and for each other.

Every year our section of churches has an annual Christmas party as a way to bring pastors and their families together for a time of fellowship. I had decided that I was going to stay home and be with Sarah, but she really insisted that I go and enjoy the fellowship of other ministers as a way to boost my spirits. So I decided to attend the Christmas party, but I was alone. I thought it would be easy and that I would enjoy being there; after all, I have gone to these kinds of things alone in the past with no problems. But this time it was different, a little harder than I expected. I saw couples having such a great time laughing and getting into the wonderful fellowship, but inside I could only think of how much I wished Sarah was with me. It becomes hard to laugh and have a good time when someone you love is sick and unable to be with you.

So many of my brothers and sisters came to me and shared such kind thoughts and prayers; it makes me glad to know that they are there; you need others when you go through hard times. I believe it to be the will of our adversary to keep us isolated when we suffer; he knows that there is strength both physically and emotionally when people touch us with kindness. I am saying all of this because it is easier to hide away and be alone when suffering, but it is important to allow people to comfort you. With that in mind, I want to thank all of you that shared your kindness with me; I am truly blessed to have friends like you in my life.

So this morning I have awakened with a grateful heart and look forward to what my Father has in store for me. I want to share with you this morning about strength and where do you get it when you need it. As I have said before, I know that God chooses people to suffer for Him. Why? Because in suffering and weakness His strength is made perfect, or rather, it is perfected through our weakness. It is when I am weak that God is called on and by being called on He is able to demonstrate His strength to us.

> But his answer was: "My grace is all you need, for my power is greatest when you are weak." I am most happy, then, to be proud of my weaknesses, in order to feel the protection of Christ's power over me.
>
> 2 Corinthians 12:9

I find that when things are going well I fail and easily fall into sinful habits. But when I am facing hardships I cry out to God for His strength and grace. I hate to say this, but I do not hear this kind of preaching in the church today. Paul here seems to be setting his heart on weakness, and today's preacher seems to be setting his heart on strength. Paul was humble, we are proud; Paul was abased, we are exalted; Paul was hungry, and we are stuffed; Paul was anointed, and we are talented and educated. He seemed to be the very opposite of what we are seeking after today. Preachers are promising that for your seed gift given to them that God will bless you with more. You will never lack if you invest in their ministry. Now, I am not against giving, and I do believe in the planting of the seed, but there is something in today's message of prosperity that seems crooked. When I hear them speak I do not leave with the feeling that I have sowed into the kingdom of God but rather into a man's works.

The secret to Paul's ministry was not his talent or education or speaking abilities but rather in his weakness; and the result of that weakness was a demonstration of the power of God in everything that he did. Without a doubt in my mind I believe that most of what we have today in the church is the demonstration of man's gifts and talents. I want what the early church had! They had the power of God: the blind saw, the lame walked, the deaf could hear. They didn't need long-term follow-up classes because when they got saved they got saved. Today's convert takes years to become ready for service, and most of the time he never really gets involved but remains a liability to the church. Stephen in Acts at the age of seventeen was already preaching to an angry mob and then laid his life down for the One he loved. David was killing giants as a teenager. Mary at the possible age of fifteen was asked to carry the Christ child. The early church didn't have time to have follow-up classes and accountability groups that would have kept them busy for the next twenty years. They had the Holy Spirit that radically transformed them into godly men and women of God.

Now, I am not against these things, but let's face it, most people have spent their entire Christian lives learning but never coming to the knowledge of the truth! What happened to having them tarry at the altar until they got a break through and were baptized in the Holy Ghost? The church has made them to be unaccountable for their actions by having them get stronger through knowledge and wisdom rather than a good old fashion spanking at the altar. Instead of eating from the tree of life that would have changed them into the likeness of Christ, we are feeding them from the tree of knowledge and the results have been fruitless to say the least. We have become wise but still in our sinful habits.

> For even though it was in weakness that he was put to death on the cross, it is by God's power that he lives. In union with him we also are weak; but in our relations with you we shall share God's power in his life.
>
> 2 Corinthians 13:4

> We are glad when we are weak but you are strong. And so we also pray that you will become perfect.
>
> 2 Corinthians 13:9

This is not the message I hear coming out of the church today. Where are the intercessors? Where are the weeping prophets? Who is crying out against the sins of your city? We want revival without paying the price; I am preaching to myself now! When David was a lonely, nobody shepherd boy, he cried out to God. When he was running from Saul, he cried out to God. One day he had finally reached the top; he had become a somebody, he was King of Israel! He had become a somebody and was too busy to spend time alone with God like he used to. Then it happened! It was recorded in Chronicles that "it was a time when kings go off to war, but David tarried in Jerusalem." He didn't feel the need to do the things he use to do when he was that poor, lonely shepherd boy. It was then that David feasted his eyes on Bathsheba and sinned against God and the nation. His pride led him to commit adultery and even murder. He never dreamed that could have happened to him, but it did! Later, again when he was at the pinnacle of his life David got bored and he numbered his troops. Remember? He wanted to know just how strong and powerful he was. He forgot that his power and strength had been given to him by God. He was supposed to stay a nobody, but he became a somebody, that was the problem! When he was a nobody he had all the power of God; as a somebody he lost everything! It's not wrong to accomplish things, but God's place in your life must never change. You need Him regardless of where you are or what you have accomplished. Greatness can install pride in your life, and that pride will rob you of the glory of God.

It is time for us to go back to being the nobody that God uses rather than a somebody without God. It's time to go back to reliance on the strength of the prayer closet, rather than our own strength and knowledge. They may be singing your praises today, but you are being set up to fall tomorrow and the devil can't wait.

> If you think you are standing firm you had better be careful that you do not fall.
>
> 1 Corinthians 10:12

Only God can keep us on the right track and His directions will always be given in the weakness of humility. Remember when Jesus said, "Blessed are the poor in spirit, for theirs is the Kingdom of God" (Matthew 5:3). To those who come to the place where they have nothing they find that God releases to them the kingdom of God.

> For the Egyptians shall help in vain, and to no purpose: therefore have I cried concerning this, their strength is to sit still.
>
> Isaiah 30:7 (KJV)

Great strength is given when you are able to rely only on the Lord.

Here's what we must do: get our first love back. Set time to be alone with Him as often as you can. The Word says, "They that seek me early will find me...when you search for me with all your heart" (Jeremiah 29:13). Finding God takes time because God is waiting for you to be serious. You have to get desperate and I mean desperate; desire and guilt is not going do it. Being sorry will not put you in the place of desperation. Guilt will only produce the feelings of "I got caught, now what should I do." But conviction will break your heart and cause you to let go of anything that hinders God from having your total heart and desire. Look at what Paul did:

> Not only those things; I reckon everything as complete loss for the sake of what is so much more valuable, the knowledge of Christ Jesus my Lord. For his sake I have thrown everything away; I consider it all as mere garbage, so that I may gain Christ.
>
> Philippians 3:8

Can you lose it all? If you can, you will find true riches. All I can say is that this is the cry of my heart and I want more, so I must lose everything that is hindering me from knowing Him. Trust me when I tell you that there may be things in the way that might be very hard to let go of. It is easy to let go of things that you have two of, not so easy when it involves something you love.

I pray that all of us can grasp the true wealth of letting go of the worldly things to have what is truly of value.

A Place Called Lodebar

Day 84—December 20, 2010

It's another cold morning here in Webster. Sarah is doing well, although she is still in some discomfort because of her kidney surgery. It is my prayer that she is able to attend our Christmas Eve service; I miss her being next to me at church.

Last night this passage of scripture came to my heart. There are so many who feel far away from God and even wonder if they could ever get back to where they used to be. They have fallen away and they long for what they use to have. If this is you, then this story is for you.

> One day David asked, "Is there anyone left of Saul's family? If there is, I would like to show him kindness for Jonathan's sake."
>
> 2 Samuel 9:1

Remember, David was now king of Israel, and Saul had been killed during a battle with the Philistines. Jonathan was Saul's son and David's best friend; he too died in that same battle. David had always loved Jonathan like a brother. Because of that love David wanted to know if there was anyone out there that was a part of Saul's family that he could show kindness to. It is a true act of love when you are willing to show kindness to someone's descendants. Remember, at one time his descendants lived in royalty.

> There was a servant of Saul's family named Ziba, and he was told to go to David. "Are you Ziba?" the king asked. "At your service, sir," he answered. The king asked him, "Is there anyone left of Saul's family to whom I can show loyalty and kindness, as I promised God I would?" Ziba answered, "There is still one of Jonathan's sons. He is crippled." "Where is he?" the king asked. "At the home of Machir son of Ammiel in Lodebar," Ziba answered.
>
> 2 Samuel 9:2-4

David never knew that Jonathan had a son! I can imagine the shock on his face once he heard this. This son who at one time had lived in royalty now lived in a town called Lodebar. Lodebar was the ghetto, the slums; and this one-time heir to the throne was barely able to support himself. All he was doing there was existing and being cared for by someone else. He no longer had the king's favor or had servants waiting on him; that part of his life was gone. Once King David heard about this his heart was moved with compassion.

> So King David sent for him. When Mephibosheth, the son of Jonathan and grandson of Saul, arrived, he bowed down before David in respect. David said, "Mephibosheth," and he answered, "At your service, sir."
>
> 2 Samuel 9:5-6

I can only imagine what Mephibosheth must have thought when the messengers came to his home and required him to appear before the king. During that time it was the bloodline that ruled the throne. Mephibosheth was the grandson of King Saul and therefore he was royalty. It was not uncommon for the reigning king to want to destroy anyone who was in the royal bloodline and it was even more uncommon that the reigning king would summon you to come to him so that he would show you kindness. It sounded like a set-up!

> "Don't be afraid," David replied. "I will be kind to you for the sake of your father Jonathan. I will give you back all the land that belonged to your grandfather Saul, and you will always be welcome at my table."
>
> 2 Samuel 9:7

What? The king was going to restore to him the land of Saul? And he was going to sit at the king's table for the rest of his life? Could all this really be happening to this crippled boy from Lodebar? Should not the king want revenge? But no, he showed love and compassion and wanted to bless this boy with the king's favor!

> Mephibosheth bowed again and said, "I am no better than a dead dog, sir! Why should you be so good to me?"
>
> 2 Samuel 9:8

Mephibosheth had developed a clear picture of how he saw himself. "I am not worth saving!" Oh, so many do this and it is so sad. They have forgotten that they are royalty by birth. Christ's blood makes you royal! Mephibosheth had been forgotten about, left crippled because of a fall, and he lived in Lodebar! Sin will always leave you feeling far from the favor of your heavenly Father. Satan is the master of doing this. He tells us that we can never leave Lodebar because if we did we would be destroyed, so we remained there!

Lodebar represents the land of failure. I believe it's a spiritual land that exists where people live when sin has overtaken their lives. It's where you go when you lose out with God. No one looks for you there; no one calls, writes, or visits. Your life has turned into one of despair and hopelessness. You have no visible future.

Then the king called Ziba, Saul's servant, and said, "I am giving Mephibosheth, your master's grandson, everything that belonged to Saul and his family. You, your sons, and your servants will farm the land for your master Saul's family and bring in the harvest, to provide food for them. But Mephibosheth himself will always be a guest at my table." (Ziba had fifteen sons and twenty servants.) Ziba answered, "I will do everything Your Majesty commands." So Mephibosheth ate at the king's table, just like one of the king's sons. Mephibosheth had a young son named Mica. All the members of Ziba's family became servants of Mephibosheth. So Mephibosheth, who was crippled in both feet, lived in Jerusalem, eating all his meals at the king's table.

2 Samuel 9:9-13

Let's look at what just happened in this passage. King David told Ziba, who was looking over Mephibosheth, that from now on he and all his servants were to serve Mephibosheth! And that Mephibosheth would eat at the king's table as one of the king's sons. Also, Mephibosheth had a son named Mica, and he too would become welcomed at the king's table!

This passage ends with something interesting. After David restores Mephibosheth his rightful place, this passage here ends this with six interesting words: "who was crippled in both feet." Why was this important to mention? This story is a story of redemption and restoration.

You and I were also crippled from a fall too, remember? The fall in the garden when Adam sinned and man was taken from royalty and forced out. Man lived in a spiritual land like Lodebar, filthy and dirty because of sin. Then God sent Jesus to the land of Lodebar looking for you and me, willing to pay any penalty to restore all that you lost from the fall. However, even though we have been restored, sin has still crippled us! This is why we must become so grateful to the King because he still loved us like this. It causes us to have to rely on Him and need Him every day! Oh, thank God, He brought in this old crippled man to sit at his table! Because of Jesus we have been brought to the table of the King; we have been placed in our rightful position and we have been given back what was lost in the fall. We are still crippled because of what we went through in life; but Christ now carries us!

> In view of all this, what can we say? If God is for us, who can be against us? Certainly not God, who did not even keep back his own Son, but offered him for us all! He gave us his Son—will he not also freely give us all things?
>
> Romans 8:31-32

Jesus gave Himself to restore all that was lost. All is forgiven! God says, "Come, eat at My table." Leave the land of Lodebar for good and head to the palace, God is waiting there for you to join Him so that He can show you His kindness.

The problem is with so many that they can never seem to let go of the past. We see ourselves as Mephibosheth saw himself. We are afraid of the King because we feel we deserve punishment rather than favor. Our sins still seem to haunt us and keep us bound to Lodebar. Look at what Paul said:

> No, in all these things we have complete victory through him who loved us! For I am certain that nothing can separate us from his love: neither death nor life, neither angels nor other heavenly rulers or powers, neither the present nor the future, neither the world above nor the world below—there is nothing in all creation that will ever be able to separate us from the love of God which is ours through Christ Jesus our Lord.
>
> Romans 8:37-39 (emphasis mine)

Notice in the passage that I italicized, what is missing? Paul forgot to say "things past." He never mentioned your past? This passage purposely said this because in Christ Jesus there is no past! Therefore, my past cannot possibly separate me from the love of Christ Jesus, my Lord.

So, it is time to come out of Lodebar and move into your palace. Christ Jesus has set you free and you can eat at His table without fear. Oh, happy day!

It is my prayer that I never forget what He did for me. There are many hurting people that live in Lodebar; they are hurting and lonely and have lost everything they once had. Sin is always destructive! When you see the addict or the homeless, remember how they got there and who keeps them there. God wants them to come to His table. Reach out and extend God's invitation of forgiveness, healing, and restoration. Let's get rid of the Lodebar communities in our cities and in our churches.

Christmas Time Is Here Again

Day 88—December 24, 2010

Christmas time is here again, and it's my most favorite time of the year. As long as I can remember Christmas has always been special. But it was always made special by those who were influential in my life. I think that is the way Christmas should be.

I love everything about the season. I love seeing manger scenes and listening to piped in Christmas songs in the stores. There is also the shopping, the family Christmas list that you make, the picking out the tree and taking time to decorate it. I also love hearing the ringing of the bell from the Salvation Army in front of the stores. I love watching the Christmas movies on TV and opening the mailbox to find Christmas cards. I can find so little to ever complain about when it comes to Christmas. But I especially love waking up on Christmas morning seeing the wonderful faces of my family gathering around the tree to give and receive the gifts to each other. What a great time of year.

I am so grateful that Sarah was able to enjoy this Christmas with me. This one I think will be my most favorite. Sarah was able to shop all by herself, something she loves to do. She will also be fixing a great Christmas dinner with all the fixings. We were so proud of our boys as they went out of their ways to make Mom feel so special this year. I know it must have meant the world to her.

But for many Christmas is not like this. Christmas for some is a difficult time of year. Some have lost loved ones or have lost their jobs and cannot give to their children the things that they wanted to give. Some are growing up in homes with addictions and oppressions and abuse. Some are in prison away from their families. And some are in foster care with no real family to be with. Christmas is fun for everyone but them. I do thank the Lord for the many organizations and churches and people who go out of their way to make Christmas special for those who suffer. We must never forget that sickness, disease, hunger, poverty, abuse, addictions, and being alone are hard. These things do not take the holidays off.

I want to share with you a little of my own childhood and what place Christmas had in my life. I can remember Christmas time as a child was always unique every year; no two years seem to have been the same. I do not remember too many Christmases prior to the age of nine. More than likely it is because at nine my father had informed my mother that he was leaving her; he had fallen in love with someone else. He decided that it was in his best interest to start life over and leave my mother with six children, all under the age of ten, to fend for ourselves. For me life seems to have started right there. I do not remember much prior to this time in my life, but I do remember these events.

It was close to Christmas time because I remember coming home from school wearing my winter coat and boots along with my older brother Marty. We were living at my grandmother's house, and my mother had asked Marty and me to sit down because she had something important to tell us. I do not have fond memories of my father growing up prior to this. He always worked and never had too much time for me. I went to my little league games alone and played outside alone. So when my mother told us that my father was leaving us, I remember that I said, "Good." It's not the typical reaction for a nine-year-old to have, but my father and I were not close. A few days later my grandmother arrived from California to be with my mother through this difficult time. My mother was only twenty-seven years old when this occurred. Imagine a twenty-seven-year-old woman having to be on her own with six children.

That day my mother loaded up the car with everything we owned along with my grandmother, and we left and headed out to adventure life without my dad. We arrived at a sleazy, nasty, dirty, old motel called the Blue Haven Motel. I remember how dark it was inside and all the locks on the door. The interior was painted with a pale blue paint and lit with dim lights; there was a small table and two big beds. My mother put us four boys on one bed and the two girls on the other, and we soon fell asleep.

That night my mom and grandma talked till near two in the morning. None of us kids really knew what she was going through. When my grandmother finally left the room to go to her own room my mother walked into the bathroom and took a bottle of sleeping pills. That night Satan wanted to take my mother's life, but God was watching over her. My grandmother had suspected something and she watched from a partially opened window as my mother took the pills. She immediately went to her room and called the police for help.

I remember hearing loud banging on the door and people yelling for my mother to open the door. I sat up in bed as my mother yelled at me to lay back down and go back to sleep. It was then that I had heard my grandmother's voice call my name and said, "Kent, this is Grandma; please open the door; it's an emergency." All was quiet after she said that and without delay I jumped up, removed a half a dozen locks, and opened the door. I did not know what was going on. They rushed in the room and grabbed my mother and carried her out. I now know that they were desperate to save her life. Grandma put us all back in bed and assured us that everything was all right.

Once at the hospital my grandmother was made to wait in the waiting room. She couldn't help but cry, hoping that my mother would survive this. While she was weeping God sent an angel to her. It was a young woman who told my grandma that she was a born-again Christian and wanted to know if she could pray for her. This wonderful woman held my grandma's hand and cried with her pleading to God to save my mom's life. She prayed for all six of us kids that God would protect us. I believe that that woman saved my mother's life that night. Her faith, love, and prayers stopped the spirit of death that wanted to take my mother's life.

The doctors worked hard to pump my mother's stomach, and by the grace of God she made it. Most of my brothers and sisters never knew this story until many years later, but I knew it. I believe that it was that night that God and Satan battled for this family, and God won.

Soon our first Christmas without my father took place. We had the first Charlie Brown Christmas tree in the neighborhood. We popped popcorn and my mother taught us how to string it and put it on the tree. There weren't a lot of decorations so we made some and hung them. I don't remember any of us kids ever thinking that we were short changed in any way. My mother did her best to make sure that the season was special for us, even though she hurt inside. She had been given a huge responsibility to raise six children all alone. Very few ever had the courage to invite my mother to visit and finding a place to live with six kids was only a miracle.

Our second Christmas things were a little better for my mom. She seemed to have her life under control and settled into the fact that her life would revolve only around her children. That year something amazing happened. We were living in Boonville, Missouri, on the second floor of a scary rundown shack. I hated

Kent & Sarah Whitecotton

it there, but that year my mother was seeing a man who had wanted to borrow money from her with a promise that he would pay her back at the end of the week. She reluctantly lent it to him and told him that it was her Christmas money for the kids. She never saw him again. Once again, Christmas was going to be disappointing and hard. But one afternoon a man showed up at our house and knocked on the front door. He seemed to be in his seventies and wore a black coat, dark clothes, and a dark hat. I remember him as if he were here today. He said something to my mom that I will never forget. He said, "The Lord has been good to my wife and me this year, and we want to help someone who is in need." He handed my mother twenty-five dollars, more than enough to give us a little Christmas. Looking back I now know that this man was an angel sent by God to watch over this family.

The third year was the best of them all. Prior to Christmas my mother had made the decision to go back to church. I was now twelve years old and I wanted to go. She packed up all six of us and headed to the Maplewood Baptist Church in St. Louis. We had moved back from Boonville and were living in this huge apartment complex. Now it is never easy going to church with a house full of kids who have never been to church. None of us were taught church etiquette so my mother had a rough time trying to hear the message. But that Sunday she responded to the altar call and gave her life to Jesus. This decision changed all of our lives to this very day.

When Christmas Eve had arrived I remember my mother saying that we did not have too much under the tree but we had Jesus, the greatest gift you can ever get for Christmas. It was the first time I can remember my mother being happy. I heard her tell us the Christmas story of the three wise men and the shepherds all coming to see Jesus. It was then that the door bell rang to our apartment and a local church had wanted to help someone for Christmas. They had a U-Haul truck parked outside with more presents than I had ever seen in my life. It was like a gift from heaven. I felt like God was saying, "Welcome home you guys, welcome home!" The rest is history.

Today, all my brothers and sisters are serving the Lord and working in their churches. What was meant for evil came out good. This life journey changed my life and has given me a heart of compassion for those who hurt.

I will never forget the sacrifice that my mother made for us. It is because of her that we were able to stay together.

Some of you reading this story have your own to tell. Some of you may be living it right now. You see, the real meaning of Christmas didn't come under the tree. It came in the manger two thousand years ago. It was the Christmas that my mother found Jesus that saved our family from destruction. It is why I am able to celebrate it today with my family. I will sit in my chair tomorrow morning and watch my own children open their gifts, all because of my mother. She means the world to me and every Christmas I never forget the story of the Blue Haven Motel.

I love you, Mom! And to my precious brothers and sisters: Marty, Cheryl, Robert, Pat, and Christine, we had a rough going, but we made it. Merry Christmas to all of you! And Merry Christmas to my Sarah; I am so glad we get to share it together with our children. I love you, my love!

Never Panic over Your Situation

Day 91—December 27, 2010

We are almost finished with the year 2010, and to me it was an amazing year of joy, frustrations, hurts, and great opportunities. You may be shocked to hear me say that! Do you ever feel frustrated? Aggravated? Useless? Ever feel like you're out of control of the situation? Don't you hate that? I hate waiting! I hate long lines in the stores. I hate long traffic lights, I hate detours, road construction, and anything that keeps me from what I think is the norm for my life. I want comfort, ease, and relaxation. I love it when everything works smoothly and hate it when something doesn't perform in the manner in which I want it to! Sarah's cancer is like this to me. I hate it! I hate waiting for her to heal from the kidney surgery. I hate not being able to take her out in public. I hate having to drive her to appointments and watch her have to take medicines and see doctors. It's the pits. But it's in conflict that God does the most work in us! Nothing grows on a mountain top and everything grows in a valley. By the way, I hate that too!

Right now we are in limbo…waiting. We know nothing about what is next or what is coming. Just waiting! Did I mention that

I hate waiting? I do! I want this journey to end quickly, and I want to get on with my formally normal life. Being out of control is not fun! Having to depend on doctors, nurses, tests results, and symptoms stinks! It takes me out of my comfort zone and makes me feel vulnerable. Have you ever felt like this? I say all this because I have learned about a characteristic of God that needs to change how I approach all of my life's situations and circumstances. And I learned about it while having all of these uncertainties surrounding me. Even though you find these truths in the Word, you still need to experience them to know how true they are and how they work. God uses our circumstances to open our eyes so that we will not just believe but experience life and not just any life! God wants you to experience His life through His Son, Jesus; to be like Jesus is the only acceptable life for God.

This characteristic that I am trying to learn is patience. God wants us to learn the value of waiting on Him. Waiting in obedience, even if there are consequences, is a great lesson to be learned. Obeying God is better than anything else we can offer Him. God is never in a rush in anything. Why? It is because He is always in control of everything all the time. Nothing surprises Him, and nothing is able to "sneak up" on His plans for our lives. Everything has to pass through His approval to be able to come to pass.

Now there is a fine line in understanding God in this area. If God is always in control then why did He allow this to happen or that to happen? Sometimes it happens because of your own doing! God has placed you in charge of all decisions concerning your life! God refuses to violate your will and therefore your choices will bring on the consequences of your decisions whether they are good or bad. If you fail to heed to His warnings then the unavoidable consequences of that sin will follow. Sometimes God allows consequences to come to us because the trial is sent to bring change into our life. Like I said, conflict brings change.

And the results of that change results in life-altering experiences and it is always deemed for our lasting good.

I hate what this leukemia is doing to Sarah, but I thank God every day for what it has done in us. God has used it for His glory in our lives. He is being seen through the trials we are in, and I have fallen deeper in love with Sarah and the boys and deeper in love with the Father as a result. He has revealed His love for me through this journey.

Do you remember the story of the three Hebrew children in Daniel three? Many of you probably remember the story from Sunday school as a child.

An order was given that at the sound of the music everyone had to bow and worship the false image that the king had made. However, Shadrach, Meshach, and Abednego heard the music but refused to bow. Now the punishment for not bowing was severe. Whoever did not bow would be thrown that very same hour into the fiery furnace. When they refused to bow they were brought before the king and given one more chance to bow or face their punishment of certain death in the furnace. This consequence left everyone with a seemingly sure decision as to what they should do, right? But remember, to bow was to violate the law of God. So a decision had to be made as to what they should do.

When it was seen that everyone in the kingdom was bowing except these three guys, they were immediately brought before the king and accused of not honoring his commands. You can surely understand why everyone would want to obey the king. But these three guys said something amazing. They said, "Our God whom we serve is able to deliver us from the burning fiery furnace, and He will deliver us out of thine hand, O king" (Daniel 3:17-18). Now that was great faith speaking! But they had more to say; "But if not, be it known to the king, that we will not serve thy gods, or worship the golden image that you set up!" Their minds were made up to do the right thing regardless of the consequences. Many times in our lives we face similar tests from God. To stand for the truth of scripture regardless of the consequences always honors God!

These three guys had two possible outcomes of this situation. The first was certain death, the second was deliverance. They seemed settled that either outcome was all right with them.

Now their decision not to bow infuriated the king. He commanded that the furnace be turned up seven times hotter than it was normally. He commanded that his most mighty of the men in his army bind these three guys and throw them into the furnace. The results were immediate because the men that had thrown them in were killed due to the heat being so hot. But, to the astonishment of the king, he looked into the furnace and questioned his counselors as to how many he had thrown in. They assured him that there were only three thrown in, but the king saw four men loose, walking in the midst of the fire unharmed. He said that the fourth one is like the Son of God.

Their obedience to the Word of the Lord had them thrown in the furnace, but the fire of the trials could not keep them bound. It was the fire from their trials that set them free. God's intention for trials is not to destroy you but to set you free. It was in the furnace that God delivered them. This story however is not just one of deliverance, it is one of obedience. God wants you to be obedient to Him regardless of whether or not you will be delivered. The true test of faith and love is always found in the decisions we make. Remember the passage about Lazarus?

John 11 tells us that Lazarus had gotten sick. Most people's reaction would be, "Oh no! What are we going to do? Hurry and run and get Jesus now!" Yes, this was serious news, and because they loved their brother very much I can understand their worries. But notice the reaction that Jesus had about the situation. He had peace; he was calm and in control.

What if His reaction would have been different? I can just see Jesus's reaction. "What...Oh no...Whatever shall I do! Come on guys, grab your stuff quickly and let's rush to Bethany before it's too late...Hurry!"

Is that how you interpreted this passage? No! Yes, Lazarus was sick, and yes, Jesus loved him very much. When he had gotten sick Martha and Mary more than likely panicked. Look at the passage again. She sent a messenger to Jesus and said, "Lord, your dear friend is sick!" She used these words to get Jesus into panic mode so that He would rush to Bethany and help her beloved brother. Mary and Martha went into fear mode and fear mode makes you worry and worry makes you act in the flesh. Fear is not a fruit of the spirit; therefore, it is always from hell! Demonic! Satan is opposite of God. He says, run...go fast...panic time... lose control! This leads you to forget about your trust in your Father and His Word. Now, there are times to rush and hurry, but only when you know the will of God for the situation.

In this passage we do not see Jesus acting in a rush. He is calm, in control, not afraid. Why? He knew the will of the Father. He knew that nothing can take God by surprise and therefore God has a plan for this situation. The plan, "This happened to bring glory to God." This situation they were in had a purpose! So He waited two days still in the same place where He was... not worried!

I am still impatient, but learning to wait on Him. I am refusing to rush out the door before I hear His voice. Let the doctors and nurses say whatever they like; they are there to help and they have done that. But I choose to follow the will of my Father because He is always in control. Therefore I will learn the gift of patience and wait on the Father in all things pertaining to me.

I can go on and on with what the Word says on this subject. I have found God to have complete power to change any situation whenever He chooses to. It is only through experience can a man truly say who God is. His Word has become alive in me because of my trials; they have tested my faith, and I have come to a complete rest in Him and His Word.

Sarah and I are going on a date today, just the two of us! We are enjoying every moment together as special; I can't wait till the lights in the movie theater go out because I am going to put my arm around her like we did when we were kids. I pray that you too will experience the things that God wants to use to teach you more about Him.

Learning to Wait—Part 1

Day 92—December 28, 2010

Today is a great day. It is another day we are given to honor the Father. I was out late last night snow plowing the church parking lot and the sidewalks, so today I am feeling the effects of that cold wind. Yesterday, I shared with you about God's patience and our need to learn to wait. I want to share more on this today, and I pray that God will help all of us to learn to wait for Him and never go forward without His blessings. I want to stop the sin of rushing that is inside of me and learn to wait on the Lord. Look at the passage here in Isaiah:

> Israel, why then do you complain that the Lord doesn't know your troubles or care if you suffer injustice? Don't you know? Haven't you heard? The Lord is the everlasting God; he created all the world. He never grows tired or weary. No one understands his thoughts. He strengthens those who are weak and tired. Even those who are young grow weak; young people can fall exhausted. But those who trust in the Lord for help will find their strength renewed. They will rise on wings like eagles; they will run and not get weary; they will walk and not grow weak.
>
> Isaiah 40:27-31

Look closely at this passage with me. It is easy to complain when things are difficult. We will always want easy answers to difficult questions. In the scripture Isaiah is telling the people that God is all powerful! He never gets tired or grows weary; He gives strength to the weak! He then tells them the secret to change. He says, "Those, (meaning not everyone but only those who are willing to do this), who trust in the Lord for help will find strength renewed." How will this happen? God will intervene in a powerful way. "They will rise on wings like eagles; they will run and not get weary; they will walk and not grow weak."

Those that wait upon the Lord do get tired, worn out; at times feel they missed the opportunity and even regret they waited so long. This is not what the Word here says, but it is how we truly feel when it comes to waiting. The amazing thing about this Word is that if you wait upon the Lord your strength will get stronger; you won't get tired and you will finish strong; and you will mount up with wings as of eagles. Why is this so significant? Because eagles are different than any other bird. An eagle soars highest and has been known to be able to even fly through a hurricane. Now a hurricane is one bad storm which leaves devastation and destruction all around. But the eagle gets through it. The psalmist is saying that God will give you superhuman strength to make it through the very worst storms just because you waited on the Lord. Others around you are running crazy and hiding in fear and get blown away from the storm. But you waited on God and the results will be clear. You will make it through. You will do so by running without getting tired; and flying through the midst of the storms that others will get blown away in; just because you waited on the Lord for strength and help.

But there is more to this passage still. He said you will run and not get weary, and you shall walk and not grow weak. You know why that is? Because those that wait upon the Lord know where they are to run. The fearful and unbelieving and impatient people run for shelter where the storms can blow them away.

They lack peace and therefore worry themselves sick. But if you wait on the Lord you receive His peace and you have His shelter. Always remember, fear is Satan's trick, not God's. God may stir your spirit with a warning light, but he does not work through His people using fear.

No one understood this more than David.

> He that dwelleth in the secret place of the most High shall abide under the shadow of the Almighty.
>
> Psalm 91:1 (KJV)

You can only find the secret place by waiting on the Lord. That is why patience is so necessary, because the last thing God wants in His secret place is someone who has failed the test of waiting. Waiting shows that you truly believe; there can be no faith without waiting. If you say you believe but fail to wait then I question what you believe. Smith Wigglesworth used to say, "I am not moved by what I see, I am moved by what I believe."

There is much to be said about being able to abide under the shadow of the Almighty. What a place to be! David knew that even the palace in Israel, surrounded by his military troops was not a safe place to be. He had to wait constantly on the Lord. It was the truth of the Lord that made David safe from all his enemies.

> I will say of the LORD, He is my refuge and my fortress: my God; in him will I trust. Surely he shall deliver thee from the snare of the fowler, and from the noisome pestilence. He shall cover thee with his feathers, and under his wings shalt thou trust: his truth shall be thy shield and buckler.
>
> Psalm 91:2-4 (KJV)

David says, "Surely He shall deliver thee from the snare of the fowler..." Even though you're under the wings of the Almighty, you still must exercise your faith. This is future tense, "He shall..."

David could exercise this faith because he knew where he dwelt; he dwelt under the shadow of the wings of Almighty God.

"His truth shall be your shield and buckler..." Truth is where you abide; get it? There is nothing more powerful than the truth. Satan does not have to give into your feelings or emotions; but He does have to give in to the truth. God's Word is the truth! All of heaven and all of hell has to surrender to it! You see, there are great advantages to learning to wait on God first. But it is not a onetime thing, it is a daily life lesson for all of us.

> Thou shalt not be afraid for the terror by night; nor for the arrow that flieth by day; Nor for the pestilence that walketh in darkness; nor for the destruction that wasteth at noonday. A thousand shall fall at thy side, and ten thousand at thy right hand; but it shall not come nigh thee.
>
> Psalm 91:5-7 (KJV)

Much of what we fear is the unknown; it's what's coming and the unknown that we are unsure of. Also, ever notice that most of us react before we know what is really going on. "What are we going to do if....?" Or, "I just know it's going to turn out bad!" All of these are signs that you have not yet waited on the Lord and found that secret place God has for us. Those voices you hear are from the devil and demonic spirits that take great joy in seeing you afraid. The danger is that the words you are speaking are helping to bring to pass your worst fears. The Bible says "Life and death are in the power of the tongue" (Proverbs 18:21). So, stop speaking like the devil and speak like God. Go and wait on the Lord and your strength will return with power.

This passage we just read is clear and it was written by God for you to remember! So stand on it, write it down, quote it every chance you get, it's a promise for you!

> Only with thine eyes shalt thou behold and see the reward of the wicked. Because thou hast made the LORD, which is my refuge, even the most High, thy habitation; there

shall no evil befall thee, neither shall any plague come nigh thy dwelling; for he shall give his angels charge over thee, to keep thee in all thy ways. They shall bear thee up in their hands, lest thou dash thy foot against a stone. Thou shalt tread upon the lion and adder: the young lion and the dragon shalt thou trample under feet.

Psalm 91:8-13 (KJV)

Did you read that above passage? The question is: do you believe it? Reading it won't put life into it, but believing and acting on it will! Look at it closely; what does it say? It says that you have angels in charge over you, watching you, protecting you, and guiding you. The Word here says they are given to you "to keep thee in all thy ways." So why are you afraid? "If my God is for me, then who can be against me?" (Romans 8:31). Why does God do all of this for us? Look at the next verse.

Because he hath set his love upon me, therefore will I deliver him: I will set him on high, because he hath known my name. He shall call upon me, and I will answer him: I will be with him in trouble; I will deliver him, and honour him. With long life will I satisfy him, and shew him my salvation.

Psalm 91:14-16 (KJV)

In these three verses God is the one speaking. He says, "Because you hath set your love upon me." The you and your in this verse is talking about you! In other words, because "you" waited on Him! Nothing shows your love to the Father more than your willingness to wait for Him!

Look what else He tells us you have, "Therefore will I deliver you: I will set you on high," Why is He willing to do this? "Because you hath known my name." He says, "I will be with you in trouble; I will deliver you, and honour you. With long life will I satisfy you, and shew you my salvation."

Take this challenge: Everywhere it says you in the above scripture, place your own name there. Like this: "Therefore will I (God) deliver Kent: I (God) will set Kent on high, Because Kent hath known my name. I (God) will be with Kent in trouble; I (God) will deliver Kent, and honour Kent. With long life will I (God) satisfy Kent, and shew Kent my (God's) salvation."

For those who think waiting for God is wasting their time I have news for you; waiting brings rewards. Moving forward without waiting is wasting your time. God is with those who wait and delivers those who wait. My waiting demonstrates my faith and releases His love towards me. Stop rushing! Learn to cry out to Him in the secret place of the Most High. I know it will change your life if you let it.

Learning to Wait—Part 2

Day 93—December 29, 2010

I have shared with you how important it is to wait on God and to never proceed without His guidance. Just about everywhere I look in Scripture I have found the importance of waiting, but not just waiting, you must wait with anticipation for the promise of God.

You might want to think this through a little. When you are waiting for God, you must be careful to understand what you are waiting for. You will be misled if you think that your waiting will give you only what you want. The purpose God has in waiting is that you will get what He wants for you and release what you want for yourself. This is why so many hate to wait! They rush out ahead of God so that God doesn't take away what they want. How many times has our rushing landed us into debt or into a crisis? Remember, you just had to have it and you ran out and got it only to find it wasn't worth it in the end. May all the guilty raise their hands! Why do so many believe that God wants to keep all the good for himself and wants us to have all the bad, leftover, used, no good stuff?

As I have previously shared, waiting is hard! So today I want to share a little more about the fruits of waiting, or as the Word puts it, the fruits of patience.

> The seeds that fell in good soil stand for those who hear
> the message and retain it in a good and obedient heart,
> and they persist until they bear fruit.
>
> Luke 8:15

Jesus was giving the parable of the sower that goes out to sow seed in his garden. In verse fifteen, he begins to talk about the seeds that went into the good soil. He said that these seeds stand for those who "hear" the message and retain it in a good and obedient heart. He also says that they persist or wait until they bear fruit. Remember, seed never goes into the ground and comes up on the next day. You have to plant it, water it, give it sunlight, and wait!

You have to have faith in the seed, right? Yes! But too many go out the next day and say, "Where's my fruit? Where is the evidence of my faith? It should have been here by now!"

Listen, in order to get fruit you must wait and while you are waiting God is working that seed in your life. You can bank on the promises of God only if you have the patience to wait. Too many of us miss God's leadings by rushing off into our plans because God didn't speak when we wanted Him too. We fail to remember that the seed is in the ground being prepared to become the fruit of our faith.

There is also another danger to be aware of. When you are waiting, be aware that Satan knows you are waiting on an answer from God. You must guard your mind against him; he will try to disguise himself by trying to answer for God. Remember the Word of the Lord says that Satan comes as an "angel of light!" This does not mean he shows up in your bedroom looking like some type of tooth fairy. No, he enters through your thoughts and tries to sound like your Father to deceive you if he can. Be aware that many go forth saying they heard from God only to later realize it was not God at all, but Satan.

Let's look at another passage:

> We also boast of our troubles, because we know that trou-
> ble produces endurance, endurance brings God's approval,
> and his approval creates hope. This hope does not disap-
> point us, for God has poured out his love into our hearts
> by means of the Holy Spirit, who is God's gift to us.
>
> Romans 5:3-5

I use to hate this scripture, how do you boast about your troubles? If you were to tell me ninety-three days ago that I would glory in the sufferings that my family was about to go through I would have said you were nuts! I felt I was too strong to be brought into this area of suffering. However, today I am able to say that I now side with the apostle Paul. I have seen too much and expe-rienced the true workings of tribulations, and I am grateful for them because they do produce patience. You may right now be going through something bigger than you are. Know that He will work in your behalf as soon as you stop working and start waiting for Him. "Troubles produce endurance [waiting] and endurance brings God's approval, and His approval created hope." I love the order of this! The hope is created through your faith making a change. You cannot have faith without having hope!

Paul ends this with assuring you of the love of God that is given you through the Holy Spirit. This is His seal of approval for your journey through the storm. He loves you enough not to keep you from the storm, because it is the storm that will bring value and character into your life as a believer, and it will rid you of the flesh and teach you of the spirit. Its lesson will bring you into a new life of knowing Christ and being like Him.

> For it was by hope that we were saved; but if we see what
> we hope for, then it is not really hope. For who of us hopes
> for something we see? But if we hope for what we do not
> see, we wait for it with patience. In the same way the Spirit
> also comes to help us, weak as we are. For we do not know
> how we ought to pray; the Spirit himself pleads with God
> for us in groans that words cannot express. And God, who

sees into our hearts, knows what the thought of the Spirit is; because the Spirit pleads with God on behalf of his people and in accordance with his will. We know that in all things God works for good with those who love him, those whom he has called according to his purpose.

Romans 8:24-28

By waiting with patience, the Spirit of God comes to help us. He even teaches us how to pray the right way!

Everything written in the scriptures was written to teach us, in order that we might have hope through the patience and encouragement which the scriptures give us.

Romans 15:4

This passage tells us why we must have God's Word deeply planted in us; if it is not correctly planted in us, we do not know what to wait for. When you wait for the wrong things your deception will bring forth fruits of the flesh and not the Spirit. God cannot stop you from making the wrong choices for your life. "There is a way that seemeth right unto a man, but the end leads to death" (Proverbs 14:12). We are warned to be careful in who and what we listen to. Your best friend that gives you all your advice is not God! I advise to seek out godly counsel because the Word tells you too, but be sure it is godly counsel and not just what you were hoping to hear!

One more thing to tell you, did you know that it is through patience that the promises of God are released?

We do not want you to become lazy, but to be like those who believe and are patient, and so receive what God has promised.

Hebrews 6:12

Do not lose your courage, then, because it brings with it a great reward. You need to be patient, in order to do the will of God and receive what he promises.

Hebrews 10:35-36

I wonder how many promises of God I have missed by being in a hurry. Those that end up with the promises of God had to stay put and hold on. When Sarah was first told she had leukemia she was told to go immediately to UMass Memorial Hospital, now! I knew in my spirit that we were not to rush; God was in control still, even with the bad news we got! This was on a Thursday afternoon. We shocked the doctors when we said we would not do anything until the church had the chance to pray for her. So we waited until Sunday, had the church pray, and said that if God chooses for her to go through this treatment then we would obey and go. I am not saying that this is a word for everyone, but it was a word for us. God uses doctors, you know! But it is at the same time not so much God needing to use any doctor or medicine, He needed Sarah and me to know Him and to know His ways above our own ways. This journey had a greater purpose than just the healing of her body! It is changing our lives!

In the book of Romans we see Paul telling us something very important to remember, "Do not lose your courage! Because it brings with it a great reward!" In other words, "do not stop believing!" Why? Because by holding onto the promise that God gave you it will bring into your life a great reward! Just don't quit holding on! Paul said that God is working patience in you and that "your patience will teach you to do the will of God and receive what He has promised!"

After God is done working in you, that is when you will get the promise! Is He finished? If not, why are you running away? How will you know when He is done? By the receiving of the promise!

You should read Hebrews 12; the chapter is like a faith booster shot. We are surrounded by so many who have proven this Word to be true. Therefore Paul says, "Let's rid ourselves of everything that gets in the way" (Hebrews 12:1). How? By running with a determination to win the race that is set before us. How are we to run it? By "keeping our eyes fixed on Jesus, on whom our faith depends on from the beginning to the end" (Hebrews 12:2). Just remember, there is an end and you can cross the finish line as a winner if you run it right.

Your eyes must be fixed only on Him; not the situation or circumstance; only on him! Where are your eyes fixed? That will show you where the problem lies; gaze on Him! This is why He came to earth to die, so that He would be there for you all the time! You are not alone in any fight, but you must learn how to battle or you will be defeated and lose the fight. Learn to walk in the spirit every day and allow Him to guide you in all truth.

Sowing and Reaping in Righteousness

Day 100—January 5, 2011

I cannot believe that we have finally reached the 100-day mark of this journey; plus, it is a new year. I am excited to be able to say that through it all He has proven Himself to be true to the Word that He gave me at the beginning. He has walked us through every step and kept every promise!

The time has also come when Sarah has to start back up with all the doctor visits. She has three for the remainder of this week. She seems to be doing very well right now, so for that I am grateful. I am really praying for this journey to find its end soon; it is very burdensome to us to have so much to deal with. However, there is no surrender flag hanging outside our front door. We are remaining strong in our faith that our Father is in control.

This past Sunday was a day of celebration for me because Sarah was able to return to church on Sunday to her rightful place as our worship leader. It was so wonderful, because even though it is just temporary, it was the fulfillment of one of many of God's promises given to us. I have His promise that she will return to her place at Faith Assembly with a new anointing, new passion, and new ministry! I am going into a new year filled with all the promises of God and I know He will complete the work which He started in both Sarah and I. This is our year!

Being that it is a new year, we need to know what the Word says so that the devil cannot lie to us. In the book of Genesis, God lays down a very important law that we must see and understand:

> As long as the world exists, there will be a time for planting and a time for harvest. There will always be cold and heat, summer and winter, day and night.
>
> Genesis 8:22 (KJV)

God is speaking to Noah concerning a promise that from that day forward whatever is planted or sowed into the ground will produce a harvest according to what is sown. This law is over everything on the earth.

Take a look at the same law being spoken about in the New Testament in Galatians:

> Do not deceive yourselves; no one makes a fool of God. You will reap exactly what you plant. If you plant in the field of your natural desires, from it you will gather the harvest of death; if you plant in the field of the Spirit, from the Spirit you will gather the harvest of eternal life. So let us not become tired of doing good; for if we do not give up, the time will come when we will reap the harvest. So then, as often as we have the chance, we should do good to everyone, and especially to those who belong to our family in the faith.
>
> Galatians 6:7-10

When a person goes through suffering or hardships it becomes easy to get off track for what God is after in their lives. When you read the book of Job you find that Job had three friends that had given him a ton of advice concerning why he was suffering. It all sounded right to some degree, but it was wrong. We many times base our advice on our own knowledge of what we think the truth is.

It is amazing to me how we can read or hear the Word of God and then live against what it teaches. For example, Jesus said to love one another. Some of the meanest Christians I know think they love others. They take no thought in giving out dirty looks and saying things behind someone's back and feel they are justified in their actions. This puzzles me! Their actions clearly show their disobedience to the Lord and their lack of understanding God's truth. What about not forgiving those who have hurt us? Do you not read the scriptures concerning this? Jesus said that if you do not forgive your brother his sin against you then God will not forgive your sin against Him. Don't you believe that He meant what He said? Then why do so many not forgive? They feel they have the right from God to hate, it puzzles me!

But let's look at this passage above and see if we can learn a new lesson for today.

First, we are given a warning not to deceive ourselves. The word deceive is a tricky word because it literally means that you can be tricked into believing the wrong thing. Many people have been tricked by the devil into believing in something even though they read in the scriptures something different. Deception is one of Satan's greatest weapons, and he is never afraid to use it. However, all deception has to pass through the eyes of God, and God says He was never fooled. Deceptions will never trick God, and you will never be able to get away with it before God, ever! So no matter what the great and mighty TV preacher or pastor might tell you, if what you hear goes against the Word of God, they are always wrong! For you to act on it or believe in it will mean that you have been deceived; that deception will not be able to be used as an excuse because you have the truth available to you through God's Word.

Secondly, this passage says to us that what you plant is exactly what you will reap. Now, he is not talking to a bunch of people getting ready to go out in the fields and plant corn. He is talking to us about our everyday life. If you are bitter, angry, mean, hard to get along with, in due time you are going to reap that back into your life. It can come back in the form of sickness, bitterness, hatred, or in many other forms of sin. The problem is many times those who sow these things have a long list of reasons why they are justified in doing so. So many people are physically and socially sick because of what they are reaping in their lives.

Now, in the same manner that you can sow bad things and reap the consequences of those bad things, you can also sow good things and reap their benefits. Whatever it is that you plant, that is what you will reap back. Let it be known to all who read this, that as parents a lot of our harvest will come out in our children. We have sown seed into their lives while they were growing up and they are now living out what we planted in them. This is the very reason why Jesus warned us to forgive those who have trespassed against us. He said that as we do not forgive then our heavenly Father would not forgive us. This is another example of reaping what you have sown. Look at the teaching of Jesus here:

> But I tell you who hear me: Love your enemies, do good to those who hate you, bless those who curse you, and pray for those who mistreat you. If anyone hits you on one cheek, let him hit the other one too; if someone takes your coat, let him have your shirt as well.
>
> Luke 6:27-29

Most people I know will say that they do this. But I see many who do not. These were the teachings of Jesus, and yet we do not see them as important because they cost us something. I believe that many times that suffering is given to teach us these lessons that Christ wanted us to learn. In suffering I am attentive to seeing from different perspectives.

Jesus tells us to love our enemies, bless or do good to those who curse you, and pray for those who mistreat you. This is what true Christians and followers of Jesus will do. In the next passage we find that Jesus now asks us to learn to give to others.

> Give to everyone who asks you for something, and when someone takes what is yours, do not ask for it back. Do for others just what you want them to do for you. If you love only the people who love you, why should you receive a blessing? Even sinners love those who love them! And if you do good only to those who do good to you, why should you receive a blessing? Even sinners do that! And if you lend only to those from whom you hope to get it back, why should you receive a blessing? Even sinners lend to sinners, to get back the same amount!
>
> Luke 6:30-34

Now we are asked to learn the lesson of giving to others without expecting to get it back. Why would Jesus say this? Because when people do not give back to us what we think belongs to us we will get bitter, angry, and resentful. Then the one who is hurt is you! In other words, He is telling us that it is better to give it away than to get bitter by not getting it back. Have you learned this lesson in your life? If you are going to lend to anyone be sure you are willing to forever let it go. This act will please the Father because you will not lose out in your soul.

It is never easy learning the right lessons when the world all around us teaches us differently. As a pastor I have seen church leaders treat other leaders with contempt and jealousy. They do not realize the seeds they are sowing into their congregations. When a leader sins, soon his followers will join in the consequences and become like their teacher.

I want to be like Jesus in my life. The path to that will take the rest of my life to accomplish, but the rewards along the way are worth any and all sacrifices. But I must commit to following and sowing the right seeds if I want the right outcome.

> Every tree is known by the fruit it bears; you do not pick figs from thorn bushes or gather grapes from bramble bushes. A good person brings good out of the treasure of good things in his heart; a bad person brings bad out of his treasure of bad things. For the mouth speaks what the heart is full of.
>
> Luke 6:44-45

One of the toughest things to ever do in life is to have a self-examination. You can test yourself by the fruit you bear. Do you have a temper? Do you have enemies around you that you can't stand? Do you have people upset with you? If so, don't go on like you are going! Make these things right or you will reap their consequences.

> Agree with thine adversary quickly, whiles thou art in the way with him; lest at any time the adversary deliver thee to the judge, and the judge deliver thee to the officer, and thou be cast into prison.
>
> Matthew 5:25 (KJV)

Make it right while you have the chance, because if you fail to the judge will cast you into prison. This prison is a spiritual one that God sends you to until you learn your lesson. So many people I know are there; the prisoners are recognized by the anger, fear, unbelief, bitterness, pride...only a true repentant heart will get them released.

Look quickly at the two verses that proceed the one we just read:

> Therefore if thou bring thy gift to the altar, and there rememberest that thy brother hath ought against thee; leave there thy gift before the altar, and go thy way; first be reconciled to thy brother, and then come and offer thy gift.
>
> Matthew 5:23-24 (KJV)

Have you done this, or are you still holding on to it? You reap what you sow! God warns us that no amount of love that you want to offer to Him is acceptable until you have made your offences right.

David said in Psalm 139:23-24, "Search me, O God, and know my heart: try me, and know my thoughts: And see if there be any wicked way in me, and lead me in the way everlasting." It's during sufferings and hardships that doing this becomes an opportunity for you. Only God knows the absolute truth of what is inside of you. I have two more scriptures I want to share before I stop. I pray that God will allow you to examine your heart for all of the truth. I also pray that the truth will set us free.

> Why do you call me, "Lord, Lord," and yet don't do what I tell you? Anyone who comes to me and listens to my words and obeys them—I will show you what he is like. He is like a man who, in building his house, dug deep and laid the foundation on rock. The river flooded over and hit that house but could not shake it, because it was well built. But anyone who hears my words and does not obey them is like a man who built his house without laying a foundation; when the flood hit that house it fell at once—and what a terrible crash that was!"
>
> Luke 6:46-49

> Israel was once like a well-trained young cow, ready and willing to thresh grain. But I decided to put a yoke on her beautiful neck and to harness her for harder work. I made Judah pull the plow and Israel pull the harrow. I said, "Plow new ground for yourselves, plant righteousness, and reap the blessings that your devotion to me will produce. It is time for you to turn to me, your LORD, and I will come and pour out blessings upon you."
>
> Hosea 10:11-12

These Scriptures show us that we have a responsibility to build our lives right. We are told to build our lives on the rock, which is God's truth, so that when the storms come (and they will come) we will be able to stand! We are also told to plant righteousness! The righteousness that is only found in the Word of God and you will reap blessings…true blessings. I have found blessings even in the midst of sufferings. God is waiting for us to plant righteous seeds that will produce godliness in us.

Discerning the Spirit of Pride in Me

Day 101—January 6, 2011

Every year our district of churches plans a wonderful prayer meeting as a way to bring us together in unity. So yesterday I decided that it would do me good to attend this. After 101 days of this journey I thought that God had to be finished with things He was wanting me to learn, but after yesterday I realized I was wrong in that assumption. Today, perhaps I have seen the worst in me. It very well may be the sin that God hates the most, and yet I have found that it is still creeping around in my heart. I am so ashamed because it has effectively disguised itself in so many forms of good deeds and Christian duties.

During the prayer meeting Pastor Bob Wise, our district superintendent, asked me to come up to the microphone and lead in a prayer over a man who was unsaved and given a very short time to live. I did what he had asked, and when I sat down I became overwhelmed with pride and selfishness in my heart. I wanted people to feel sorry for me like I was feeling sorry for myself. The feeling was overwhelming as I looked around the room wanting to be seen or noticed.

This became like a blanket over me, and I remember I wanted to leave because I felt I needed more from these men and women than what I was getting. What shame came over me when I realized what God was trying to reveal to me. That nasty giant of pride and selfishness was in me deep in my heart, and I was forced to reckon with it like David who was facing Goliath. This sin is worse than any sickness that you can go through because it is the very sin that disrupted heaven and forced Satan and one third of the angels to be cast out. This sin is serious! It is the one sin that Satan wants you to have and it is so easily disguised in us as something that it is not.

Today I want to deal with this sin; it is one that has crippled churches, brought down ministries, and shipwrecked countless saints. It is the sin of pride. Nothing carries more long lasting devastation than pride, because the root of pride is what fuels almost every sin and hinders God from delivering those who are bound by sinful habits. It was the very sin that caused Satan to fall from heaven, and it will do the same to you. It will steal from you the truth you were meant to have and cause you to become blinded by things that are meant to destroy you.

Look at these following passages to see what I mean:

> Why are you so far away, O LORD? Why do you hide yourself when we are in trouble? The wicked are proud and persecute the poor; catch them in the traps they have made. The wicked are proud of their evil desires; the greedy curse and reject the LORD. The wicked do not care about the LORD; in their pride they think that God doesn't matter. The wicked succeed in everything. They cannot understand God's judgments; they sneer at their enemies. They say to themselves, "We will never fail; we will never be in trouble." Their speech is filled with curses, lies, and threats; they are quick to speak hateful, evil words. They hide themselves in the villages, waiting to murder innocent people. They spy on their helpless victims; they wait in their hiding place like lions. They lie in wait for the poor;

they catch them in their traps and drag them away. The helpless victims lie crushed; brute strength has defeated them. The wicked say to themselves, "God doesn't care! He has closed his eyes and will never see me!"

Psalm 10:1-11

The passage here opens up with a question to God asking "Why are you staying far away from us? Why are you hiding when we are in trouble?" The answer was because of their pride. Their pride caused the poor to be persecuted. It caused the wicked to boast and to bless the greedy; they even reject the Lord. The proud would not seek after God; God is not in his thoughts. All of this is caused by their pride, but there's more: He says in his heart, I shall not be in trouble—his mouth is full of cursing and deceit and fraud. Worse of all He hath said in his heart, God doesn't care: he has closed his eyes; he will never see me. They were being deceived, and it was because of their pride.

What exactly is pride? It is when you have lost your dependence upon God and you rely on yourself. It is exalting yourself above others or raising your nose up against the poor and needy and refusing to reach down to their level. I have found pride to be like a sneaky, old attorney that lives inside of each of us. Every time we do wrong he shows up just in time to defend our sinful deeds with excuses and reasons why our sin isn't as bad as someone else's. He is the one who screams out, "Others should be punished, not my client!" Rather than allowing our sin to face the eyes of the Lord, he creates loopholes that sneak through our convictions and render us innocent when we are without a doubt guilty. The proud shut out the needs of others because his needs are more urgent. They rush to be heard at the cost of others not being as important as they are. They are like the people who see the oppressed and rather than feed them or help them they make laws to get them off the streets. Sinful pride is always self-exalting and blind to everything around you. When a proud person sees someone doing well rather than admonishing them, they find fault in the way they did what they did. Pride never asks for help, because it needs help from no one. This wicked sin is the first in line for self-promotion and the most critical of the successes of others. It is so deadly of a sin that like cancer it usually has over taken the whole body before a cure can be found to save them. It is not a wonder that God says that He hates the proud.

Look at these other scriptures that help us to define its true nature:

> To honor the LORD is to hate evil; I hate pride and arrogance, evil ways and false words.
>
> Proverbs 8:13

Do you hate pride like God hates it? I once heard it said that pride is like bad breath; you think everyone has it but you. It was pride that kicked Lucifer out of heaven. Pride always pushes itself to the front and allows you to think you are more than you are. It refuses to see the better in others because it is blinded by the good in itself. It is exactly opposite of what the apostle Paul says, "I know that good does not live in me—that is, in my human nature. For even though the desire to do good is in me, I am not able to do it" (Romans 7:18). If there is nothing good found in me then why am I so convinced that I am better than anyone else? Pride is so deceptive that it can make us think that we do not even deserve to suffer like others do.

In the next few verses of Proverbs we are told that pride brings shame. It is found in the mouth of fools; it goes before destruction and leads you to have a haughty spirit that will result in a fall.

> People who are proud will soon be disgraced. It is wiser to be modest.
>
> Proverbs 11:2

The word modest actually means humble or abased. It means that we not place ourselves above anyone else.

Proud fools talk too much.

Proverbs 14:3

Proverbs tells us that the proud are not quiet. They don't mind letting you know just how much they know. Always bragging about their accomplishments and comparing their works with those around them as more superior.

> It is better—much better—to have wisdom and knowledge than gold and silver. Those who are good travel a road that avoids evil; so watch where you are going—it may save your life. Pride leads to destruction, and arrogance to downfall. It is better to be humble and stay poor than to be one of the arrogant and get a share of their loot. Pay attention to what you are taught, and you will be successful; trust in the LORD and you will be happy.

Proverbs 16:16

Now we are warned about what is really of value and the way we are to go. We are told that wisdom and knowledge have more value than gold and silver. That's hard to believe in the natural sense but in life it is true. We are also told to avoid the road of evil—that road is the road where the house that pride is located. Pride will lead you to destruction and your downfall. These are warning signs for us to heed too.

The key to avoiding this disaster is to choose what others avoid; choose to stay humble and even poor rather than to have company with the spirit of pride.

> The LORD says to Edom, "I will make you weak; everyone will despise you. Your pride has deceived you. Your capital is a fortress of solid rock; your home is high in the mountains, and so you say to yourself, 'Who can ever pull me down?'"

Obadiah 1:2-3

Obadiah warns us through the events of Edom that pride is deceptive and makes us believe we are more than we are. The main danger of pride is that it is the root of almost all sin and it hinders deliverance from sin. Many a great church, ministry, and leader have been brought down because of pride. Pride allows you to hide your sin and yet rebuke it in others. Pride makes you judge other's failures harsher than you would judge your own. It allows your sin to continue and the sin in others to face swift judgment. It refuses to show mercy and kindness and worse of all it is the seed of hell. Many have fallen to her evil desires.

> Do not love the world or anything that belongs to the world. If you love the world, you do not love the Father. Everything that belongs to the world—what the sinful self desires, what people see and want, and everything in this world that people are so proud of—none of this comes from the Father; it all comes from the world. The world and everything in it that people desire is passing away; but those who do the will of God live forever.
>
> 1 John 2:15-17

> God resists the proud, but gives grace to the humble.
>
> James 4:6

The only person that God resists in the Bible is the one who is proud. A murderer has a better shot at making things right with God than one who comes in pride.

> For from the inside, from your heart, come the evil ideas which lead you to do immoral things, to rob, kill, commit adultery, be greedy, and do all sorts of evil things; deceit, indecency, jealousy, slander, pride, and folly—all these evil things come from inside you and make you unclean.
>
> Mark 7:21-23

This is one subject that I could go on and on about because the Bible has a lot to say about it. In Revelation, we see the power of pride that will be in the church of the last days:

> To the angel of the church in Laodicea write: "This is the message from the Amen, the faithful and true witness, who is the origin of all that God has created. I know what you have done; I know that you are neither cold nor hot. How I wish you were either one or the other! But because you are lukewarm, neither hot nor cold, I am going to spit you out of my mouth! You say, 'I am rich and well off; I have all I need.' But you do not know how miserable and pitiful you are! You are poor, naked, and blind. I advise you, then, to buy gold from me, pure gold, in order to be rich. Buy also white clothing to dress yourself and cover up your shameful nakedness. Buy also some ointment to put on your eyes, so that you may see. I rebuke and punish all whom I love. Be in earnest, then, and turn from your sins. Listen! I stand at the door and knock; if any hear my voice and open the door, I will come into their house and eat with them, and they will eat with me."
>
> Revelation 3:14-20

The church of the last days will be lukewarm because of its pride. They feel no need to walk humble before God because they have need of nothing. What a wretched place to end up for the people of God! I challenge you to repent of your pride and not sit in the seat of the judge. Humble yourselves before Him and He will exalt you. God has a great work to be done and pride will hinder you, not exalt you.

Do you know what caused God to destroy the cities of Sodom and Gomorrah? It wasn't their homosexuality! It was their pride, their fullness of bread, and their abundance of idleness. Sounds like America to me.

> Behold, this was the iniquity of thy sister Sodom, pride, fullness of bread, and abundance of idleness was in her and

in her daughters, neither did she strengthen the hand of the poor and needy. And they were haughty, and committed abomination before me: therefore I took them away as I saw good.

Ezekiel 16:49-50 (KJV)

So, where do we go from here? I suggest we go to Matthew 5-7 and study the teachings of Jesus on the Sermon on the Mount. Then live what He taught. Breaking pride is not easy, and it will more than likely be a lifelong battle. But living life and not recognizing this demon is worse. We must humble ourselves to God and submit to His ways if we are going to beat this spirit.

Today I am grateful that God revealed this to me. I am saddened that it is in me but committed to allowing Him to use our trials to keep me humble.

Jesus Walks in Storms

Day 107—January 12, 2011

Today Sarah got her test results back from a painful bone marrow biopsy. They showed that there were no problems anywhere in her body and that her leukemia is still in remission, even though it hasn't been treated for the past seven weeks because of the removal of her kidney. There is no leukemia in her body! So she has been just about cleared to continue treatment for her leukemia. The next step is that they will be restarting her chemotherapy and preparing her for her bone marrow transplant. This process will be done by taking stem cells from her body and using them during the transplant procedure. Even though this is a sign of everything coming to an end it is also the most severe of treatments thus far.

<hr/>

I have noticed a trend in people who suffer. Many allow their suffering to shut them down or during it they give up all together. Not us! We have set our course and we will remain faithful to His calling and plan for our lives no matter what the sacrifice required. Sarah had informed me that she is going to finish the race strong, and I believe her! So we have no time to indulge in self-pity. It's the call of the kingdom that is our priority, and

Sarah feels the same way. I hope you do not take this wrong. I am not trying to be a hero or callous about the situation. Suffering is real and it is confusing. There will be times when your faith runs out and you need a refill in a hurry. This is all right, and I believe that everyone will go through that. But you can still have your eyes focused on the prize of a well finished race.

For some who suffer they will have the strength needed to finish well, but others will need the strength of others to finish. Like the story of the man whose five friends brought him to Jesus. The man was too sick to come on his own, and as far as we know he may not have had any strength whatsoever to ask for help. So his friends took him to Jesus. They could not get to him because of the crowds so they took him up on the roof and opened it up and then lowered him down right in front of Jesus. Now that is faith; but not faith coming from the one who is sick but from those who loved him. When your loved one is too sick to have faith, then you must have faith for him. It will work just as well!

So, if you are discouraged today, then the only thing you can do is turn your eyes to Him, the author and finisher of our faith. Trust His Word that says, "I will never leave you or forsake you" (Hebrews 13:5). And stay faithful! Many fail during adversity because when tested they have their eyes on the wrong things. To stay focused on Him is the key and He will allow you to know for sure that He will get you through. To prove my point, check out this horrible situation that the disciples found themselves in:

> After saying good-bye to the people, he went away to a hill to pray. When evening came, the boat was in the middle of the lake, while Jesus was alone on land. He saw that his disciples were straining at the oars, because they were rowing against the wind; so sometime between three and six o'clock in the morning, he came to them, walking on the water. He was going to pass them by.
>
> Mark 6:46-48

These poor disciples were really in trouble; a very powerful and unexpected storm arose while they were heading home, and it seemed that they were going to die. Now remember that these guys were trained fishermen who were very experienced on the sea. But this storm came and it was fierce, more than they were used to handling.

From the shore Jesus seen them struggling and without warning he just starts walking on the water toward their boat. Notice, Jesus wasn't panicked. He wasn't running hysterically saying, "Here I come, don't worry, I am right here, I will save you!" Not at all! He was calm and just starto walking towards the boat right in the midst of that raging storm.

This passage is interesting because it says that Jesus did see them toiling, yet it then goes on to say that, "He was going to pass them by." What? Pass them by? Why? He sees them struggling and fearful and yet He was going to pass them by? Why? It doesn't make sense that Jesus, who loved them so much, would have done such a cruel thing. Look at the rest of the story:

> But they saw him walking on the water. "It's a ghost!" they thought, and screamed.
>
> Mark 6:49

The reason why they screamed was because all fishermen knew that if they ever saw a spirit while at sea during a storm it meant that they were done for. This caused them to be very afraid and it made them cry out in fear.

> They were all terrified when they saw him. Jesus spoke to them at once, "Courage!" he said. "It is I. Don't be afraid!" Then he got into the boat with them, and the wind died down. The disciples were completely amazed.
>
> Mark 6:50-51

When Jesus was outside the boat, everything was stormy and fearful; fear will keep Jesus outside of your situation. Do not be afraid, but look in the midst of the storm for Jesus because He is nearby waiting to be invited into your boat. Once inside the boat there is peace and everything becomes normal.

The end of the verse above said something that was not good, "The disciples were completely amazed." Why? What was there to wonder about? They had already seen so much and heard so much, yet they still failed to believe and trust completely in it all. Maybe the answer is in the next verse:

> Because they had not understood the real meaning of the feeding of the five thousand; their minds could not grasp it.
>
> Mark 6:52

How often we forget that God has come through before. In fact, the Bible tells us that the things written in scripture were written for us so that we might believe. If God did it then He will do it now because the Word says that Jesus Christ is the same yesterday, today, and forever.

When God does something great and we fail to remember what He has done our hearts will get hard. The same goes for when we fail to believe His Word. We have allowed ourselves to forget the Word; our hearts have hardened. Our joy must come from the promises of the Word; even though we do not see the results visibly, that means nothing, because His Word stands alone! Remember, if His Word is true then it is all true, and it will come to pass just as He said it would. Even though there is a storm around your boat, fear not because somewhere out on the water Jesus is walking and waiting to be asked to get in, just look closely!

The question, however, still remains. Why would Jesus have passed them by? He was waiting for them to see Him not as a spirit, but has their Lord. You must stop the toiling and the fear and look to Jesus; get Him in your boat and the storms will cease. You have to see Him the way the Word of God describes Him.

Your faith has to stretch into the truth of God's Word otherwise you will struggle during the storms of your life.

You want to know why I have peace? Why Sarah is not fearful? Why we are able to continue on? Why we are not afraid? Because we brought Jesus into our boat and He calmed the seas of fear.

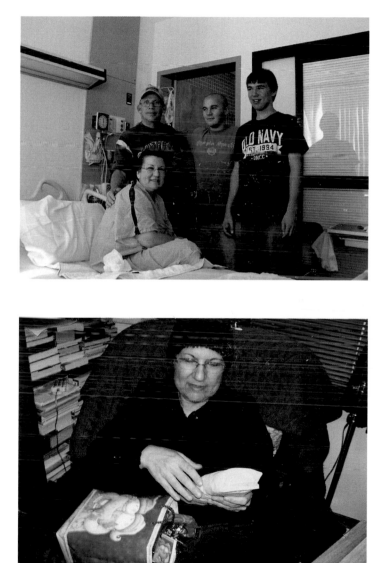

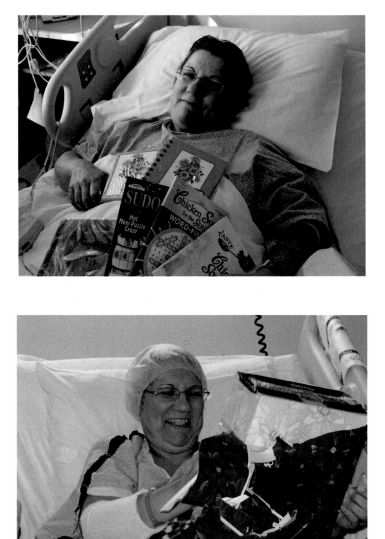

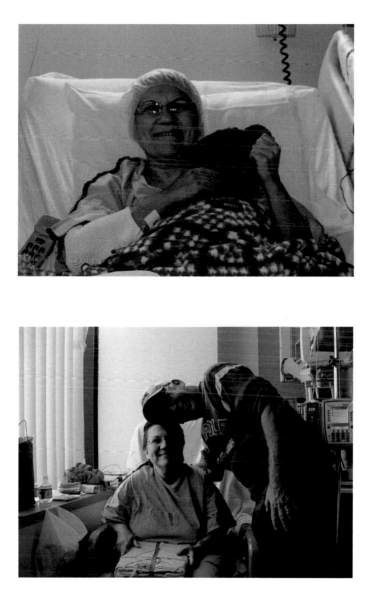

Dreams from God
Do not Die

Day 117—January 22, 2011

Many of you were wondering how Sarah's doctor visits went yesterday. Well, it pains me to tell you all the things that are getting ready to come her way. We met with her doctors that will be getting the stem cells from her, and they shared with us the procedure that she will be going through. They will be surgically inserting a catheter into her chest sometime in the next week or so. Then they will be starting her on another round of chemotherapy to bring her blood counts down. After that they will wait until her blood counts reach a certain level and then they will extract her stem cells. This is a very long and drawn-out procedure, but the good news is because she does not need a donor it will mean a less chance of rejection during the transplant. We look forward to when this is completed. Doctor Nath says that this is it! Once this is done and we do the transplant we will be finished for good. Sarah will be cured!

***

Yesterday we had another big snow storm! During this past week we have had over three feet of new snow, and there is another big storm on the way for later in the week. I love snow and it's pretty to see, but after a while you look forward to it all going away.

As I was getting ready to plow my driveway the garage door started opening. Thinking it was one of my boys coming out to help I was shocked when the door opened and there stood Sarah with her hat, coat, gloves, and scarf on. She tells me she is coming out to help me clear the snow. Now, I have been married to her almost twenty-six years, and she has never once come out to help me clear the snow. So needless to say I was a little confused; she is suppose to be resting. It only took me a few seconds until I realized why she was here. I saw it in her eyes, a passion to not allow anything to take her out of the life she has been given. She needed to feel useful again, so she came out to help me. I have tears in my eyes just thinking about what was going through her mind. I am writing this with a heart of thanks because this woman God has given to me who has refused to lose or give up. She has made up her mind that leukemia will not take over her life.

⚜

I have never met anyone who didn't have a dream, we all have one for ourselves and hope that one day we fulfill it. Some of you have been given dreams by God or had dreams of doing something great for Him. But you got sick or distracted by something unexpected. It is a common thing for many to even give up their dreams when they suffer sickness and they allow all their dreams to die, but not Sarah! She is refusing to stop dreaming or to stop running the race that God has set before her.

During these past 117 days I have had people sit back and watch us, expecting us to fall apart. Hard to believe that, but it is true. They tell us they can't believe that we are still holding up so well. Sarah and I thought that staying faithful to God was the normal behavior of a Christian. Christians should never quit or give up because we have the strength from the Lord to go through anything that comes our way. This is true! It is why we have found ways to get through everything we have faced thus far. Even though dreams have got to be put on hold it doesn't mean they have to be put off for good. God has a plan for each of us and a purpose for our lives. Sufferings are God's way of bringing us towards our purpose that God has for us. Does sufferings change our dreams? Sometimes, but not always. But it does refine them to perfection in the purpose of God's plan for us.

One of the greatest stories in the entire Bible is the story of Joseph. It's a story about a dreamer who had all but lost his dreams; at least that is what he thought.

> Joseph, a young man of seventeen, took care of the sheep and goats with his brothers. He brought bad reports to his father about what his brothers were doing. Jacob loved Joseph more than all his other sons, because he had been born to him when he was old. He made a long robe with full sleeves for him. When his brothers saw that their father loved Joseph more than he loved them, they hated their brother so much that they would not speak to him in a friendly manner. One time Joseph had a dream, and when he told his brothers about it, they hated him even more.
>
> Genesis 37:2-5

Joseph was a daddy's boy, self-indulged, and treated better than everyone else. It's hard to like a guy like him. He was a tattletale, a snitch, someone that you would have liked to beat up at school. He was also a dreamer, which made matters worse. This caused friction at home with his family. You see, there are times when God gives us dreams, and these dreams turn into expectations for our lives. We begin to follow them in hopes of achieving them one day. But with Joseph, his dreams were about people bowing down to him, and that can make people really mad at you!

With Joseph, however, God gives him a dream; and even though Joseph was young, impressionable, and undisciplined God shows him a little of his future. What God did not show him was what it was going to take to get him to the place where this dream could be fulfilled. The fulfillment of God's dream in him was going to have to go the route of great suffering because whom much is given much will be required.

Look at the reaction of his family when Joseph tells them his dream,

> He said, "Listen to the dream I had. We were all in the field tying up sheaves of wheat, when my sheaf got up and stood up straight. Yours formed a circle around mine and bowed down to it." "Do you think you are going to be a king and rule over us?" his brothers asked. So they hated him even more because of his dreams and because of what he said about them. Then Joseph had another dream and told his brothers, "I had another dream, in which I saw the sun, the moon, and eleven stars bowing down to me." He also told the dream to his father, and his father scolded him: "What kind of a dream is that? Do you think that your mother, your brothers, and I are going to come and bow down to you?"
>
> Genesis 37:6-10

So, after reading that you can kind of understand why everyone was a little upset with Joseph. That day, a dream began to live in him; it was a dream that he did not understand or comprehend because God had only told him a little. God never told him what would lead to this dream becoming a reality. Inside of Sarah and me lives a dream too; just like each of you who are suffering or watching someone else suffer. That dream is still breathing in Sarah and me, and it is why Sarah refuses to stay still. You too must lift up your eyes to find strength in God because God wants your dream to live. However, the life of our dreams needs to go through the purpose and the plan of God so that it can be fulfilled in God's way. At seventeen Joseph was not able to fulfill the dream God had planned because Joseph himself was not ready. You can tell this by how everyone reacts to his dream. Joseph thought he was something and when you think you are something you are never ready for what God has for you.

The story goes on to tell about when Joseph's father sent Joseph to go looking for his brothers. The father was worried because they had been gone so long. So Joseph headed out to find them. After an extensive search he finally sees them off in a distance. However, his brothers saw him as well. They despised him, all dressed up in his coat of many colors.

> They saw him in the distance, and before he reached them, they plotted against him and decided to kill him. They said to one another, "Here comes that dreamer. Come on now, let's kill him and throw his body into one of the dry wells. We can say that a wild animal killed him. Then we will see what becomes of his dreams."
>
> Genesis 37:18-20

Poor Joseph, I think he thought that everyone loved him; after all, he had the coat, he had his father's favor, and he had his dreams. Little did he know what his brothers had stored up for him.

> When Joseph came up to his brothers, they ripped off his long robe with full sleeves. Then they took him and threw him into the well, which was dry. While they were eating, they suddenly saw a group of Ishmaelites traveling from Gilead to Egypt. Their camels were loaded with spices and resins. Judah said to his brothers, "What will we gain by killing our brother and covering up the murder? Let's sell him to these Ishmaelites. Then we won't have to hurt him; after all, he is our brother, our own flesh and blood." His brothers agreed, and when some Midianite traders came by, the brothers pulled Joseph out of the well and sold him for twenty pieces of silver to the Ishmaelites, who took him to Egypt.
>
> Genesis 37:23-28

This is bad! Sound like the end of Joseph, the end of his dreams, his goals, and even his life. He was just sold as a slave and he was on his way to Egypt. He was not going home to be with his father; he was not going to put on his coat that his father had made just for him. No more home cooked meals or special treatment. All that part of his life was over forever!

This sounds like the effects of sickness, doesn't it? Everything was going great until this happened! Now what are we going to do? These are times that the real test comes; what are you going to do? Your decision at this point will determine the course that God will choose for you to travel. The more you fight the more that is going to come your way.

During the past many months I have watched in semi-amazement as people waited for us to quit and fall apart. They watched for us to give in to Sarah's disease and surrender our dreams. Someone even said to me, "How can you find the strength to go on with all that you're going through." Where in the Bible are we as Christians told that we are not suppose to suffer? Who said that things were only suppose to go well for the believer? These so called high class preachers who are preaching a "blessing only" gospel have misled us into a lie that tells us that the Christian life is a life of ease, comfort, and total joy. No wonder people get mad at God when they go through hardships; it is easy to get mad at God because He did not line up to what the preacher they listen to said.

Friends, it is the suffering and hardships that will refine your dreams and your gifts. Don't you know that everything that comes your way has to pass through the approval of God Himself! That's right! God has to approve what comes into the believer's life because it is God that is working in you to perfect you for His glory! That is why we are to never quit in the midst of our sufferings. We are being prepared for the fulfillment of our dreams. This fulfillment means changing our dreams into His dreams! That is why so many want to "kill the dreamer." We almost despise those who never give up and who keep dreaming even when the dream looks dead. I have watched my Sarah fighting to dream more; not allowing herself the pleasure of quitting. Quitting would be easier and demand so much less expectation and so many wouldn't blame her if she did. But no! There she was dressed up with a snow shovel in her hand ready to step back into her dreams. This disease has caused our lives to change, but the dreams still live on.

So, whatever became of Joseph? You will have to read it and find out. The story is written in the book of Genesis 39-45. I will tell you this, God used sufferings, hardships, and faith to transform this "daddy's boy" into a man of God. He saved a nation from starvation and God fulfilled all of his dreams. Look at how Joseph saw what had happened to him:

> Now do not be upset or blame yourselves because you sold me here. It was really God who sent me ahead of you to save people's lives.
>
> Genesis 45:5

Isn't it great to know that God has a plan that we do not see or understand? If only we had known the plan of God we would have never gotten mad at Him.

This is why Sarah got all dressed up and came outside today. She knows that there is a plan of God working in our lives and she is allowing her faith to demonstrate that. We pray for each of you who are in a struggle in your own lives to see the plan of God. Rest and put your confidence back in the Lord. When Joseph went to Egypt there is not one time we read in Scripture that Joseph ever doubted God! Not one place! No wonder God fulfilled his dreams.

Breaking Pride and Releasing Grace

Day 120—January 25, 2011

It has been officially four months since this journey began…it seems so much longer. I think journeys are meant to feel longer than they really are so that we rid ourselves of the hindrances that get in God's way, especially because with God one day is like a thousand years and a thousand years is like one day. Starting next week the journey will take on a new road, one that hopefully will lead us home. Sarah will be preparing for the bone narrow transplant, and it will mean going through the trials of isolation and weakness again. I hope we are up to it; after all it has been so nice having things back to normal and having Sarah back to the way she was before. But I am ready, and so is Sarah, and we will bring Him glory while going through it!

Today I want to share a little with you, especially to those who have long-term struggles. Some struggles are self-inflicted and God has to deal in different ways to change you. Sometimes He will use the long arm of the law to break your sinful habits; other times he will use mercy to accomplish his will.

Others are fighting long-term illness and sickness, and the battle has turned into a full-blown war. Just when one battle ends another fight begins. You are tired and weary from holding on and at times you wish it all to end.

Some have had to go through the loss of someone through death or tragedy. The pain of this type of loss can send you into a lifelong world of despair.

And there are some of you who are like me. You are forced to stand on the sidelines and watch someone you love suffer.

With each of these God has grace that He wants to give you. That grace will without a doubt get you through whatever you are experiencing. So just how do you get to that place of receiving the grace you need? The Bible says in James 4:6, "God resists the proud, but He gives grace to the humble." In this passage, we find two things that God is going to use when He allows us to suffer. One is resistance and the other is grace. God will use one or the other in getting His will done in our lives. The key to the method that the Lord will use is based on how much pride He has to break through in your life. This is a very important thing to remember, because when God has to deal with the pride in our lives He is forced to use harsher methods to break the hardness that has developed around the heart. Because pride is so deceptive in us God has to use harsh methods to reveal to us where this pride is living. It is through suffering that God can take a person and cause them to see just what little power they have and how much they need the Lord.

It is a must to understand that it is only when we are humbled that God can begin and complete the work that He started in us. This very well could determine the length of the trials we have to face in our journeys. If a person has a lot of pride in them then it will take a lot of work to destroy the strongholds they have built.

I believe that pride was an issue with Job. His pride led him to believe that he did not deserve to suffer because he was such a good person. That could explain why God did not answer him until chapter thirty-eight. By then his pride had been smashed and broken and He made him able to hear the Lord speak even from a storm.

Humility is a complete surrender to your own will, your own desires, and your own plans. Just because we decided to follow Christ does not mean we have all of the worldliness out of us. There are things in you that God is after to get out of you so that you will be ready for heaven.

Listen, I am not trying to be tough; suffering is hard, and only those who have been there know just how hard it really is. It is easy for those to say, "Just get over it!" It is only because they have not been there. I am broken as I write this because so many are fighting to hold on. Many spend their days in pain, despair, loneliness, and discomfort. So, my question for you to remember is: "What has the Lord said to you when this all first began? Did He tell you that you would make it? Did He give you a scripture of faith for you to hold on to? If so, dig it up now and stand on it. He gives us promises that he intends on fulfilling. He is not a man that He would lie, what did He tell you?"

I believe that there comes a time in every trial that you come to the point of quitting, you want to stop fighting and raise the white flag of surrender because you have lost hope. I believe that it is at that point that you have crossed over to the place where the finish line is in view. It may be hard to see because you have blurred vision, but it's there nonetheless. You have officially exhausted your own efforts and you are at the place where God is now in control. This is the place where pride is being dealt with. Your feelings of self-confidence are gone and you have exhausted all your own resources. It's just you and God now! So now, recall His promises and use what strength and faith you have left and cry out just one more time. It is at this point that grace is ready to be released because the resistance of pride is out of God's way.

Look at the scriptures I have for you today:

In my distress I called upon the LORD, and cried unto my God: he heard my voice out of his temple, and my cry came before him, even into his ears.

Psalm 18:6 (KJV)

They cried unto thee, and were delivered: they trusted in thee, and were not confounded.

Psalm 22:5 (KJV)

O LORD my God, I cried unto thee, and thou hast healed me.

Psalm 30:2 (KJV)

For I said in my haste, I am cut off from before thine eyes: nevertheless thou heardest the voice of my supplications when I cried unto thee.

Psalm 31:22 (KJV)

Then they cried unto the LORD in their trouble, and he delivered them out of their distresses.

Psalm 107:6 (KJV)

Look at these verses; it's the results of coming to the place where we have nothing left but desperation. No hope left that you can see, all you got left is to cry unto the Lord. No pride left, complete humility before God releases help.

Coming to the place of total despair and desperation is the starting line to finishing the journey. Try it! Take these scriptures as your own; they were written for you to have a clear picture of God; it is your strength in written form.

Never forget that your Father cares for you. It is the reason why he would rather break the sin in your life now than have to judge you for it on the day of judgment. You may not want to go through the fires of testing, but when it is over you will be of great value. So run with patience and run with joy, knowing that "All things work together for good" (Romans 8:28). Place yourself in His hands and you will have the peace of the Lord today. His promises are precious if we will hold on to the end.

Stop Working and Start Resting

Day 128—February 3, 2011

Sarah has finished her latest round of chemotherapy and should be coming home from the hospital today. She is doing well and she can't wait to get back into her own bed, however, there are more treatments; she is not able to work; she is not able to do the things she used to always do. Nothing has been normal for her for the past 128 days. Having her sick means I have twice the amount of things that has to get done: laundry, cooking, cleaning, church business, visiting her in the hospital, and of course the snow removal...and lots more that I am too tired to remember.

For most people that I know the past few years have been a real struggle. It has been easy to say that when it rains it pours. Some have lost jobs, have had major family issues, and even struggled with sickness. I do not know why it all comes at once, but it usually does. I also know that the time that it takes to recover from major life struggles is astronomical. Is this punishment from God or a challenge of our faith?

From my view I see that the world is in a tailspin. The government does not know what to do. The economy is a mess; families are falling apart; the church is helpless and unsure what to do.

No one seems to have a good enough answer for the problems we are facing today. We are fighting to fix what is broken, but we do not have the right parts because what is broken is not physical it is spiritual.

We are living is perilous times like the Bible warned us about in the book of Timothy. But the solutions do not come from Congress, it comes from the Word of God. How can we expect to receive the promises of God in any other way than obedience to the Word of God?

Now we know that there is a great difference between believing in God's promises and acting on God's promises, right? I know you believe them to be true, but are they a first response or a last resort? Oh, how many times do I choose God's Word last! For me, I first try and exhaust all my great and wonderful ideas. I think I can fix the situation, so why bother God with this? I then wait until all my great ideas fail and I am left frustrated and aggravated and defeated. This always happens when my ideas go first. You see, just because something worked somewhere else does not mean that God wants you to use it where you're at now. God wants you to seek Him for every situation and not lean on past accomplishments or successes. He has you in a new place even though it may seem familiar to you. You still must learn to wait on the Lord and never assume you have the right direction for the situation.

My problem is that I know that my own will is strong, and that is dangerous. It is why God uses life's situations to keep me in need of Him. This is not about God having a power trip over us, it is however about the fact that Satan wants you disillusioned with God, and therefore you will turn your worship over to him rather than God. Does Satan want your worship? Yes! Read the story in Matthew about the temptation of Christ. Satan said to Jesus, "All this I will give to you if you will just bow down and worship me!" If you're not trusting in God you're trusting in Satan, and he may promise you the world and all its glory, but it will demand your worship. Worship is allegiance and trust. Who you trust is who you worship.

Do I like it when things are hard? No. When they get hard I do not always make the right decisions, and I then have to bear the consequences. This is the problem of the church today and the country. We have stopped relying on the Word of the Lord and now we trust common sense; this is always a great mistake.

William Bradford, the governor of the Plymouth Colony of pilgrims, insisted, "Those who believe in the Holy Scriptures are bound to observe its teachings. Those who do not are to be bound by its consequences."

Much like the captivity of Israel, we too are in captivity to the economy, to spiritual darkness, and to our own good works. God has a place of rest for us to enter into; all of us. This place is a place where we cease from all our labor and allow the finished work of Jesus on the cross to take over. It is a place where my faith in Him overrides my good judgment and great ideas. It is a place I stay in when the world all around is in chaos. Look with me at this wonderful promise in the Word.

Hebrews 4:1:

> Now, God has offered us the promise that we may receive that rest he spoke about. Let us take care, then, that none of you will be found to have failed to receive that promised rest.

Here we have a verse in the Bible that tells us about a promise of rest that is offered to us by God. Now, we know that God's promises come through patience, obedience, and faith. Patience allows us the opportunity for God to work in us so that the promise will be a gift from God. Obedience to the requirements of the promise allows God to test our allegiance to Him as our supplier of all the things that we need. And faith demonstrates our dependence upon Him and His Word.

This verse does give us a stern warning, it is a warning for us to not miss His promised rest. In other words, God doesn't want you to miss out on this.

> For we have heard the Good News, just as they did. They heard the message, but it did them no good, because when they heard it, they did not accept it with faith. We who believe, then, do receive that rest which God promised. It is just as he said, "I was angry and made a solemn promise: 'They will never enter the land where I would have given them rest!'" He said this even though his work had been finished from the time he created the world. For somewhere in the scriptures this is said about the seventh day: "God rested on the seventh day from all his work." This same matter is spoken of again: "They will never enter that land where I would have given them rest." Those who first heard the Good News did not receive that rest, because they did not believe. There are, then, others who are allowed to receive it. This is shown by the fact that God sets another day, which is called "Today." Many years later he spoke of it through David in the scripture already quoted: "If you hear God's voice today, do not be stubborn." If Joshua had given the people the rest that God had promised, God would not have spoken later about another day.
>
> Hebrews 4:2-8

Why are we not in this place as a church? Because we do not know that it really exists. Our unbelief has hidden it away from us and therefore we are not aware of it. Unbelief is a death sentence to the spiritual life.

Os Guiness gives a very helpful definition of doubt in his book In Two Minds. He says,

> When you believe, you are in one mind and accept something as true. Unbelief is to be of one mind and reject that something is true. To doubt is to waver between the two,

to believe and disbelieve at the same time, and so to be in "two minds."

That is what James calls, in chapter 1, a "double-minded man," or as the Chinese say, "Doubt is standing in two boats, with one foot in each."

F.B. Meyer once said that "Unbelief puts our circumstances between us and God, but faith puts God between us and our circumstances."

The only way to bring life to the promises of God is through true and genuine faith. It takes more than just thinking that God's Word is filled with good ideas and good stories. We must go back to knowing that is it the very Word of God speaking to us.

This passage in Hebrews tells us that God has a place of rest for us. Do you believe that? For you to believe it you must seek for it until you enter into it.

> As it is, however, there still remains for God's people a rest like God's resting on the seventh day. For those who receive that rest which God promised will rest from their own work, just as God rested from his.
>
> Hebrews 4:9-10

There is the key to entering the door of the promise: You must want to enter. How? By faith. Belief is not easy; to have it takes work. Why? Because it is not in our human nature to just believe in everything we read and hear. We are skeptical and often hesitant. This belief must be firm and unwavering; otherwise you will not enter into the fullness of God. The curse of Christianity is unbelief! It cancels everything God wants to do and everything He can do; that is why God calls unbelief a sin. The biggest sin we can ever make is unbelief! The Bible says that God resists the proud and He gives grace to the humble.

> Let us, then, do our best to receive that rest, so that no one of us will fail as they did because of their lack of faith. The

word of God is alive and active, sharper than any double-edged sword. It cuts all the way through, to where soul and spirit meet, to where joints and marrow come together. It judges the desires and thoughts of the heart. There is nothing that can be hid from God; everything in all creation is exposed and lies open before his eyes. And it is to him that we must all give an account of ourselves.

Hebrews 4:11-13

This is the power of the promise of God's Word! It is sure and it is powerful to act. Never underestimate it or neglect what it says. You're a fool to do so because this Word, unlike any other word ever spoken or written by the pen it is backed up by all of heaven.

Let us, then, hold firmly to the faith we profess. For we have a great High Priest who has gone into the very presence of God—Jesus, the Son of God. Our High Priest is not one who cannot feel sympathy for our weaknesses. On the contrary, we have a High Priest who was tempted in every way that we are, but did not sin.

Hebrews 4:14-15

This is what you have in your corner—Jesus Christ the Righteous. Paul says this is enough for you to want to hold on to; this is the profession of your faith and you're not to give up! He is your reason for trusting in what God's Word says. He went through it all Himself; all the heartaches, sufferings, and physical torments. He bore all our sins and failures and every disappointment. Why? He did it so that He would be able to help you get through yours. He didn't have to do it. He chose to so that you would have the comfort and help you need when you need it. And because He did it without sinning He is all the more able to help you. Had He sinned there would be little consolation for us; after all, who wants to hear about those who didn't make it? We hear from them all the time. Because He succeeded you have this final promise:

Let us have confidence, then, and approach God's throne, where there is grace. There we will receive mercy and find grace to help us just when we need it.

Hebrews 4:16

This is the reward. Come, obtain, find. Come boldly, He said. Don't be afraid and do not worry that you have failed or that you're in need. What a wonderful grace that we have been given; if only we would have the faith to enter into it.

One more thing; before you leave God's throne room, be sure to get your mercy. Mercy is only given to those who have failed. How do we fail? Unbelief! Not going to God first! After you get your mercy from God you will find your grace. There will be just enough to get through today's storms.

You ready to give up? Stop fighting a winless war and turn to Him. He will guide you out of your storm and set your feet on solid ground.

The Call of a Servant

Day 131—February 6, 2011

I was e-mailed this cute little story today:

A farmer had some puppies he needed to sell. He painted a sign advertising the four pups and set about nailing it to a post on the edge of his yard. As he was driving the last nail into the post, he felt a tug on his overalls. He looked down into the eyes of a little boy. "Mister," he said, "I want to buy one of your puppies." "Well," said the farmer, as he rubbed the sweat off the back of his neck, "These puppies come from fine parents and cost a good deal of money." The boy dropped his head for a moment. Then reaching deep into his pocket, he pulled out a handful of change and held it up to the farmer. "I've got thirty nine cents. Is that enough to take a look?" "Sure," said the farmer. And with that he let out a whistle. "Here, Dolly!" he called. Out from the doghouse and down the ramp ran Dolly followed by four little balls of fur. The little boy pressed his face against the chain link fence. His eyes danced with delight. As the dogs made their way to the fence, the little boy noticed something else stirring inside the doghouse. Slowly another little ball appeared; this one noticeably smaller. Down the ramp it slid. Then in a somewhat awkward manner, the little pup began hobbling toward the others, doing its best to catch up. "I want that one," the little boy said, pointing to the runt. The farmer knelt down at the boy's side and said, "Son, you don't want that puppy. He will never be able to run and play with you like these other dogs would." With that the little boy stepped back from the fence, reached down, and began rolling up one leg of his trousers. In doing so he revealed a steel brace running down both sides of his leg attaching itself to a specially made shoe. Looking back up at the farmer, he said, "You see, sir, I don't run too well myself, and he will need someone who understands." With tears in his eyes, the farmer reached down and picked up the little pup. Holding it carefully he handed it to the little boy. "How much?" asked the little boy. "No charge," answered the farmer. "There's no charge for love."

The world is full of people who need someone who understands.

What a wonderful story. People who suffer know that they have limitations in life. There is a need for dependence from those who understand them. Every day they are passed by and forgotten by people who maybe just do not understand. For the past several months I have learned that people with disabilities or sickness are among the most wonderful people I have ever met. So many of them, of course, never have the opportunity to reveal this because we have failed to let them speak. We have shut them up by ignoring their existence and because of that we have silenced wonderful people who need to be heard from. Seeing needs around us is the whole purpose of Christ saving and delivering us. Our salvation came with a price, and that price is to be like Jesus. Only when we are like Him are we demonstrating true Christianity

The movie Radio is a true story about a young man with mental disabilities who was lost in the system of life. His mother worked all day, and he wandered alone through the neighborhood pushing a grocery carriage minding his own business. He was constantly teased and made fun of by those needing a good laugh. No one understood him or cared to know him. They all assumed that he was unreachable and had nothing to offer their world in which they lived.

I loved this movie because one person dared to reach out to this person. He reached him with simple love and acceptance. This young man turned their world around. He became loved by thousands all because someone reached into his life and allowed this young man the chance to be who he always was.

In my church, we have a nine-year-old young man named Jacob who is autistic. When he first came here over a year ago he was all over the place. Sometimes even the service was disrupted because of him. At first I wasn't sure what to do. While I was praying over the matter the Lord spoke to me and said, "I sent this boy here to teach your church how to love." Now this young man is a church favorite. He helps the elderly in and out of the church, prays for people who are sick, loves everyone who he meets…he has taught us how to love. The boy who at one time ran the aisles during service now worships on the front row. He just had to be given the chance.

Why is it that we assume that disabilities make someone useless? Or when people get old they need to retire? Does God have a chapter somewhere that tells us what the age limitations on being useful is? Or what physical requirements might be needed in order to be a part of the church? Who sets these boundaries anyway? They are set by those who do not understand or do not see through the eyes of Jesus.

Now, I agree that not everyone can lead worship or play an instrument. Just ask my church. I have tried to lead worship in the past and I know that is something I am not called to do. That is just not my gift. Our Jacob has found his gift to our church; he is our spiritual greeter. If you were to come here you will see a young man with flaming red hair approach you and he expects a hug. If you need help or assistance he is always the first on the scene. He can make our ushers look bad if they are not careful. He sees the simple needs of those he meets, and he meets them.

So many people miss the true understanding of what it means to serve the Lord. It does not come in a title or a gift. It comes by being available when needed. I believe in the joy that comes from serving others. Serving others means that you find opportunities to bless others and minister to them. You bring out their best and allow them as well as others to see that they are useful and needed.

Instead of our churches being filled with only people we like and accept, we should see it filled with people who need God. God is looking for servants who will serve Him to those who need Him. Christian servitude needs to be given to those who need the Lord. Once you have the Lord your attitude should change from a receiver to a giver. Jesus said that it is better to give than to receive. Why? The rewards of giving are greater than the rewards of receiving.

> This, however, is not the way it shall be among you. If one of you wants to be great, you must be the servant of the rest; and if one of you wants to be first, you must be the slave of the others—like the Son of Man, who did not come to be served, but to serve and to give his life to redeem many people.
>
> Matthew 20:26-28

In the kingdom of God everything is opposite of the world. In the world, we want to be served, and we avoid doing anything that might cost us something. But the kingdom of God is a kingdom of serving others over ourselves. This was the example given to us by Jesus when He left heaven to come to earth.

> Don't do anything from selfish ambition or from a cheap desire to boast, but be humble toward one another, always considering others better than yourselves. And look out for one another's interests, not just for your own. The atti-

tude you should have is the one that Christ Jesus had: He always had the nature of God, but he did not think that by force he should try to remain equal with God. Instead of this, of his own freewill he gave up all he had, and took the nature of a servant. He became like a human being and appeared in human likeness.

Philippians 2:3-7

This was the apostle Paul's admonition to all believers concerning Christianity in its highest level. Love each other; serve each other; do nothing selfishly; consider others over yourselves; have the attitude that Christ had when He came to serve and not be served.

He ends this by showing us the reward of Christ's actions of serving. God raised Him up and gave Him a name above every name. But He had to walk the path of obedience all the way to the cross; no short cuts.

Unfortunately this is not the path taught in today's Christian circles. Like the Pharisees of the Bible, we are always looking for the best seats, the best foods, and the places of honor. We do not like to serve or wait on others and we demand that we are treated with respect, all in the name of Christ. But this is not what this scripture said to do! Christ was never first or sat in honor or royalty. He served others and honored God.

The greatest one among you must be your servant. Whoever makes himself great will be humbled, and whoever humbles himself will be made great.

Matthew 23:11-12

We must follow the example of Christ if we are to honor Him. Learn the lesson of the servant and serve one another so that God will exalt you in due time.

The Sounds of the Church Bells

Day 135—February 10, 2011

Today I am here with Sarah in the kitchen enjoying a cup of hot tea before heading to her doctor's appointment. During the past 135 days we have had to learn to live in a daily, if not hourly, time of uncertainty. This disease makes and decides your daily routine and determines what your day is going to be like, so many do not understand that. You assume you are always in control or at least supposed to be in control, but you are not. I have to change my plans according to what Sarah might need, but that is all right. I think it is a true act of love and I am glad God is teaching that to me. When someone is sick they need to know that there are people who love them that are going to be with them through the tough times they face. It is also like that with serving Christ. We must learn to direct our lives around the desires of the Lord and never assume that the day belongs to ourselves.

For the past two nights the Father has been dealing with me about something that I know is close to His heart. It's souls, people! Literally multitudes of lost, hurting souls surround every church in America, and yet there seems to be little to no concern for their well-being. This includes my church as well. Within three miles of this church in Webster are 26,500 souls, and within five miles it jumps to 46,000 souls. I am not looking at this number for the purpose of church growth opportunities, but rather seeing it from the eyes of my Father, who wishes all men to be saved. It must break His heart to see so many who are lost, hurting, and searching in all the wrong places for the life that only He can give.

As I walked into the house from my car last night, I heard the church bells ringing from one of the local churches here in Webster. It is one of the many things I love about this town. The sounds of the beautiful, old hymns could be heard for miles away and no doubt literally thousands are able to hear its beauty. However, I could not help but think just how many people have tuned them out and can no longer enjoy the sounds of these old hymns. To them the sounds have only alerted them to the fact that another hour has past here in Webster.

So many miss the words and the passion for which these old hymns were written. They have shut the door tight and refuse to have anything to do with the church and what it is offering. After all, the church has been stained with its own problems—accusations of scandal, abuse, fraud, and all the rest. No wonder few have confidence in the message that it's offering. We have become little more than the owners of fancy buildings filled with stuck up people who have shut the hurting out. You say, "Pastor Kent, you are being too hard!" Yes, I know I am, but rest assured I am speaking to myself as well. I feel that as a church we have lost sight of the Great Commission and the true compassion of Christ. We do not seemed alarmed anymore about the unprecedented amount of violent crimes that we read about every day in the paper. We are not alarmed at the amount of worldliness that has crept into the church and about the lack of power we posses. I am alarmed! I want to sound the wake-up call for us to return to the altars of sacrifice and call out upon the God of Abraham, Isaac, and Jacob. Like the prophets of old who cried out for God to rend the heavens and pour out revival. I am not looking for a "Bless the Saints" revival. True revival does not bless the saints, it wakens them! It commissions and calls them into battle like a mighty army of well-trained soldiers. He commissions them to the altars to wait for the commands of its Commander and Chief, Jesus Christ,! It is a revival that will wake-up the church to their callings to reach the lost, deliver the afflicted, and love the hurting. I long for a revival like the early church possessed! One that brought deliverance with them everywhere they went. They became the very voice of deliverance and hope everywhere they went! They didn't just encourage the sick they prayed!

This message to you must hit your own heart. When I speak of the church I am not talking about the building in which you go and worship. It is not the combination of your congregation that is the church. It is you! You are the church of the Lord Jesus Christ. You! We are great at passing the buck to the leaders and the denomination. We must take a deeper look at personal responsibility to the fact that in us dwells the power of the living, resurrected Christ. If we do not learn to live it then He sent the Holy Spirit in vain and Christ's death means nothing.

Look at what happened to Israel after they had been in captivity and bondage for over four hundred years.

> Years later the king of Egypt died, but the Israelites were still groaning under their slavery and cried out for help. Their cry went up to God, who heard their groaning and remembered his covenant with Abraham, Isaac, and Jacob. He saw the slavery of the Israelites and was concerned for them.
>
> Exodus 2:23-25

If you read this chapter you will notice in verse twenty-two that Moses was living in the wilderness hiding because he had committed murder. He had set up a new life with his wife and child and became comfortable. This is important to remember because Moses was their coming deliverer.

I believe that God is ready to send to our city a deliverer! That deliverer is the awakened, living, resurrected body of the Lord Jesus Christ. The church is going to wake up and become the hope to those who need it. Why? Because God has heard the cry of our cities! I can hear the cry of the city of Webster! The addicted are crying out for deliverance; the sick are crying out for healing; the lost are crying out for hope. Can you hear them crying? Maybe you have gotten to the place where the sound of the church bells are so familiar that you can't hear them anymore. But I hear them loud and clear. Rise up and fill your calling! This is the time for the church to awaken out of its slumber and rise to its destiny.

The children of Israel had to first get desperate and learn the power of crying out to God. It was when they cried out that a child named Moses was born; hope is born out of tears and desperation. Self-confidence and ability only delay the deliverance that only God can give to you.

If you look at the life of Moses you will see the heart of God. Moses started out living the life of luxury as a son of Pharaoh; after seeing a Hebrew man abused he murdered an Egyptian. He then fled for his life and ended up living in the wilderness, far away from anything and anyone that could link him to his past. For the next forty years He lived in a wilderness tending to someone else's sheep. Then one day he was out tending the flock when he saw something strange. It was a bush on fire! As he approached it He heard the voice of God telling Him to take off his shoes for the ground that he was standing on was holy ground! It was there that God spoke to Moses to go back to what he had come out of and bring deliverance to God's people! God always brings us back to what we were delivered from because we are familiar with the hurts of those who are there.

Jesus suffered because suffering brought Him into our needs. He makes intercession for us because He is familiar with our pain. This is the reason why God wants us to become the deliverer in our cities because we are familiar with their suffering.

It was breaking God's heart to know that the people of Israel were crying out and yet there was no one to go to them. Look at what happened next:

> Then Moses answered the LORD, "But suppose the Israelites do not believe me and will not listen to what I say. What shall I do if they say that you did not appear to me?" So the LORD asked him, "What are you holding?" "A walking stick," he answered. The LORD said, "Throw it on the ground." When Moses threw it down, it turned into a snake, and he ran away from it. Then the LORD said to Moses, "Reach down and pick it up by the tail." So Moses reached down and caught it, and it became a walking stick again. The LORD said, "Do this to prove to the Israelites that the LORD, the God of their ancestors, the God of Abraham, Isaac, and Jacob, has appeared to you."
>
> Exodus 4:1-5

"What is in your hand?" For too long the church has failed to see what they had with them. It is true that you cannot go forward without knowing what it is you have to offer; it is important to know that what you need, you already have. Moses had a stick! That was it, just a stick! It had no magic laser or buttons that transformed it into anything special; it was just a shepherd's staff made of wood from some tree. However, once he was willing to let it go it became more than a stick; it became an opportunity to make someone believe. I believe that this represents our testimony. Every one of us has experienced the power of God in setting us free from our own sins and failures. This is like the staff that Moses had, if we will just take it and lay it down before those who are lost it will become a powerful message that will open their hearts.

Satan has convinced us that our staff is nothing more than our past that should be forgotten and kept hidden. He knows that what is in your hand is powerful! His plan is to shut you up and make you see that you have nothing to give. But you do! Like Moses, he wants to send you to the backside of the desert and leave you there forever, but God is speaking to you through the burning bush in your heart to take your shoes off and listen to what He has to say to you.

> Then the LORD said to Moses, "Reach down and pick it up by the tail." So Moses reached down and caught it, and it became a walking stick again. The LORD said, "Do this to prove to the Israelites that the LORD, the God of their ancestors, the God of Abraham, Isaac, and Jacob, has appeared to you." The LORD spoke to Moses again, "Put your hand inside your robe." Moses obeyed; and when he took his hand out, it was diseased, covered with white spots, like snow. Then the LORD said, "Put your hand inside your robe again." He did so, and when he took it out this time, it was healthy, just like the rest of his body.
>
> Exodus 4:4-7

God does something to help Moses understand just how urgent this matter was. Israel, His beloved treasure, was crying out in pain and affliction and the only way to them was through Moses. Friends, man is lost! Diseased with incurable sin and man has become a spiritual outcast. The only hope man had is for someone to take deliverance to him.

In this passage, God shows Moses what was even in his own heart—leprosy! It must have been a shock for Moses to see what God sees in us. We too have suffered but we seem to forget what was in us. We forgot what He delivered us from.

Only a man yielded to God can bring man back to God. The blood of Jesus is the remedy and the cure for man, but it has to be applied by those who have experienced its power. Only you and I can do it! Why? Because at one time we had this disease in us and God gave us the cure. How did He do it? Through someone else! Someone came to you and showed you the love of Jesus! That love when it went into you and cleansed you by His blood also infected you; you therefore have become a carrier of the deliverance of Jesus Christ. His Blood now flows through us and is the cure for fallen humanity. It is a great sin to not use it on those who need Him.

Look at Moses's final excuse:

> But Moses said, "No, LORD, don't send me. I have never been a good speaker, and I haven't become one since you began to speak to me. I am a poor speaker, slow and hesitant." The LORD said to him, "Who gives man his mouth? Who makes him deaf or dumb? Who gives him sight or makes him blind? It is I, the LORD. Now, go! I will help you to speak, and I will tell you what to say."

> Exodus 4:10-12

Tell me, my friends, what excuse do you have left for not telling the lost about Jesus? What excuse do you have for not reaching out to the disabled? What excuse do you have for being too busy to help someone? He's given you the message of your testimony (the stick); He's given you the reason why you must go (the leprosy); and He's given you the word's to say (the speech). There is one more thing He gives to you. He gives to you His presence. He promises to go with you and empower you to do this work. Will you go? I'm going!

Sarah is going to the hospital today for her daily check-up. She had a lot of bleeding from her nose and gums for most of the night. It is primarily due to her very low blood count and she will more than likely need platelets. God is good and His faithfulness is evident every day. We are standing on very precious promises!

To My Sweet Valentine

Day 139—February 14, 2011

Today is a special day! It's Valentine's Day! It's the day to show love to that special person in our lives.

Unfortunately, today my love is back in the hospital at UMass Memorial, room 802. Her treatments are still being done, and even though special days and events arrive, we are unable to celebrate them in the manner to which we would like. Due to the leukemia I have not been able to kiss her, and even hugs come rarely, and when they do come they have been so very special to me.

Today I want to honor this very special woman that God gave to me. On February 23 of this year, we will have been married for twenty-six wonderful years. So today is dedicated to the one person who helped me make it and been by my side through everything; to my Sarah in room 802!

This is a letter for Sarah. I remember the day I met you. I had moved here from Texas and had only been in New England for a very short time. I had taken a position at the Grace Assembly of God Church as a youth pastor and I was not used to the New England way of life, neither were they used to me!

After a few months of getting my feet wet I met a guy named Dan, and he invited me to go with him to an old-fashion tent meeting in Haverhill on a Friday night. I was at first not inter-ested in going because I had so much to do, but he persuaded me and I went. We arrived at the place where they had a huge tent set up and several people crowded inside to be a part of this old-fashion style preaching and singing; it was great! I loved old-fashion tent meetings, because I grew up on services just like them. Soon after I got there I remember seeing you for the first time. You were standing in the third row of wooden chairs sing-ing and raising your hands to the Lord, and I could tell you loved the Lord. You had that blue jean skirt on and that beautiful long hair, and I knew at that moment I wanted to find a way to meet you. I had a hard time concentrating on the service because I had my eyes fixed on you.

When the pastor finished preaching and gave the altar call I saw you respond, and I rushed up so that I could stand behind you, hoping by some miracle I would have the chance to say hello. We sang several choruses and the service had finally ended. I remember you turning around and saying, "You have a very nice voice!" I knew then that you were either tone deaf or that you were the one for me. I found out that you and Dan knew each other. He then invited you to join us at Friendly's Restaurant for ice cream. I was thrilled because I had the chance to be with you. You were so beautiful, and I couldn't take my eyes off of you.

The next day I couldn't wait to go to the tent meeting to see you and hopefully find a way to sit next to you. You were even more beautiful that night than the previous night. Your eyes sparkled and your smile mesmerized me.

The next night I sat by the telephone trying to find the words and the courage to call and ask you out on a date. I just knew you would say no. You were so beautiful and wonderful; way too special for me. But when I asked you to go out you invited me to dinner at your house. I drove to your house like a madman; I couldn't wait to see you. I was, however, afraid of meeting your folks and getting the third degree, but they were so nice and treated me so well. That night you made turkey cutlets, but I had no appetite; I was like a lovesick puppy. I never wanted to leave that day; I felt that I had found the one I was searching for.

After I left your house I went home on cloud nine that night. I called you for another date! Remember? We went to Bishops together, and it was there that I held your hand for the first time; I was crying inside because I was so happy. I was actually holding your hand! You were my dream come true.

By the end of our first week together I remember I wanted to ask you to marry me. I wanted to spend the rest of my life with you. We went to a Mexican restaurant, and you had Mexican food for the first time. I loved being able to sit next to you and explain what you should order off of the Mexican menu. I was so in love! On the way home I decided that now was the time! So I pulled over to the nearest parking lot and got you out of the car and said, "Sarah, would you marry me?" Not too sure what you were going to say; but you said, "I'd be honored to!" I could not believe it! You were going to be my wife, my best friend, and my lifelong companion. We were going to go through everything together. I was the most blessed man that ever lived! I felt invincible and knew that nothing could ever go wrong from this day on! You said yes!

I was walking on cloud nine, and then three days later I fell off of a three-story roof, shattered my elbow, and broke my nose. I ended up in the hospital, the same one your dad worked at. I don't know if you ever knew what I thought about on that day. I was a mess, and I thought you would walk in that room and say this is over. But you didn't! You came every day to be with me and you comforted me!

I remember the day you came in, and you were smiling ear to ear and you handed me a piece of paper that said "February 23rd" on it. When I asked you what it meant you said, "It's the day that I want to marry you!" I couldn't believe it! I was not dreaming; this was real. Sarah, I want you to never forget how much

I loved you! I wanted this wedding to be special for you, and I wanted it to be a dream come true for both of us. February 23, I couldn't wait!

It ended up taking me several months to completely recover from that fall, and it was you that nursed me back to health. You stayed with me every day, standing next to me and being there for me.

The day of the wedding finally came. I was dressed four hours early! I couldn't wait any longer; this was going to be the best day ever. I remember standing in front of the congregation and hearing the wedding march begin to play. There you were, so amazingly beautiful in that beautiful white dress; you were the most beautiful thing I have ever seen in my life. I watched as your father escorted you to me. You were going to be mine after today! I was so happy, and I could see it in you as well.

The time came in the ceremony for you to sing a special song to me. I will never forget the words to that song as long as I live. "This is the day that the Lord has made, and I am so glad he made you." I saw such love in your eyes as the words flowed from you.

The dinner soon followed, and we sat together at the head of the wedding table. We were the center of everyone's attention. I still remember your mother clinking the glass every five minutes so that we would kiss. Little did she know that she did not have to clink the glass, I would have kissed you without ever being told to. After the ceremony and the food and all the smiling we did, the time had finally come to leave the church and head onto our first day as a married couple. This was it Sarah, our lives together officially started as we drove out of the church parking lot.

Our honeymoon was great; Hilton Head Island, South Carolina! I was now a married man and married to the most beautiful woman ever! The honeymoon was wonderful! We lay in each other's arms for the first time. I remember waking up and seeing you lying there next to me. You were still asleep, and you were so beautiful to look upon.

We soon had to go home and begin living our lives together. I am heartbroken to have to bring this up, but you already know that things didn't stay so wonderful. The passion of our love was being tested by our very own hurts from our past. We both had a secret life that had been brought into our marriage. I admit that I was a lousy husband! I am so sorry for what I put you through. I pray that you would forgive me for those years!

I was not the wonderful husband that you had hoped for. I was selfish, self-centered, and had no clue on how to be a husband. I watched as you were being drawn away from me knowing there was nothing I could do to bring you back to me.

Soon our son Brandon was born to us, and I hoped that he would bring us back to each other. At first it was working; I saw us happy again because we were going to be parents, but soon after he was born I think we drifted even farther apart. Sarah, I didn't know what to do or how to fix things; I tried to and I wanted to. You soon got sick and tired of hearing me say, "I'm sorry," and "I will change," but that was all I knew to do. I know I was blowing it but I couldn't help myself; I couldn't find the way out. I was crying out inside and I wanted to fix everything, but didn't know how. You needed a man in your life, and I was just a boy.

Both of us come from broken homes and had no idea what we were really getting into. We soon learned that love was not enough; it took more to keep a marriage healthy, and neither of us seemed to know where to begin to fix the problems.

Well, I am so glad that God knew how to fix everything. I resigned as the youth pastor of Grace Assembly and we started attending New Life Christian Center in Haverhill. It was there that we met Pastor Ken and Gloria Kashner. Our first morning service there was very hard to sit through for me. It was like Pastor Kashner was telling everything about me. I couldn't understand how he knew all of this. Did Sarah call him? This was an encounter for me. That morning God ambushed me with the truth of who I was.

Through Ken and Gloria Kashner, God brought true healing into me. The strongholds of pride and selfishness were being attacked, and I felt that I was learning how to really love you the right way. It took many years for me to breakdown the enemy's strongholds, but you stayed after me. I know that you could have left me Sarah, I would have deserved it. But you stayed! You willingly walked through everything with me and stood by me regardless of the consequences.

It is never easy to let God take down your walls, because you feel vulnerable and open for everyone else to see. But since pride is the strongman that keeps us in our old ways, God has to bring into us humility to counter this sin in us.

Then you became pregnant with little Jeremiah. About a month before he was due you decided to climb up a ladder and help me work on a roof. What were we thinking? It was shortly after that your water broke and we both knew that Jeremiah was soon to arrive into our lives. You were so in love with our little man. He was so defenseless and small. I knew what you were thinking because you had carried him inside you for so long. He was a part of you, and I remember you holding him with a smile from ear to ear. Due to his prematurity you had to go home without him. I know it was hard for you to do that. I used to love watching you hold him and talk to him in a way that I knew only he understood.

We now had two boys and a marriage that God was healing. It took God a long time to get completely through to me; thanks for waiting and not giving up! It was during this time that we had left youth ministry and took our first church in Manhattan, Kansas. It was the worst two years of my life. Little did I know that God was still pulling junk out of my life. We soon realized that the best thing for us to do was to go back home to Haverhill and be with our families. After returning I soon figured out that God had more to do in us. I often thought that He would never finish with me; I would be an eternal mess! But now I know that God plans on dealing with our lives until we leave this earth.

Soon after returning we were blessed with son number three, Isaac. Remember the night on the couple's retreat and after we went to bed and all of a sudden we both started laughing and we couldn't stop! It was that night that I saw for the first time that God was truly completing a healing in our lives; God was doing a great work in both of us. It was also that night we gave Isaac his name because Isaac meant laughter. God broke through and we laughed at the marriage retreat for hours together. We were falling back in love, and I had my girl back, and she had me. We were going to make it! That was seventeen years ago, my love! And you are still here! Thanks for staying! I have made it my life's goal to be a great husband and father. Through the wisdom found in failures and the wisdom from God Himself, I am learning every day to heed to the Holy Spirit and to obey His voice.

Little did I know that the testing of God was not over. You were diagnosed with a deadly disease, acute myeloid leukemia and renal cell cancer. For almost a year I would have to learn to love you in a more special way, a deeper love that would have to look into your heart to see the woman I so love. Although your appearance would change, I would see you in your eyes and your smile. You were there as always, refusing to ever give up or fall apart. Your sickness became my inspiration to write this book and to fall more deeply in love with you. I also knew that it was a part of His wondrous plan to completing His work in us both. Even though I have been unable to touch you and to kiss you, I want you to know that all of my hugs and kisses belong only to you. They are being stored up and saved for the day when there will be no restrictions on you. You are my lifelong partner, for better or for worse, in sickness and in health, till death do us part!

We are now surrounded by three grown boys, a great church family, and an awesome amount of friends and family. When things get hard you have become amazing! You're the best thing that has ever happened to me, and I love you with all my heart.

I am now looking forward to what God has in store for the two of us. Soon this cancer will be completely behind us and we will be able to move forward into a new life together. We will begin to see the results of all of our testing and I am looking forward to seeing them together with you.

Ephesians 5:25:

> Husbands, love your wives, even as Christ also loved the church, and gave himself for it.

Happy Valentine's Day, with all my love, forever! Kent.

Learning to Trust the Love of the Father

Day 148—February 23, 2011

Happy Anniversary, Sarah! Twenty-six years and we are still going strong! I am so glad we get to celebrate together without the distractions of doctors, hospitals, and nurses! I am also excited because the journey is winding down and we are almost done.

They have been able to extract four million stem cells, and now the transplant is close. We are excited about it getting here, but we have been informed that it will be the worst part of the journey. It is our prayer that God will only continue what He has already done and that she will go through under His watchful eye.

When I was a young boy, I had always dreamed about leaving home and experiencing the world. I wanted to see what was out there and didn't want to be told by others what to do. I hated being told what to do, where to go, and how to do it. I wanted to be a somebody and have the freedom to make all of my own choices.

There were also times later in my life that I became overwhelmed because of the choices I was allowed to make on my own. These choices began to make great demands on me and became difficult to follow through with. The results were that all I wanted to do was to get away and run as fast as I could away from the life I had created for myself.

There are times when we are in situations that are over our heads. Our jobs are too demanding; our families are falling apart; we are not in love with the person we married anymore; we have become bored with life in general. We begin looking for the way out thinking that a change would solve everything. This is what my father did when I was nine years old. He jumped ship and swam to another land, one where he could start over and leave everyone else to fend for themselves. Now, I love my father and he made some drastic mistakes in life that he has repented for, but the consequences come nonetheless.

Life is always going to have great difficulties in it, and there will be a time when starting over is the only option you have. My father quit for his own benefit, and he unfortunately had to suffer the consequences that came with that choice. He missed watching us grow up, getting to know his grandchildren, experiencing the successes of his children, and so much more.

I am writing to challenge each of you to be cautious that you do not make the same mistakes in your life. Cherish what you have! Losing it could be so much worse later in your life than you think.

I am well aware that many people are facing great uncertainty. You have been taken out of your comfort zone and placed into a new place. This may have been caused by a loss of a job, or by a tragedy you had to face, or even just by time going by. You are at a place that you are looking for a change.

Look with me in the book of Luke at a familiar story that just might help us see what I am talking about:

> Jesus went on to say, "There was once a man who had two sons. The younger one said to him, 'Father, give me my share of the property now.' So the man divided his property between his two sons. After a few days the younger

son sold his part of the property and left home with the money. He went to a country far away, where he wasted his money in reckless living. He spent everything he had. Then a severe famine spread over that country, and he was left without a thing.

Luke 15:11-14

It wasn't all that long ago when most of us had great jobs, great families, and great lives. Gas was below two dollars a gallon, jobs had benefits and pay increases, and kids went to college. We could even boast that America had moral values of knowing the difference between right and wrong. But something has happened; things have changed, and we seem to be spiraling downward out of control. What is happening? It's simple! We have left our Father's house. We decided a long time ago that no one was going to tell us what to do. We wanted the freedom to make our own choices and to do what we wanted. We wanted to have God as a convenience rather than a Lord over us. Then, when things got out of control, we have found that all the things we went after are gone. The famine has taken everything, and now we are in need.

We have said to God, "We do not want you in our schools!" What have we received in return? School shootings, rebellion, murder, rape, violence, and out-of-control teens who are violent and rebellious. And this is happening from our elementary grades all the way through college. We must realize that without God there is no standard of righteousness, no boundaries; man is not held accountable to anyone. He becomes hopeless and therefore fails to have a future; his dream dies. Without God, the Ten Commandments do not make sense, and without them we have no code of proper conduct.

We have taken God out of our government. Laws are passed to please the people's sin. Instead of banning abortion we give the people a choice. The murder of the unborn is out of control; there is no value of life anymore. It is sad to say that much of the country couldn't care less; after all when God is left out of the picture there is no concern for what is right and wrong anymore; as long as I am happy nothing else matters.

We have taken God out of our homes. Many used to go to church and Sunday school, but not anymore. We have gotten too busy. The kids have sports to play, and Dad needs to cut the grass, and it's the only day we get to sleep in. Plus, we are too tired. We love God, but do not need to be in church. We become religious without the accountability of a relationship with God Himself.

All of these are the deceptions that Satan is using to bring America into bondage and captivity. We have been lured away from God and because of this we are now caught in a famine. There is nothing left; the kids are home, but not here. Mom and Dad are here, but no longer in love...the spark is out. The things that were supposed to bring us together are now tearing us apart.

The answer for all of us is simple. Like the younger son in the above story, we have spent all that we had and we are now in want. So we must stop and find the right solution. The danger is this: there are many temporary solutions but in time they will all lead you back to the same place you are in now. You must choose the right one! Let's look into this passage of scripture a little deeper.

> So he went to work for one of the citizens of that country, who sent him out to his farm to take care of the pigs. He wished he could fill himself with the bean pods the pigs ate, but no one gave him anything to eat.
>
> Luke 15:15-16

This young man did what he thought would be the way to get through the mess he was in. He joined himself to his surroundings and he got a job feeding the pigs, but it never changed him. He was still in need. He still had to eat, and what he ate was the same food that was given to the pigs. Life on his own did not get better; it got much worse! This is always the results of our wanting to be in charge of our lives and not allowing God in it. We never get what we were promised.

To make matters worse, if you choose the wrong solution you only end up prolonging the purpose of the famine. God allows famine or suffering for a great purpose; to get you to come home to Him. Look at what this young man decided to do.

> At last he came to his senses and said, "All my father's hired workers have more than they can eat, and here I am about to starve! I will get up and go to my father and say, 'Father, I have sinned against God and against you. I am no longer fit to be called your son; treat me as one of your hired workers.'"

> Luke 15:17-19

Go back to your Father's house! That was it! Go back to the place of blessing, warmth, and love. What he once despised he now craved. You might be reading this and feel that this story relates to you a little. Trust me. What God is after is you. He wants you to come back into the fold of His dear Son. Famines are allowed by God to make us see the end results of life without Him. Something changes when we are back in the Father's house; there is love there. It's like a refreshing wind that no one can describe because it goes deep inside of you. In your Father's house, peace returns even when there is a storm raging around you. The famine has made you see what you truly had from the beginning; it was right!

So this is exactly what this young man in the story did; he went back to his father. He went back humbled and was willing to be nothing more than one of his father's hired servants. He was returning changed, hopeless, and humbled. He wasn't returning the same man that he was when he left. This is the effects of suffering and trials that we go through. It changes us and makes us ready to be in the Father's house. Never did he expect what he was about to receive.

So he got up and started back to his father. He was still a long way from home when his father saw him; his heart was filled with pity, and he ran, threw his arms around his son, and kissed him. "Father," the son said, "I have sinned against God and against you. I am no longer fit to be called your son." But the father called to his servants. "Hurry!" he said. "Bring the best robe and put it on him. Put a ring on his finger and shoes on his feet. Then go and get the prize calf and kill it, and let us celebrate with a feast! For this son of mine was dead, but now he is alive; he was lost, but now he has been found." And so the feasting began.

Luke 15:2024

The devil will always lie to us concerning the Father's love for us. We feel it's too late; we've gone too far, nothing is left there for me; they don't want anything to do with me. These are all lies! The Father is waiting for us, longing for us, missing us. This story isn't so much the story of a straying son as much as it is the story of a loving father who is desperate to get his son home where he is safe. He couldn't care less what it took to get his son back because he loved his son.

The Bible warns us that the wages of sin is death! We are also told that "Sin is fun for a season, but the end is death." God will never force you to return to Him, but He will try to draw you out especially during a famine. His love for you is evident by His wanting to draw you back to Him by sending Jesus to pay the penalty for your sin. Remember, the end result of sin is not just wanting, its death, hell, torment, eternity. This is what God wants to save you from. The famine was sent to save you, not to lose you.

I pray that God will bring you back to Him. Return us all to our first love and to the place of true love and passion for God. The end is near, time is too short, and God is waiting.

Preparing for the Inevitable

Day 155—March 2, 2011

Since Sarah has gotten sick I have talked about many issues that face those who are suffering. I have also learned that not everyone's outcome will be the same. When someone we love is sick the one thing we fear the most is death. Death is the dreaded news that no one ever wants to face, because we are never ready to say good-bye.

Today I want to touch on this subject, although I fear that it is not going to be an easy one to talk about. I know it is sensitive, but death is coming to everyone, and we must not only prepare for it but we must understand it. In God's eyes death is not the worst thing that can happen to us. If we are Christians, God calls death a reward. Death for those who do not know Christ is called damnation and torment. God's Word declares that He is not willing that any perish but all come to repentance. This perish is not the death of leaving this earth, it is the death of losing your soul on the day of judgment.

So, I am going to do my best to try and share with you a little about my own thoughts concerning this matter.

Nearly three years ago my wife and I lost both our fathers. My father at age sixty-nine went in for surgery for his knees and the worst that we thought would happen was that he would lose one or both of his legs. I remember talking to him the night before he had the surgery and we teased each other about the operation. It was good to laugh with him, because for thirty years I had no contact with him. I had allowed anger and bitterness to rob me of knowing him. About ten years ago an act of forgiveness brought my father and me back together, and although we knew we could never get back the lost years we decided to start fresh and move forward together.

The next morning at around 8:00 a.m. my phone rang and it was my father's wife, Mary Anne. She called to inform me that last night my father had gotten a blood clot that went to his heart and he passed away. I was in shock; I could not for a second believe what I had just heard. This was not possible; the surgery was a success and my dad and I were supposed to have the time to make up for all those lost years. I was not ready to say good-bye! I guess deep down I thought you could live forever.

As I tried to recover from the shock, I had the horrible task of calling all my brothers and sisters and giving them the news that Dad had died during the night. No one could believe it. We had no warning or even an opportunity to say good-bye. For many of my brothers and sisters there were things in the past that had been left undone. Most of them felt that the relationship of father and sibling was never made right between them and their father. Sometimes you end up waiting one day too long, and then it's too late. Saying and hearing words like "I love you" and "I forgive you;" words that needed to be said, but now it was too late. My father's death left a lot of hurt among my siblings. No one planned for this to happen, but it did because death is usually uncontrollable. No one has the timetable before them as to when their time is finished. That is why we are told to redeem the time; what you have available for you today may not be here tomorrow.

I miss my father deeply, but I often wonder just how much was left undone that could have been resolved. There were many things left unsaid and much left to do to make up for so many lost years. I do not know why God took him when He did; his death left a lot of unanswered questions in all of us. It wasn't until the funeral in Dallas, Texas, that I really found out the kind of life my father had lived. I soon found out just how little I knew about him and wished that God would have given us just a few more years together.

The following September my wife's father had also passed away. Things were quite different with him compared to my own father. Sarah's father, Chuck, was my best friend in the whole world, someone I could talk to and unload my cares on. I loved both of these men very much, but Chuck was a godsend to me. He became my mentor and my teacher about life and love. Shortly after I had met Chuck, in 1985, he had a massive heart attack and almost died while at work. He was forced to go through a quadruple by-pass operation to save his life.

Chuck's health had remained bad for a long time; besides a bad heart he also had severe diabetes. As he got older he had lost all feeling in his feet and in 2007 he had endured his second major open heart surgery. I never thought of what life would be without him because for more than twenty years he was always there for me. He had become the father I never had while growing up. He was also the rock in his family and all of us depended on his wisdom to get through tough situations.

I remember when I had first met Chuck when I started dating Sarah. After I had proposed to her I was told to call him Dad. That was unbelievably hard for me to do because I have never considered myself as having a dad. I did my best to never be in a situation of having to get his attention so that I never had to use that name. I guess deep down I was saving it for my own father, hoping that one day he would come back into my life and reclaim his title back as my dad.

Chuck did his best to try and win my affections by always being there for me when I needed him. He was never pushy or forward and he never demanded anything from me. For that reason he soon earned the coveted title of "Dad" from me. I never regretted it and to this day I have never changed my feelings.

He was Dad to Sarah and me and Papaw to my three boys. The summer before he went to be with Jesus we spent at the Reservation in Salisbury, Massachusetts. We all knew that time with Dad was limited and we wanted to have as many memories as we could get. I remember Brandon and me pushing Dad in his wheelchair to the edge of the water on the beach. The water here was freezing year round, but Dad couldn't feel it. We teased each other and laughed together as a family should, we took extra time to make sure Dad was having a great time. There wasn't anything anyone of us would not have done to make him happy. He had always been there for us and even though I only held the title of son-in-law no one ever knew that; I was treated like a son.

But one day the news came from home, Dad was not doing well and the family received the call that you never want to get. We needed to get to the hospital as quickly as possible because doctors have told the family that Dad was ready to go. At least that is the news that Sarah and I had gotten. The truth was that Dad was already with Jesus. We arrived at the hospital hoping to say good-bye to a great man, but it was too late. He lay there on the bed still and cold. I wanted to cover him up so that he would be warm, but it really didn't matter. How could this be happening? My best friend was gone. We all cried. We loved him very much, and who would not miss him? He had taught me how to love a father again and I hated the thought that we would have no more father and son discussions and special times of laughter. There were many questions that ran through our minds that day. Sarah's mother stayed very strong as well as the rest of the family. It was hard to just sit there and see Dad lying there so still. I expected him to sit up or at least say good-bye.

I understand what it feels like to lose someone you love. You feel abandoned and alone; you're not able to bring them back or change what is going on. You have to settle with the fact that they will not be riding home in the car with you and you will never be able to call again for advice when things are difficult.

The funerals of these two men were quite different in my mind. My father had left my mother when all six of my brothers and sisters where under the age of ten. Life was hard for a single mother and even harder for kids to grow up without a dad. I vowed to hate my father for what he had done to us. As painful as it is to tell you about this you must hear it. For thirty years I lived a hurting life as a result of hating my dad. I took it out on my wife and I was a lousy husband as a result. I took it out on my sons, my friends, and my work I did for the Lord. I was angry, prideful, arrogant, self-centered, conceited, self pleasing, and self-serving. I think I was out to prove to my dad that I could be a somebody without him. I was wrong; unforgiveness ruins you and it becomes the open door for sin to creep into your life. That is the reason why Jesus commanded that we forgive one another because failure to forgive will ruin you and destroy you for years to come. It will go into your children and into their families. It must be stopped and the only way to do that is to be the one to forgive it all first. I am not saying this to hurt my father, but it is a reality in the lives of many people including mine. You cannot continue to live your life holding onto this hurt. I thank the Lord that I had found the grace about six years before his death to ask for forgiveness. My dad and I became close even though we realized that the relationship we could have had was never going to come. Life had taken us both in different directions so we had to settle for moving forward from where we were rather than going back to the beginning. We settled for being father and son and letting all the past go; this allowed us to have the relationship we had. I loved my father very much, and his death was something I could accept because of the forgiveness we gave to each other.

But for many of my siblings the opportunity to do that never came. My father's funeral was sad for them. I watched them trying to cope with knowing things were not right between them, and now it was too late.

For many of you reading this you must ask God to help you make things right before it's too late. One day your parents will pass on and you will have to live with all the pains that are not healed. My dad's funeral was sad to me because we missed too many chances to be close. My sister told me that she waited for many years to hear Dad call her "princess" and never heard it. My brother Pat wanted to hear Dad say "I'm sorry" but never felt he heard that either. I knew that my father did love them all very much, but like them he too had a difficult time knowing how to heal the past. There seemed to be no way to heal it any longer because Dad was gone. Will this be your story? Death does not have to end like this. Words like, "forgive me, I'm sorry, I was wrong," may not be enough to heal at first, but they are a start. Once you start, do not stop. Hurts take time to heal and persistence is hard to maintain, but it will be worth it. With my dad's death came some healing for all of us. It allowed us to see that we really did love him, and we all decided that we could forgive. My father made mistakes that he could never heal, but we are guilty too. We have to be willing to release those who have hurt us and forgive them in the same manner we want them to forgive us.

My wife's father had a different story to tell. Sarah's father died with no regrets as far as I could see. He made things right while he was here. He pulled himself away from the hours he spent watching TV and the extra shifts at work to take time to be with all of us. I watched as he took his son, Johnny, aside and spent quality time with him at men's retreats to try and re-build their relationship. He made each of his grandchildren feel that they where the most important grandchild that he had. It took effort and time to make this work.

When Chuck passed away I was asked to do the funeral. I was honored but afraid. This man in the casket was bringing hurt to my family right now. They all missed him so much and I wasn't sure that I could bring them the peace that they all needed. I remember showing up at the church and standing before all the people that had come to pay their respects to this wonderful man that I loved so much. At the funeral, I recalled to everyone just how much they meant to him. He loved his kids and grandkids and especially his wife, Millie. Dad wanted everyone to know about Jesus at his funeral, so I shared about my father's God. Both our dads knew the forgiveness of Jesus. This is the one thing that brought all of us peace, because we knew we would see them again. At my father-in-law's funeral I gave an altar invitation for salvation and well over a hundred hands were raised into the air. I felt it was a life lived well and ended well.

This is the story of two men, two lives, and two different stories. Both were great men and both had different outcomes at the end. I believe that we should always be prepared for the day we die. Not just with funeral arrangements but by making sure we are in right standings with each other. Right before God, and right before man.

I have people in my church who have parents that are close to the end; maybe you have someone too. I challenge you to forgive them and release each other from the torments of the past. Let there be no regrets. Use words to tell them you love them. Laugh together and recall old memories. Encourage each other to focus on Jesus. If they do not know the Lord, share it with them. This should be done with each other every day. You may not have a tomorrow to go so say I'm sorry and do it today. Love much and always forgive!

Sarah is doing very well today. She has been given time off from treatments to prepare for her transplant. I tell her every day how much I love her. I also want you to know that when I forgave my father God healed our marriage. Let Him do the same for you.

A Book Deal

Day 158—March 5, 2011

Sarah and I went to see her doctor yesterday for a consultation. They want to start the transplant in three weeks. The doctor told us that she would be in the hospital for one month and it would take approximately a hundred days for her to completely be through it. He also told us that this would be the most difficult part of the entire journey for her. We have come to learn that the end of a race is always the most difficult. It's the final lap that seems to take the most effort because you have used all you have left. This is where you have to dig deeper than you ever have before to find the strength to finish well.

I also have great news that I want to share with you. At the beginning of this journey I felt that God had spoken to me to begin writing this journal and posting it on Facebook and e-mail so that everyone would be able to know how things were going with Sarah. Many of my friends told me that it was very moving and inspiring to them when they read it, and some had insisted that I consider seeing a publisher to turn it into a book. I wasn't so sure about that, although I had found a real love for writing down what was going on in me. I was flattered that so many were enjoying it and it did kind of help push me to continue, but a book? Who would want to read a book written by a guy who could barely pass English in high school?

Well, Sarah has always been the push in my life when I stalled. She along with her mother encouraged me to look into it. I prayed and asked the Lord that if this was His will. Then I needed a miracle, because I had no clue where to start.

I am writing this because I want to share with you a little bit about dreams and passions. Three years ago when I was sitting on the board of my old church and we were looking for a pastor, we interviewed a man who had written and submitted articles to the Pentecostal Evangel that were published. I had e-mailed him and said I had always wanted to write and see if it could get published, but I was unsure how to go about it. He told me I was wasting my time. He said only a few of us had the gifts and talents it takes to do this. Now understand; this guy didn't even know me. He never read anything I wrote and never heard me speak, never sat together for coffee, nothing. I felt shot down and of course I never wrote anything, I just believed what he said.

Many of you have experienced similar things in your lives. People have shot down your dreams and you listened to what they said and because you never tried you never knew for sure if you could fly. It is better to try and to fail than to never try. When I first started writing this blog I was writing about six hundred words in my blog every day. After writing for nearly a month it went to 1,200 words, and now my blogs are over 2,100 words. I did not do this on purpose; it just happened and developed that way. I was asked to send articles to our weekly town paper, and they are printing my articles every other week. I know this was a God-thing for me and people wonder where I get the time to do it, but it flows out from my heart every time I sit down at my desk.

What are your dreams? Start out small and see where it leads you. Allow God to direct you. The Internet has become a great tool for sharing dreams and seeing where they lead you. But God wants us to be at our fullest potential, not half way or even three quarter way is sufficient with God. He wants us at full potential and full speed, but guided by the Holy Spirit. You will always have enough grace for what God has for you to accomplish, but only if you pursue the dream.

Now, what should you do if your dreams crash and burn? Re-evaluate. The greatest lessons are learned through failure, not success. Failure can become a tool of great accomplishments for your future. You must quit only if you have realized that you are pursuing the wrong dream. Otherwise you keep going. Failure is not a sign that you should stop. Timing is one of God's important lessons in life and many times it is where we fail. Wrong time! Wrong place!

Also, guard your passions carefully. Your dreams are usually hidden in your passions.

Many years ago a test was done among several teachers and students across the United States. The teachers were gathered together and told that they were chosen to teach the country's most gifted children because they were the most gifted teachers. They went through great efforts to inform these teachers that they were highly sought out to do this task. Then these researchers did the same among the high school students. They told them they were the country's best. After a school year had past they studied the test results and found that the students excelled way beyond what they ever imagined. They literally scored among the highest test grades in the country. The teachers were ecstatic as well as the students. After all, they were the countries best, right? Wrong! After the results came in these teachers and student were told that they were not the countries best and brightest, but rather just plain average. But during the year they were made to believe that they could do more and they did.

Belief is a powerful tool if used correctly; it produces passion and faith. How many times have I seen people live way below their potential because they were told they could not go that high.

Parents make grave mistakes in calling their children stupid and dumb. I have heard them tell their kids that they were worthless and would never amount to anything. What a grave mistake they have done. It kills the passion of creativity and will render them useless in dreaming dreams. What they could have become or accomplished was aborted because their confidence was stolen.

What is your dream? I challenge you to begin to pray about reaching higher for God. If you're a Sunday school teacher then dream about having the best Sunday school class in the church and then in the city. If you're a pastor, dream about having the place that everyone wants to check out. It will require you to change and to learn from others, but they will only enhance your passion. I have a dream for my church. We are going to be the best church that Webster has ever seen. We are going to get better in every area from the ushers, to the classes, to the ministries we offer, to the worship, and to the preaching every area at top level. It all starts with a dream. That dream will lead to passion, and passion will lead to opportunity, and opportunity will lead to fulfillment.

That dream you have may take time to manifest completely, but don't give up. Hide it in your heart like Joseph did. His brothers tried to kill that dream but couldn't. God sent Joseph on a journey that would eventually help bring his dream to pass. Even in prison the dream was still in motion because it was God's dream. Joseph had to allow himself to flow with what God was allowing for his life, and in so doing he ended up at the place for the dream to begin. Do not give up when it feels like your dream is dead, it very well could just be ready to start to live.

By the way, in two more days it's Sarah's birthday. Like I have said previously, these days have made special events more special. I get to celebrate this special time with her along with our three boys. And, because her counts are up we get to take her out to eat! This is always something special for us!

By the way, Tate Publishing sent me a contract to have my blog published and turned into a book...Never stop believing!

Eyes Back on the Prize

Day 170—March 17, 2011

I have learned many lessons from this journey we are on, but perhaps none more important than the lesson of self-pity. It has been easy sitting in my chair feeling sorry for Sarah and myself because of her leukemia. Trust me; it's not hard to do. Every day there are people who face devastating hurt, loss, and suffering far greater than I have ever imagined. Car accidents that instantly change the lives of families; sickness that renders people helpless; death that leaves people empty; although I cannot possibly prevent any of these things from happening nor am I able to explain why they are allowed to happen, I do know that I am needed everywhere I go to help heal the pain. If I forget that then I will be swallowed up by the demons of self-pity and I will miss my calling of bringing Jesus to this world.

As you know, the world is in chaos all around us. Many of you remember reading about the thousands that died in a 9.0 earthquake and tsunami in 2010 that devastated the country of Japan. It was the fifth most devastating earthquake ever recorded in history, and in just a moment's notice their lives were drastically changed forever. Thousands of children lost their parents; families were destroyed; people lost everything they owned; a nation was brought to its knees. For most people the thought of something like that happening never enters into their minds. We know it's possible, but we never think we would ever be in that kind of a situation.

We seem to know how to block it out so that we are able to function without being concerned about disaster. But every day people face its possibility. Suffering and hurting are all around us; people are daily diagnosed with disease that they never expected to affect them. Or a car accident that changed their life for the worse. No one knows what tomorrow may hold for them. Therefore, I must guard myself against personal self-pity and look around me, because the battle rages on.

However, we do know the future; it is found in God's Word. There will be a day that we will stand before God and have to give an account for our lives we lived here on earth. Look at what the apostle Paul tells us:

> For all of us must appear before Christ, to be judged by him. We will each receive what we deserve, according to everything we have done, good or bad, in our bodily life.
>
> 2 Corinthians 5:10

This is the one verse in the Bible that should make us want to change the way we live and the way we respond to the needs of others. One day your life will be open for all to see; everything you have done will be visible. The only thing that it will not show is the things that you wanted to do but didn't. Your level of giving, loving, caring, serving, and all the rest will be open to the eyes of the Lord to judge. Before Sarah got sick, I found it easy to feel that I do enough; I fed the hungry, gave clothing to those who needed it, I shared my faith everywhere I went, and even tried to show kindness to those who needed it. Now that sickness literally came into our own lives I see it in a deeper way. It's not stuff that always demonstrates compassion; it is touching, hearing, crying, laughing, reading to someone, visits, and smiles. These things are more valuable than anything physical.

Now I feel that it is a daily decision that I must make to be available to give, care, serve, and love those who are brought into my path. But I want you to know that the only true way to do this is to have the heart of Christ. To see through the eyes of Jesus is to allow the Holy Spirit to lead and to guide you every day. This will lead to Him purging out the selfish heart that you have developed and replacing it with His love. Nothing starts apart from loving Christ first. Look at this amazing chapter that David wrote about his own battle with God:

> God is indeed good to Israel, to those who have pure hearts. But I had nearly lost confidence; my faith was almost gone.
>
> Psalm 73:1-2

David is describing the fact of the goodness of God. He is confident that God is good to those who possess a pure heart; that is a heart that sees things only in the way that God sees them. It is not pure according to the way I see them because my heart has been tainted by sin and is partial to my wants and desires.

However, like many of us who go through difficult times, he had lost his confidence, and his faith was almost gone. Have you ever been there? If you have then you know that the one thing you need is faith and confidence working together in your life to allow you to see past the storms you are facing in your life. Otherwise you will be swallowed up in life's mess with no vision on how to get out. David was at that place in this chapter. Like us, he got tired of the life he was given to live and began to notice the lives that others had around him.

So many seem to have it better; they have better houses, better cars, better children, better jobs, happy lives; all I have is the mundane average boring life that seems to go nowhere. You are stuck in wanting what others have and wondering why you have to go through the trials you're in when others around you do not.

The question is: How do you get yourself in such a place? We have all been there at one time or another. But how did it happen? David tells us how:

> Because I was jealous of the proud when I saw that things go well for the wicked. They do not suffer pain; they are strong and healthy. They do not suffer as other people do; they do not have the troubles that others have. And so they wear pride like a necklace and violence like a robe; their hearts pour out evil, and their minds are busy with wicked schemes. They laugh at other people and speak of evil things; they are proud and make plans to oppress others. They speak evil of God in heaven and give arrogant orders to everyone on earth, so that even God's people turn to them and eagerly believe whatever they say.
>
> Psalm 73:3-10

Look at how it all happened. First, He was jealous; he saw people with things he did not have and he noticed that things apparently went quite well for them. They didn't seem to have the issues and problems that he had. Have you ever looked at the wealthy and said, "They have it made," or "I wish I had what they had?" I have. What I would do to have no more worries or problems financially. They seem not to have any problems and nothing to worry about and so naturally we envy them and think that while the world is suffering they are living on easy street.

The second thing that happened is that he got his eyes off of the Lord. You see, it is easy to think that the life of the Christian is hard, because it is. We are required to look at the future and not the present; to care for others more than we care for ourselves; to give and not to expect anything in return; and to love unconditionally. What I mean by that is we are not to be of this world; we are to be pilgrims just passing through. Our future is heaven, and that is our destiny and our life. The rich live for today and that's it; but we live for what is coming waiting until the day when the Lord calls us home to live with Him.

You see, God may be showing you His mercy by allowing you to go through struggle. That mercy is because He knows the end of the wicked, and he does not want you to envy them because their joy will soon fade away. Like the earthquake in Japan, in just a moment's notice everything you have could be swept away. You will then be left with nothing. But those of us who love Jesus are never left with nothing even if we were to lose all we presently have.

When man settles down here on earth and becomes dependent upon this world, he soon forgets God. It was seen in the lives of Abraham and Lot. When the choice came to choose where they would go, Lot chose Sodom because of the way it looked. It represented the world and all that the world possessed. He ended up conformed to their way of life and barely escaped its destruction; however, his family did not escape, the love of the world cost them their lives. The effects of the world don't happen instantly— it's gradual, but it is progressive.

The acts of those who love this world are done with an evil heart because they say, "God doesn't notice." It becomes easier to fall into the pit of sin and slime because earthly rewards become so tempting. Like Eve in the garden who was surrounded by more than enough, yet the temptation to have more became overwhelming and enticing. It lures you away without your knowledge or permission. It is like a snare hidden in the brush, and once you're in it the trap snaps shut and you're caught. Look at the rest of David's words:

> They say, "God will not know; the Most High will not find out." That is what the wicked are like. They have plenty and are always getting more.
>
> Psalm 73:11-12

We all feel the temptations to go against what we know is right. Small compromises will soon have great paybacks and those who have done so will be forced to pay the piper. I have witnessed this all around me, and we all have the danger of being lured away by its seeming promises of happiness. The worst part is that we have convinced ourselves that God will not see it or find out what we did. We have even convinced ourselves that what we are about to do can be forgiven and so we do it. Even David felt the temptation.

> Is it for nothing, then, that I have kept myself pure and have not committed sin? O God, you have made me suffer all day long; every morning you have punished me. If I had said such things, I would not be acting as one of your people.
>
> Psalm 73:13-15

These thoughts become enticing when you're struggling in life. David knew better than to ponder on these thoughts, but he did, and those suffering think about it often as well. Those who struggle financially or physically or emotionally end up questioning God as to why they have to go through such things and think it unfair that others around them don't. After all, God is all powerful, and He could yank me out of this if He truly loved me, right? Why do the wicked prosper? Maybe it is because of the mercy of God and because of their choices they have no future; or maybe it is because God wants to test your loyalty to Him by allowing you to choose.

> I tried to think this problem through, but it was too difficult for me until I went into your Temple. Then I understood what will happen to the wicked. You will put them in slippery places and make them fall to destruction! They are instantly destroyed; they go down to a horrible end. They are like a dream that goes away in the morning; when you rouse yourself, O Lord, they disappear.
>
> Psalm 73:16-20

It is amazing how clear the purpose of our situation becomes when we understand God! When you realize that God is close to those who have a need for Him, and as a Father, God wants our dependence to be always upon Him. He loves to be called upon, and He is generous to those who love and wait for Him. As long as we look to the wrong place to find our fulfillment we will never understand or receive from the Lord.

There is one more thing to note here, our desire to be like them would change if we knew what happens to the wicked. Understand, just because someone prospers does not make them wicked! Abraham prospered and he was not wicked; his prospering was a result of his obedience to God. There are two ways to prosper in this life; one is through obeying God and that life represents a life of prospering through blessings coming from God. These blessings are given by God and returned back to God by giving to others. The other way is prospering by going against God's truth and His Word. Your wealth is through deception and your own good works. Instead of using your wealth for others you hoard it for yourself; it becomes the only thing that makes you happy. Like the story of the man in Luke 12:

> Then Jesus told them this parable: "There was once a rich man who had land which bore good crops. He began to think to himself, 'I don't have a place to keep all my crops. What can I do? This is what I will do,' he told himself; 'I will tear down my barns and build bigger ones, where I will store the grain and all my other goods. Then I will say to myself, lucky man, you have all the good things you need for many years. Take life easy, eat, drink, and enjoy yourself!' But God said to him, 'You fool! This very night you will have to give up your life; then who will get all these things you have kept for yourself?'" And Jesus concluded, "This is how it is with those who pile up riches for themselves but are not rich in God's sight."
>
> Luke 12:16-21

It is so easy to forget God when things go well. Are you sure you want what they have? We always think that if we had it we would not be like them; they use to say the same things! The life they have is a trap waiting for innocent victims to take the bait.

> When my thoughts were bitter and my feelings were hurt, I was as stupid as an animal; I did not understand you. Yet I always stay close to you, and you hold me by the hand. You guide me with your instruction and at the end you will receive me with honor. What else do I have in heaven but you? Since I have you, what else could I want on earth? My mind and my body may grow weak, but God is my strength; he is all I ever need. Those who abandon you will certainly perish; you will destroy those who are unfaithful to you.
>
> Psalm 73:21-27

Sometimes, like David, we have to snap ourselves back into reality; not an earthly reality, mind you, but a kingdom reality. David did that! He realized just how stupid his thoughts were concerning God. Strength comes from truth! When you realize the truth you will understand the purpose and the intention of God. Look at how he ends this:

> But as for me, how wonderful to be near God, to find protection with the Sovereign LORD and to proclaim all that he has done!
>
> Psalm 73:28

Stop looking at others; they will have their own reward. Look directly to the Lord and you will find peace. One day you will stand with Him in eternity and hear the words, "Well done my good and faithful servant!" These are words that will be worth any journey. One last thing here:

> As a deer longs for a stream of cool water, so I long for you, O God. I thirst for you, the living God. When can I

go and worship in your presence? Day and night I cry, and tears are my only food; all the time my enemies ask me, "Where is your God?" My heart breaks when I remember the past, when I went with the crowds to the house of God and led them as they walked along, a happy crowd, singing and shouting praise to God.

Psalm 42:1-4

In this psalm, David writes the secret to his own walk with God. He tells us the story of the deer that would hide in the brush near the brook because to go out and get a drink during the heat of the day would leave him vulnerable to predators. So the deer would hide until the evening hours when it was safe to go and drink. While the deer waited he would pant for that cool water and wish he could have it. While he waited he would never take his eyes off of the prize that he so longed for. This is how David describes his passion for God. He wanted God and longed for God passionately. At times when he felt away from God his tears became evidence of his longing for Him. He was not content to be without God or to be away from God so it left an emptiness inside him. So when he felt that way he would pursue in a manner of passion, like a deer longing and waiting and wanting to return to God.

When David found God, it brought out the praise and the voice of joy within him; even in the circumstance he was in. I struggle to believe that you can have a grumpy or selfish attitude and be in the presence of God. His presence is evident by the joy and praise of the one who has found Him. Do you long for God, or are you caught up in wanting to be in the world that you're surrounded by? Regardless of what you're going through, even if it is suffering, you are better off than the wicked any day. It's time to offer your praise to God!

You Must Learn the Value of Personal ME Time

Day 177—March 24, 2011

The final leg of our journey is ready to begin. As of today, Sarah is cleared to begin her transplant. She has passed her heart test and pulmonary test and her visit to the dentist showed she had been brushing every day because there were no cavities. The news is both joyous and sad for us because we know that the next part of the journey is going to be the hardest.

I have so enjoyed the past several weeks having Sarah here with me. She has been able to lead worship at the church and go grocery shopping and we have enjoyed being able to go out to eat together as a family—all the things we enjoyed before only now I must admit it is way more wonderful. During the past several months I felt constantly like a newlywed and looked forward to hearing her voice and seeing her smile every day. Never again will I take her for granted. So on Tuesday morning we will meet with her doctor for our consultation and then proceed to the transplant.

Lately I have had the opportunity to talk to many people who have been overwhelmed with the things going on in their lives. Some are going through foreclosure and having to rearrange their whole lives and have to take their families out of their comfort zones. Some are going through stress with marriage and responsibilities of raising their children. Some are struggling with their jobs and the cares of life that have become overwhelming at times. I too feel the stress of the long journey with Sarah and the responsibilities of pasturing a church and raising three boys. It is easy to be overwhelmed with all of these things. I mean after all, who hasn't been where we are? When we get stressed out we need some Personal M-e Time and a lot of it. Stress always comes from seeing things from your own eyes and not from the eyes of the Lord. It is therefore important that we break away from things and get alone with God without any distractions. It's Personal Me Time that will re-direct you and get you on the right path.

This needs to be a must for every Christian as a way to re-focus on the Lord. If you start out early before everything in life begins to overtake you, I promise the days will become productive, restful, and rewarding. Your strength will be renewed and life will keep its zest. I have done this routinely and it does work! Trying to live in this world without the counsel of God is foolish and exhausting. Look at these passages of scripture and see what I mean.

> Be merciful to me, O God, be merciful, because I come to you for safety. In the shadow of your wings I find protection until the raging storms are over.
>
> Psalm 57:1

David was running for his life from King Saul; yet David never mentions this when he writes this psalm. He only sets his sights on God and not on the situation he is in. This is something you must always remember. To work things out on your own when you are in a tough situation will only make matters worse. God has our answers if we will take time to wait on Him.

> I call to God, the Most High, to God, who supplies my every need. He will answer from heaven and save me; he will defeat my oppressors. God will show me his constant love and faithfulness. I am surrounded by enemies, who are like lions hungry for human flesh. Their teeth are like spears and arrows; their tongues are like sharp swords. Show your greatness in the sky, O God, and your glory over all the earth. My enemies have spread a net to catch me; I am overcome with distress. They dug a pit in my path, but fell into it themselves.
>
> Psalm 57:2-6

David was not in la-la land; this situation was real and exhausting for him. His enemies were after his life, and they were not going away empty handed. I want to interject here and say that I have witnessed how God will raise up our enemies intentionally to be against us so that we are forced to re-focus on what is truly important. There is no growth on a mountain top; men usually fall when everything is going well, and having everything going your way very well might become your downfall. It is in the furnace of trials and confrontation that steel is formed and gold and silver are purified. David became Israel's true king in the desert running from Saul not in the palace being served. So, how does David deal with the situation he is in?

> I have complete confidence, O God; I will sing and praise you! Wake up, my soul! Wake up, my harp and lyre! I will wake up the sun. I will thank you, O Lord, among the nations. I will praise you among the peoples. Your constant love reaches the heavens; your faithfulness touches the skies. Show your greatness in the sky, O God, and your glory over all the earth.
>
> Psalm 57:7-11

David settles his situation with God. He comes to the place of rest and trust and fixes his eyes on the Lord by having Personal

Me Time with God. His problem is still out there, but he refuses to stare at it any longer or listen to the voices in his head that bring him fear and unrest. He knows he has to face it, and so rather than worry he rests in the Lord. How does he do that? He fixes his heart on God. He does this through singing and praise, worship, and trust. He tells everything inside of him to wake up, because it is time to praise the Lord. Much like Paul and Silas did at the midnight hour in Acts while imprisoned. It is time to refocus and see the Lord. As soon as David starts singing, his songs changed his emotions and his heart. He refused to see anything but God. Try it! Turn on some praise music and sing loud enough to drown out the doubts and fears in you. God is still in control, and He has the outcome in his command; you just praise Him!

Here is another passage written by David while being chased by Saul.

> O God, you are my God, and I long for you. My whole being desires you; like a dry, worn-out, and waterless land, my soul is thirsty for you. Let me see you in the sanctuary; let me see how mighty and glorious you are.
>
> Psalm 63:1-2

The dry land represented a place of struggle. David wanted the refreshing of the presence of God that he used to enjoy when in the sanctuary. He was tired of the struggles he was facing and missed the mountain top experiences he once enjoyed.

I believe that this is an important place to come to; it will cause you to seek after what you will find to be the answer for life's entire struggle.

> Your constant love is better than life itself, and so I will praise you. I will give you thanks as long as I live; I will raise my hands to you in prayer. My soul will feast and be satisfied, and I will sing glad songs of praise to you. As I lie in bed, I remember you; all night long I think of you,

because you have always been my help. In the shadow of
your wings I sing for joy. I cling to you, and your hand
keeps me safe.

Psalm 63:3-8

There he goes with that praise thing again! So even though David
was away from the sanctuary he decided to bring the sanctuary
to him. He began to praise and worship and bless the Lord. He
said, "My soul shall be satisfied." This worked! Following after
the Lord brought rest and peace in the midst of his struggle.

One more passage:

I love those who love me; whoever looks for me can find
me. I have riches and honor to give, prosperity and success. What you get from me is better than the finest gold,
better than the purest silver. I walk the way of righteousness; I follow the paths of justice, giving wealth to those
who love me, filling their houses with treasures.

Proverbs 8:17-21

This is a promise to you from God, Himself. Seek after that
which is better. Your job is not your means of support; God is.
Now don't go and quit your job, but go and allow Him to go with
you on your job. Let God use you there as a missionary and a
voice from heaven. Ask God how to turn it into a ministry, and
then you will love being there because you will know that He had
sent you.

Finally, turn the side of your bed into your prayer closet; every
day start there and end there. Get your marching orders and your
P. M. Time in proper perspective. Jesus said, "Seek first the kingdom of God and all these things shall be added unto you."

Trials do not mean God is not with you! It means that God is
trying to get your attention. Maybe He misses you!

Who Decides What is Acceptable?

Day 178—March 25, 2011

Three days left before Sarah has to meet for her consultation for the transplant. We are not sure when they will begin but are assuming it will be next week. So Sunday at our church it is going to be a special day to pray with her and believe God to continue that which He has already started. We will have the blessing of her leading worship and the opportunity to pray for her to recover quickly.

Do you have any pet peeves? I have a few. I have a few questions for you to think about today. Have you ever been made fun of? Teased? Laughed at? Bullied because you're too small to fight back? Have you ever been told that you are ugly? Overweight? Stupid? Or maybe you were always picked last for sports because you were unable to compete on the same level as everyone else? I have met countless people who have lived a never-ending nightmare of hurt and rejection because they were different than those who made the rules. Some suffer because it comes from home where parents use words as weapons to bring their children into submission. Some of it was at school or on the bus. Many have gone through their entire school years as the object of other people's pleasures that were designed to belittle them so that they could look more impressive to others. Do you not know what kind of lifelong hurts are the results of this? They were people who could have accomplished so much more had someone believed in them and encouraged them. Instead they were beat down just because you refused them because they were not like you.

I have seen parents push their children to the edge of ruin because they didn't measure up to their expectations. Or parents that thought "tough love" was the only way to raise good children. So the child grew up never getting to enjoy being a child. They had little toys, little laughing, and little expression of who they truly were. The times when they did well the parents never praised them because that was what was expected of them. Instead of praise they get critical construction; criticism on how they can improve and do even better the next time. They could never give enough.

There is a young man who goes to my church who is in high school. He is shorter than everyone else and always has a lot to say. Because of his stature he is picked on every day at school. Everyone wants a piece of him because they know he could never defend himself. When this young man first started coming to our church, he was loud and always getting told to settle down because he was always clocked in at a hundred miles per hour. When he gave his heart to the Lord I began to notice in him something very special—I saw myself when I was his age. Outwardly moving, but inwardly hurting. I so wanted to be accepted, but no one gave me the chance to fit into their pre-made world. This young man is no different than anyone else. He just wanted to be loved and to have friends like everyone else did. During the past two years I have watched this special young man mature in the Lord and become hungry for God. His life is changing faster than I can calculate, and he is no longer off the walls. He has become a dear friend to me, and I see the call of God on his life. I want to be a part of his life because I feel that one day he is going to touch the world.

I am working hard to get the people of my church to love the unloved; to love the people that society says no longer fits in; to reach out to them as Jesus did and to use love as a tool to bring them to the cross that will change their lives forever.

When I was a youth pastor I remember reading the alarming statistics of teen suicide. It was the number two leading cause of death among teenagers in America. Imagine that! We are not talking about cancers, sicknesses, or some unheard of disease here. We are talking about a teen taking his or her life on purpose. Why? Many did so to avoid the teasing they were receiving; many did so because of things going on at home; maybe it was wrong expectations that they had; or the feeling of not fitting in. They were never told that things could get better or that they were loved. Instead they lived in a world that they never could measure up too. They faced things that no one took time to explain to them. Others seem to have the answers that they were searching for, but little did they know how wrong they were. Some hide hurts behind sports, bullying, teasing, looks, clothes, academics, and so much more. They are never told that they lived in a fallen world that needs Jesus. No, instead they are convinced that they just do not measure up. That leads me to the next question. Who makes the rules on how you are to fit in? Is there a secret rule book somewhere that says you have to be a good athlete, or you have to weigh in at a certain amount? Does it give you the guidelines to what is acceptable or not acceptable? Does anyone have a copy of that book so that I could see it? I would love to use it in a Sunday school class so that kids will no longer be picked on in school. Someone please tell me what is going on here? I am tired of seeing kids lose their childhood to be the subjects of other people's stupidity. Someone needs to stand up. Youth pastors need to wake up; churches need to open their eyes.

Hurry before another child gets hurt or lost into the wrong value system somewhere.

This crisis has even happened in our churches. There are cliques of people who only allow a certain type of person to come in their circles. Their thoughts are: we do not want the homeless because they stink and have dirty clothes; we do not want the disabled because they are too disruptive and could have a meltdown; we do not want the youth who are troubled because they might steal something that we never use; we do not want the addicted or the broken or the different races, because they are different than we are. They will disrupt our flow. They might hinder the move of the Holy Spirit!

Are we really thinking like this? I think if we reached out to them that just the opposite might happen. We just might release the Holy Spirit back into our churches. We might have a move of God that will shake our cities. To see the worst of the worst set free is what Jesus came to do, so why are we afraid of that?

So who makes the rules for acceptance? What are your rules? You say you love people, but do you reach out to them? There are two things I want to talk about in this: One, how do you love those you do not understand? And two, how do you learn to accept love when you've been teased all your life?

Let's look at the first one first. It is hard to love someone you do not respect. Many children grow up believing that they are better than others and because they are able to receive things from their parents that other kids did not get, they felt that they were on a higher plateau. These are the kids that get spoiled and pampered their whole lives. They are not used to losing in games because their parents never let them. In order to make sure their winning ways continue they will often change the rules so that they benefit over everyone else. When they cry, the parents come running and cater to their every whim. Once in school they struggle to handle the possibility that they could come in second place. They became so convinced of their superiority that only first place with little to no effort is acceptable to them. When this is not accomplished they become the ones who belittle others and tease those who are not at their level. It helps them to feel like they are the people they have come to believe they are. This is sad because in some ways it is not always their fault, but someone gets hurt none the less.

Some kids grew up with abuse at home. Abuse can be given in many ways. There is verbal abuse, when they are yelled at and verbally torn down. They can never do enough to please their parents at home. They are called stupid, worthless, morons, and every other name that the abuser can think of. That child begins to take their pain out others, and by hurting someone else they feel better.

Then there are the emotionally abused. They are those who get the silent treatment and those who have to become the parents of the home at very young ages. They do not have the joy of living normal lives at home and playing GI Joe and Barbie with their friends. They can never join sports or hang out with their friends at the mall because they are needed at home. They will never enjoy the fun of an all-night sleepover because they could never bring anyone into their home. They have no money to buy the latest gadgets and gaming systems, and most of what they own used to belong to somebody else. They hide in the shadows of the school hallways hoping that no one notices the holes in their shoes or the fact that the clothes don't fit right. They are tired all the time because the demands of taking care of the home are overwhelming. They have the potential to make straight A's or to succeed in sports or cheerleading if they only had the time. They go home and have to cook, clean, shop, and take care of mom and dad. In many of these cases the home is broken with only one parent there. There are even some cases where mom has a different guy in the house every six months, so they have to protect themselves from the choices made by the parent. They dream of the day when they will turn eighteen and are able to get away from it all. Many young girls in this situation end up pregnant as young as twelve years old just so they have someone to love in the way they want to be loved. They live their lives with no confidence, no dreams, and no future that they can see. Many will never go to the prom or have Dad there to help them learn to drive or to get his loving instructions for their lives. They will most likely drop out of school, live on the streets, spend time in jail…this is not right! They were never meant to go in that direction; life was supposed to give them more. I think we, the church, failed them as well. We never went after them and checked on their well-being. We should have brought Jesus to the parents and allowed Him to heal them.

There is also the physically abused. They are the ones who get the back of the hand from an angry father when they make too much noise. They are also the victims of sexual abuse. Young girls who have lost their innocence on the bed of a lust-filled father or relative; it can drastically change that child's life and scar her forever. It's not just girls who have this nightmare, it is boys too. Nothing can bring back what has been taken, and the emotional pains last for life. There are no good excuses for touching a child, rather it be emotionally, physically, or verbally.

The saddest thing is that those who have experienced such things usually end up abusers themselves. They become carriers of the nightmares they experienced. Some show it by overeating, violence, isolation, education and achievement, crime, hurting themselves and others. Some show it by acting out and becoming bullies; and some by becoming overachievers. All of these types of people are hurting and in many cases in the process of finding healing for themselves they have to hurt in order to feel a little relief.

Now I am no psychiatrist. I am just tired of seeing the devastation of the devil's work all around me. It is time to bring true healing to the hurting and throw away the book of acceptance.

To begin to love one another and to treat others the same way we want to be treated.

What can you do? Love one another as Christ has loved you. Learn how to accept those who live in the shadows. Be a friend to everyone. Love unconditionally. When you see someone who is standing away, invite them in. Try not to judge them until you've walked in their shoes. Take the time to hear their story and then allow God to use you to help them find their way. Learn to stand up for the truth found only in God's Word. That truth is to love one another as much as you love yourself. Learn to sit with those whom no one would sit with. Maybe, just maybe, we can break this curse and not allow it to continue anymore. Never judge anyone by their clothing, piercings, wheelchair, length of hair, or weight. Some people will not let you just rush into their lives and start fixing everything that's wrong; that is a privilege that you have to earn through loving them first. It will take time for that door to open and only by truly loving them will you be willing to wait.

What about those who are the victims? Seek counsel from your pastor. Ask God to send you a good friend, one who in time can know your story and minister to you. Never tell your story until you know you are loved by the one you tell it to. Stop living as the victim and believe everything God's Word says about you. You are loved by God. He wants to take your hurt away that is why he died on the cross. His death was done to free you and to release you from your hurt. But you have to accept it.

I pray that one day the church will become the rescue mission it was called to be; that the doors of acceptance will be opened, so that the ministry of deliverance and healing can take place. Try to stop watching the hurting from your rearview mirror and learn to stop and pick them up.

I am ending this message hurting, because I was one of those people I mentioned above. I was rejected because of being different. We were poor and had just enough to eat. My father jumped ship and left my mother with six children all under the age of ten. My mother had very little work experience, so she had to work nights at a sleazy truck stop so that we could eat. She had to be mom and dad for our entire childhood, doing her best to take care of us. She was forced to live many years in a life of sacrificing and doing things she rather not do just to keep us together. Thanks, Mom! She made sure that we were always in by dark, and even though the house was chaotic most of the time we knew we were loved. By mother ended up raising a house full of ministers. She kept us in church even when we fought her. The key to her success was a small church in St. Louis, Missouri, that accepted us just like we were. We didn't have to prove anything to them. My mother would never miss a church service even during a snow storm that led to us crashing into a cemetery. This little church allowed us to grow up making mistakes and being ourselves. Thank you, Pastor Leroy Maxey, and all the people at Evangel Temple in St. Louis, Missouri, for loving us through the most difficult time in our lives. You made it possible for us to live. That church sent and paid for all of us kids to go to church camp in Mountain View, Missouri, where most of us found the Lord. I am indebted to all of those who were there for us so-called rejects. Thanks for loving us when we put you all through so much.

I pray for those who are still suffering from any of the things I mentioned. If you are in a church that does not see you I hope you find one that does. We are all part of the same body of Christ, and we need each other for that body to work correctly. You are loved!

The Transplant

The transplant was to be the final stage of Sarah's treatment of her leukemia. I wanted to share with you all exactly what she went through during this time and let you know that she is now doing very well.

On Thursday, March 31, day 184, she went to the hospital to begin an intense three-week final treatment that would include six days of chemotherapy followed by the stem cell transplant. As usual it was very hard driving her there and dropping her off knowing that she was about to experience three very difficult weeks. The hope was that we knew that this would be it and she would finally have reached the end of treating this.

After five days of chemotherapy they told us that she would now have a very intense dose of chemo. This one, unlike the others that took only about an hour or two, would take twelve hours. It would also have severe side effects on Sarah, which included pain from her mouth to her throat and into her stomach.

On April 7, 194 days after this all began, they began the transplant. The procedure was really quite simple. When I arrived in her room they had told me that it would begin at 4:00 p.m. They had raised her bed up as high as it would go and hooked her up to all the appropriate monitors and machines. I watched Sarah face shine while lying there; she always keeps a great attitude no matter what she is going through. I was glad to know that this was nearly over for her, but sad to think that the next few weeks were going to be really hard. Celeste, one of the nurses on the floor, was in charge to doing the transplant. She is one of the bubbliest nurses on the floor always smiling, laughing, and joyful. I love seeing her when I visit Sarah because of her charisma and zest for life. We have grown accustomed on this floor to great nurses like her who always take the time to bring joy to their patients.

The stem cell transplant is actually very simple; it involves taking Sarah's own stem cells that they had already collected and putting them back into her through her IV. The entire process takes less than two hours, and although it is a very risky procedure, there is very little risk of rejection because they are her cells. I sat next to Sarah and held her hand, and we smiled at each other, feeling confident that this journey was almost over. We talked about being able to go home soon and not have to ever come back here except to visit. We also talked about this book, and we both prayed that God would take it and use to help others to find Him. We were interrupted several times as Celeste would have to take Sarah's temperature after each bag of stem cells was completed. And soon it was finished. The transplant was over and Sarah was feeling really good.

About 9:30 p.m. I decided it was time to head home, feeling confident that this was a job well done. It wasn't long when the side effects started showing. We were warned many times by Doctor Nath that this final treatment would be the most intense; he was right. Sores developed in her mouth and throat that became so bad that she could not stand the pain. Her nurses worked hard to do whatever they could do to bring her a little comfort, but I knew that there was little they could do to help her; she was forced to ride this out for the next week with every day being worse than the day before.

When Saturday morning came on April 16th, nine days after the transplant had begun, I had a work day planned at the church and had to go help clean out our church flower beds. I decided to go and see Sarah before I even had a chance to take a shower or get cleaned up. I had completely forgotten how dangerous it was for her to breath in what was on my clothes and it was that afternoon that she hit her all time low. The fever returned and she had the worst night of the entire journey. At 9:00 p.m. she had called her mother, our son Brandon, and me complaining about everything she was going through. This was so unlike her. She cried for the first time, telling me that she was not improving at all, but rather getting much worse. She had difficulty breathing, could not even take oral medications, and the morphine was causing her to have bad dreams when she closed her eyes. To make matters worse she even felt that I was to blame for coming in with all of that stuff on my clothes. I felt horrible about what I had done, and even though the nurse assured me that she was safe due to the amount of antibiotics she was on, I still knew that it was my responsibility to protect her from all of this. All I could do was to pray and ask God to keep His promises to her.

That night I posted on Facebook and e-mail for everyone to pray for her because she really needed it. That very night, something amazing happened. About 10:00 p.m. she called me back, and she was a different person. She talked different and acted different. I could not believe that this was happening. Her fever broke instantly, she felt better and began to do what she had always done before; she began to encourage me. This was my Sarah!

Sunday was a much improved day. Although she could not eat yet because of the pain in her throat, she was feeling much better. Monday came, and she was even doing better than the day before that. Her white blood cell counts were going up every day, and they are ready to release her as soon as she can take her medications orally. Can you believe that? Just two days ago she experienced the worst day of the whole journey, and now they are talking about release. Her doctor told me that she is producing her own bone marrow. That means that the transplant is working!

On Wednesday, April 20, 2011, Sarah was released from the hospital, and thus far she is completely cured of her disease. The journey is still far from over. Before they released her, one of the nurses, Marion, had to sit with both of us and explain to us what we needed to do to protect Sarah. She has a rough road ahead of her for the next year until her immune system can return to normal, but she is doing great.

There are many things we have learned through the past 204 days. The first thing is I now understand how important change is. I firmly believe that it is only through conflict and struggle that true change can be produced in us. Most people want to change and plan to change, but rarely do change. Like me, there were many things I had planned to work on in my life so that I would be more Christ-like. I would make commitments and promises only to realize years later that nothing had ever changed in me; I was still the same. I now see change that was forged in my heart as a result of this journey; change that came through conflict and faith being mixed together. The testing of my faith has created something of great value in me; something priceless.

> For God, who commanded the light to shine out of darkness, hath shined in our hearts, to give the light of the knowledge of the glory of God in the face of Jesus Christ. But we have this treasure in earthen vessels, that the excellency of the power may be of God, and not of us. We are troubled on every side, yet not distressed; we are perplexed, but not in despair; Persecuted, but not forsaken; cast down, but not destroyed; Always bearing about in the body the dying of the Lord Jesus, that the life also of Jesus might be made manifest in our body.
>
> 2 Corinthians 4:6-10 (KJV)

This journey has brought light out of darkness. We have seen the results of our faith and know that God has brought us into a new place with Him. The process took conflict in order to produce change so that the glory of God could be released.

There were also other things that have happened because of this journey. During the past months I have had the opportunity to share my faith with more people than ever; I have also prayed for more people than ever; people want to listen to what I have to say now because they realize I have been down that road. I have found a gentleness in my life and a heart of compassion that just somehow showed up. I no longer feel that I am working to make things work, but rather I have just been in the right place at the right time, and things just happened. It is the reward of a well-finished race. Sarah and I have laid everything about our future down and committed to walking in the obedience of Christ every day.

Another thing is, even though I prayed for a miracle for Sarah when this first happened, I didn't get the instant miracle that I wanted. That instant miracle was a sign of my lack of understanding the purpose and plan of God, not my faith! I thought that I deserved a miracle so that we would not have to suffer anything or go through anything. No one likes to suffer, and when we do have to suffer we fail to realize just how much stronger and better we really become by going through it. I talk to people now every day who open their hearts up to me because they watched how Sarah and I went through this suffering. I now feel that miracles are given to those who do not need change, and suffering is God's method of creating newness in each of us. Even though I would rather have gotten a miracle, I am so thankful for the suffering, because through it my life and the life of my whole family has changed! I am so grateful to God who knew from the beginning what we needed and loved me enough to take me through it.

Why do people suffer? I am no longer sure that anyone can have the absolute right answer to this question; there are just too many variables to consider, but I do believe that in each of those who have to suffer God has a reason. Some suffer so that God can build character in them; suffering can protect us and release us from pride, selfishness, and sins of the flesh and spirit. It creates godliness in us. I am not so certain that God just wants to test us to see if we're faithful; I believe His purposes are bigger than that. He tests us to create long-term godliness and a Christ-likeness in us that is tested and purified with godly fire.

Some suffer for the glory of God, like those who are persecuted for their faith. No one would dare say that those who died for their faith had no faith, right? So why did God allow them to die?

Some suffer as a result of sin and disobedience to God; they made choices that came with consequences. We cannot blame God when a person becomes addicted and suffers the effects of an overdose.

There are also some who suffer and no one knows why. Cancer, accidents, disease, and even natural disasters cannot be explained until we all get to heaven.

What should my attitude be like when I am forced into suffering? Or how should I respond if someone I love has to suffer? You respond with trust. Trust may be a higher form of faith than just knowing what His Word says. Trust relies on God over the outcome of the trial. The reason why this is important is because the outcome may require us to suffer loss or to gain an outcome that is painful to bear. Therefore only those who truly trust the Lord with all their heart are able to maintain their faith in a God who will never fail them.

Once again I would like to strongly emphasize that your outcome may not be what you were praying for, because we do not always understand the true purpose and plan of God. Satan will always try to use your trial to pull your heart away from God and cause you to doubt His Words. You must not lose your trust in Him. The apostle Paul said, "I have suffered the loss of all things that I might win Christ" (Philippians 3:8). If you keep your heart in trust toward God, the reward for the trial in time will be made evident in your life.

For Sarah and me the suffering we endured was done for the purpose of bringing in change for our lives. Changes for us have come in so many different forms and ways that it is still yet undetermined what all has happened in us. Change is never for sure until it has been tested through time and circumstances. In other words, we do not know the full outcome of what has been done in us; only time will reveal that to us. Time is the key factor of determination; then and only then will you know the extent of what God has done in you.

There is one last thing I want to say. I want to thank Sarah for showing me how to finish a race well. I love you more than ever; you are my hero.

Sarah's Final Words

It is now been one week after my release from the hospital. I have received my transplant and Dr. Nath says that this is it. I just have to have a few more bone marrow biopsies to make sure I am clear of any cancer. I am feeling good. My strength is returning day by day.

This has been a seven-month journey so far. I have to say that the grace of God was there for me each step of the way. I have kept my eyes on the Father and allowed Him to do what He felt was best for me at this time of my life. I feel like I am on a new path of life. I don't know what's ahead, but I am looking forward to it.

I am reminded of the scripture found in James 1:2-3, which is: "My friends, consider yourselves fortunate when all kinds of trials come your way, for you know that when your faith succeeds in facing such trials, the result is the ability to endure." I can honestly say that I tried to walk this out in my journey to the best of my ability. I found that the only way I could do it was that I had to keep my eyes off of myself and totally on God. He sees the big picture, so I just felt the need to be still and know that He is God. Verse four of James goes on to say, "Make sure that your endurance carries you all the way without failing, so that you may be perfect and complete, lacking nothing." As my faith was being proved by the trial, I had to let God have His way in my life so that in the end I could be fully developed in my faith.

I have learned so much about myself through this journey. First, that I am able to bear much more than I thought I ever could. I always used to think that I could never endure the thought of ever losing my hair. I took much pride in my hair and spent much time making sure it looked its best. I have found that there are much worse things in life than going bald. Hair is such a fleeting thing. God knows exactly what we can bear. He knew I could do it. He had to let me see it for myself. We should never say that we could never go through this or that. God is able to keep us and get us through anything He calls us to go through.

Second, I learned that the love of God is so deep and it is beyond what I ever imagined it could be. Sometimes we as Christians get caught up in trying to be good. But I heard Joyce Myer comment today that we need to separate our "who" from our "do." God loves us for who we are, not for what we do. Jesus already did everything that needed to be done for us to be accepted in God. We just need to let God's love flow through us and stop trying to "work" for our salvation. These past seven months I have just rested in the love of God.

Third, I learned that no matter how bad a situation looks, if we let God come in the center of it, He can turn it all for good. My marriage has been transformed through this trial. I have never felt so loved and adored from my husband as I have since this trial began. I have also seen so many people touched by the fact that they see me living out the scriptures. Being a pastor's wife, I think people thought that my life was perfect. Now they can see that I am human and that I am not exempt from trials of life.

I am so thankful for all the people God put in my life through this journey. I have met some wonderful and awesome doctors and nurses along the way. I have found that there were so many people across the nation that were praying for me, people I didn't even know. They just heard about my story and felt compelled to pray and let my husband and me know that they were there for us. I am so thankful to be part of a church that has stood by my family during this long journey. I am thankful for family that has stood by my side. My mom called me every day just to say hi and see how I was feeling for that day. I am thankful for my three sons who did what they had to do to help me get through this journey. I can't say enough about their love and support. And for my husband who has stood by me through the ups and downs of this journey. Thank you, my love, for your unconditional love. And lastly, I am thankful for my Lord and Savior who gave me the grace and peace for each day of the journey. Lord, I give you my life completely. I have come to trust You and know You in a way I never knew I could. You are the rock upon which I stand.

Kent's Final Words

I want to sum everything up in one final chapter. The best way to do this is to share John 15:1-2:

> I am the real vine, and my Father is the gardener. He breaks off every branch in me that does not bear fruit, and he prunes every branch that does bear fruit, so that it will be clean and bear more fruit.

We must understand that God allows pruning so that we will produce true fruit. When I prayed that God would use me He immediately began pruning the branches that had no value. He is the gardener and knows what He is doing when it comes to being spiritually productive. He will begin to remove things out of our lives that are useless. But what happens when He wants to remove something that we demand to keep? We say, "No, that is mine, and I will not give it up." I am sure that you are like I am and have had this happen to you.

The progress of God begins to stall until He is able to get us to surrender. This is where trials and suffering play such a huge role in us. As I write this last chapter I just heard of devastating tornadoes that has ripped through the south parts of the United States. Over three hundred people were killed. My mother and sister live there and have seen the devastation first hand. This town in Mississippi was a predominately Christian town. You may say, "Why did God allow this to happen to them?" I then began to hear the testimonies of people who have reached out to help the suffering. Prayer meetings began everywhere and people began to help one another. Some who have lost everything were among the first to respond to reach out to their neighbor. How were they able to do this? They may have lost things, but they did not lose God. True pruning does not rob you of God, it only removes what is not important. Things are replaceable, but being Christ-like requires pruning. It is the removal of the useless branches that help the plant to grow.

Last year I decided to try my hand at planting a garden at the church. The fruit was going to be given to those in the church who needed it. I had several tomato plants that had just started producing small tomatoes. One day a neighbor came over who was an expert at gardening. He always had a great garden every year and I wanted one like his. When he stopped by he asked me if he could come by later and prune the tomato plants for me. I said, "Sure, I don't mind." The next day when I went to the garden to water the plants I was shocked at what I saw. My neighbor had stripped them bare. He removed all the branches and leaves, they looked horrible. I felt he had sabotaged my garden. He killed my plants; that guy ruined my tomato plants!

Well, I did not want to say anything to him to get him mad so when I saw him I just thanked him for helping me out. He then proceeded to tell me what he had done. He said that all of those excess branches and leaves were robbing the plant of nutrition and water. They were useless to the plant and by removing them the buds would receive much more resources to produce bigger and better tomatoes.

Sure enough, about three weeks later I was enjoying huge tomatoes, bigger than I had ever imagined. He was right. This is what God wants to do in us. He wants to remove those things that are robbing us of His strength and power so that we bear bigger and better fruit for Him. So do not weep at the loss of material possessions; rather lay them down as offerings at the feet of the Lord. Anything lost that God wants you to have will return back to you multiplied. Remember the end of the story in the book of Job? God gave him back his children, but not just the ten he lost, he got twenty back from God. God keeps great records of the inventory of our lives and knows what things we need even before we ask Him.

Sarah and I know that there are people who have gone through things much worse than we have. Their suffering lasts for years and years. Their dreams and passions are no longer important to them because they can no longer envision them. To each of you Sarah and I want you to know that we pray that you will still look to the Father. He is still there for you through all you're going through. I pray that God will surround you with those who will pray you through to the Father and will be the resource of faith and hope.

To those of you who have read our journey, I challenge you one last time as I have done throughout this book, "Touch your world!" You are needed to demonstrate the compassion of Christ wherever you are and by whatever you do. Start with a smile and then a kind word. Be willing to help your neighbor and forgive those who have hurt you. Love others the way you want to be loved and visit the sick and the afflicted. Be the first to help the disabled when they are in need. Reach into your pocket to feed the hungry. This is what Christians do!

I know that Sarah and I have been pruned for such a time as this. So much of what was hanging onto us has been stripped away and we are ready to bear fruit that glorifies our heavenly Father!